CENTRAL LIBRARY
828 "I" STREET
SACRAMENTO, CA 95814
JUN - - 2000

Dreambirds

Dreambirds

THE STRANGE HISTORY OF THE OSTRICH IN FASHION, FOOD, AND FORTUNE

ROB NIXON

**PICADOR USA
NEW YORK**

ISBN 0-312-24540-8

First published in Great Britain by Doubleday, a division of Transworld Publishers Ltd

First Picador USA Edition: March 2000

10 9 8 7 6 5 4 3 2 1

For Anne.
And in memory of my father, Bob ('Babiana') Nixon.

Acknowledgments

Special thanks go to my agent, Bill Hamilton, for his sustained enthusiasm, as well as to Marianne Velmans at Transworld for her early encouragement and acute editing. I would also like to thank George Witte for his support and for the book's sub-title.

I owe a debt to friends – Catherine Bush, Clifford Hill, Kathleen Hill and Kate Sterns – for their insightful responses to this book while it was taking shape. My appreciation goes, in addition, to the many people who spoke to me on my travels about the world of ostriches.

For providing quiet, reviving places to work I am grateful to the Blue Mountain Center, the MacDowell Colony, Virginia Center for the Creative Arts and Yaddo, as well as to Eileen Pagan.

My deepest debt, as ever, is to Anne.

Author's Note

A few names in this book have been altered. Most remain the same.

We cross the desert with remnants
Of some earlier image in mind,

That is all a living man
Knows of the promised land.

GIUSEPPE UNGARETTI

Hope is the thing with feathers.

EMILY DICKINSON

Part One

Chapter One

Dad died three days ago; we buried him this morning. His going has brought us all home: five brothers and sisters, strangers and relative strangers, together in the same country for the first time in twenty-four years. Only my brother has remained here in Port Elizabeth, Africa's southernmost city. The rest of us spread or fled north, east and west to New York, Cape Town, Sydney, Henley-on-Thames. Five children, four continents. I worked it out this morning while preparing for the funeral: collectively, we've put 22,000 miles between us and the first place we called home.

It's typical – and right – that Dad is absent. That's exactly how I remember him: dashing off regardless of the occasion, excusing himself, disappearing over the horizon on one of his perpetual schemes. If he's gone now, it's because he's so busy. 'Back,' as he always said, 'in a jiffy.'

We're sitting in the bedroom in our church clothes, too heavy for this late summer weather. We're sipping tea and trying to get to know each other. And trying to find ways of supporting Mom, today (and most days) the bravest woman around. We've pulled open Dad's drawers and surrounded ourselves with photographs: mounds and mounds of them, the foothills of the past.

Each cupboard we poke into is a jumble of slides and prints. He took them pell-mell, faster than they could be labelled or organized. Family groups, elephants at feeding time, mountain peaks he had climbed, parks he had helped preserve, choirs to which he had added his tentative tenor. But mostly we uncover pictures of indigenous plants: flowers (some still unknown to science), trees shot from far off and close-up images of the delicate deltas of leaves. That's where he composed himself: behind the camera, in front of foliage. Fiddling for focus, tinkering with a viewfinder, switching lenses and filters, trying to get just the right aperture on his shutters. Then he'd be off again, back into the darkroom.

Mom shuffles photos absently, fingering them but looking away. Then she pulls one out, glances at it, and passes it to me upside down, like a dealer distributing cards. 'Rob, do you remember this? Do you remember how hot it was? Do you remember what you lost that day?'

Yes, I do.

I see a small boy perched high on the back of an ostrich. A boy with dangly legs, his hands full of feathers, his knees tucked beneath the wings. He's looking down, afraid of heights, unsure of all this altitude. To keep the bird from bolting, someone has slipped over its head a white hood that says 'Bleached Flour', like some cartoonist's spoof of the Ku Klux Klan.

I see I am wearing my hot pants. My shortest shorts. This was Mom's innocent term, her way of talking. She would say: 'It's pretty steamy out there, my boy; why don't you just slip into your hot pants?'

The ostrich handler must have stepped up then (he's obscured in the picture, reduced to a saggy hat) and whipped off the bag. The bird shot out of the starting block and thumped me to the ground. The hat man caught my ostrich and was kind to me. It bothers me that I can't see his face. But I can picture it: warmly creased in the manner of the mixed-race 'coloureds' who worked those desert farms. The man hoisted me back into the high, hot nest of feathers: '*Luister nou* – now listen here,' he whispered in Afrikaans, 'when you're up there, sit low and lean back. You can't ride it like a horse, otherwise you'll go right over the top.' And off I went, this time staying on, running topspeed round and round the ring.

4

The stretch of South Africa where I grew up boasts a century-old tradition of ostrich ranching. The giant birds were as integral to my boyhood landscape as hogs to any Iowa child or lambs to a Welsh one. I grew up on the edge of the Karoo, a huge scrub desert whose name derives from a San or Bushman word meaning Big Thirst. The Karoo sprawls for a quarter of a million square miles – an area as big as Texas or five times the size of England. In this desert world, the ostrich has been an object of reverie for generations, a glamorous creature inspiring elaborate dreams.

If you cross the Karoo, driving west from Port Elizabeth, you arrive at Oudtshoorn, a town that has long been the global epicentre of everything ostrich. At the end of the nineteenth century, ragtag bands of Lithuanian Jews, fleeing the pogroms, beached on South Africa's shores. Some trekked inland towards Oudtshoorn, where, among the aloes and prickly pears of the Karoo desert, they turned to farming ostriches. Oudtshoorn was the Afrikaans name for the village that these refugees came to know by another name: the Jerusalem of Africa. The place became, for them, an oasis of hope. Whole villages in Lithuania acquired fabulous stories about this Jerusalem of Africa where Jews could grow wealthy in the desert herding gigantic geese.

Within a decade or two of arriving in the Karoo, some refugees had metamorphosed into wealthy ostrich barons. A bunch of barons – Jews, Afrikaners, Englishmen and Scots – built feather palaces from the proceeds of the plumes: huge, eccentric mansions that mixed the wildest excesses of Ottoman, Victorian, Greek and Gothic architecture.

Those were the glory days of the feather trade. From the 1880s until World War One, the elegant plumes were more than an accessory to style: on boas and opera cloaks and cascading from hats, they became a fashion fundamental. To satisfy the tastes of natty dressers in America and Europe, and the demands of music hall and cabaret, the South African ostrich population swelled and swelled, until by 1913 one million birds were being bred for their feathers. The plumes soared in value, becoming, ounce for ounce, more precious than gold.

Our family trips to Oudtshoorn were a major boyhood adventure. There was something about the place. Magical, but disturbing. The streets were broad enough for oxwagons to turn in, piled high with plumes for foreign dames. I got to glimpse those ladies in Oudtshoorn's ostrich museum: pink mannequins wearing feathery clothes that looked like if you sneezed they'd come tumbling to the ground. I loved to visit those ladies in their glass cages, though I never stayed for long. They looked desirable but wrong.

I could tell that Oudtshoorn had been touched by far-off places, by the glamorous north end of the earth. I knew them only as names: Paris, New York, London, St Petersburg, Vienna and Berlin. As a child, the history of this ostrich town felt different, spoke to me through traces and trinkets of a fabulous beyond.

The Jerusalem of Africa became my imaginative oasis, allowing me a whiff of mystery through the coquetry of feathers. But the town at large was severely Calvinist. I shrank, even then, from this other Oudtshoorn which bristled with soldiers and church spires. Later, I would recognize it as a one-mistake town. South Africa's hinterland abounded in such towns: places where, in a flash, you could become a life-long casualty of some unmentionable act – a dalliance behind a shed, an abortion, a hint of homosexuality, cross-racial intimacy of any kind. Places where, if you were black, your destiny could be sealed by gossip about a glance, an in-surrectionary look at a white man, or a flash of illegitimate desire. One-mistake towns like Oudtshoorn seemed to produce sad, purgatorial people, trailing the Main Street, reminding everyone that if you slipped you would be made to live the error of your ways.

So the Oudtshoorn of my childhood became two towns rolled into one. An enchanted place, full of giant birds, feathers and fantasies of Parisian fashion and cabaret. But it was always also this other thing: a place of tarnished magic and an as yet unspecified unease.

Oudtshoorn lies about 200 miles west of our Port Elizabeth home. But if you took the desert route, as we usually did, there was nothing in-between, nothing except a few dry hamlets, a couple of inbred families in each. We would set off in our Opel Kapitan, a big bulbous car with the colouring and lethargy of a camel. Like every car and camera Dad ever owned, it was third-, or fourth- or fifth-hand. There were no floor gears: the gearstick grew out of the steering-wheel, which meant you could pack a driver and three people on the bench seat up front.

Our Kapitan was the envy of every petrol attendant at every gas station we visited. We would watch the gauge sliding towards empty; wait for Dad to pull in at the next Mobil or Caltex sign; and then sit back while the haggling began. An African would saunter up, beaming but drowning in those billowing blue overalls attendants were made to wear. 'Morning, boss. Best taxi-car in the world, boss. This car is a must-have, boss. Hard to get, boss. Look at this rust, boss. Too old for a whiteman, boss.' There Dad stood, shaking his head and shifting his feet, quietly refusing, utterly ill at ease.

I had visions of him one day, as the gas sizzled into the tank beneath us, poking his head through the window and announcing: 'OK, you lot. Pile out. We're walking from here.' Not because he cared to sell, but just to spare himself these jabbing reminders that – despite his heroic efforts and Mom's – we were not quite middle class.

In truth, he couldn't sell. The Kapitan's taxi potential made it ideal for our family. We were a multi-generational, nine-tiered construction, like one of those parking garages that spirals up and up. I was the ground floor. My younger brother, Andy, must have felt he was destined to be the basement. Up above me, was my sister Marion; on the levels beyond her, Sheelagh then Ruth. Next came Mom and Dad, then Mom's mom, and right at the top, where the spiral was exposed to the sky, you would find Mom's mom's father, whom we knew as Gaffy.

I was much older before I ever heard the phrase 'head of the family', but it was an idea I never quite understood. Our family never had a head or a ceiling. Dad was lost in the middle somewhere. As a child, I half-expected at any minute, from a coughing recess of the house, that yet another ancient would emerge. 'Good morning,' he would say. 'You must be Robert. Let me introduce myself. I'm your mother's mother's father's father.'

I don't recall how many of us filed into the Kapitan that day I first learned the rudiments of ostrich riding. Gaffy, I'm sure, didn't come. He often stayed home: he was on the brink of turning one hundred. A cricket fan, he was dead set on scoring his century. 'Slow but steady,' he would say. 'I'll let the other chaps hit out.'

He certainly wasn't going to throw it all away on a trip to see some darn fool ostriches in this heart-stopping heat.

So Gaffy wasn't there. But his watch was.

I never figured whether he gave it to me as something valuable, an heirloom for the oldest boy, or because it didn't work too well. It was a wonky watch. It had an immaculate round face, fine numbering as delicate as a hair and a bold, brassy shine. But the long hand was bent and scratchy. It would get snarled up and then spring forward, so the minutes didn't always arrive on time. But it was my first watch and I loved it; loved it enough to invent all forms of business that required someone to announce the hour. It was a watch with a history and now it could transport me into adulthood.

Gaffy had brought it from the old country when, in 1910, at age forty-five, he'd emigrated to South Africa as a painter-decorator. He came from a Scottish border hamlet called Biggar, some miles south of Edinburgh. 'Biggar,' Gaffy would say, 'is far smaller than you think.' It wasn't a good joke, and, in his dotage, he made it far too often, but when I heard it for the first time I remember laughing and thinking, with

8

pleasure, that I was catching on to the tricks adults played with words.

So the watch went with me on the ostrich trip. It was a blistering Oudtshoorn day; so hot we could have fried an egg – maybe a chicken even – on the rooftop of our Opel Kapitan. The steel concertina watch strap started pinching and sweating in the heat. I took it off, cradling the watch in my palm. After the ostrich ride, we were given a tour of the farm. At one of the paddocks, I noticed a tatty ostrich hen pecking at the earth. Finding the stone of her fancy, she ate it; picking out a second and a third, she arched her neck to swallow. I asked our guide about her odd behaviour: was she sick, like when Blacky, our cat, eats grass?

No, he explained, this was normal. To stay alive, an ostrich has to keep three pounds of stones in its gut for grinding its food into submission. The stones serve as surrogate teeth: this is a creature with molars in its stomach.

'Did you know they eat diamonds too?' He paused so we could grasp that fact.

'One of the first and biggest diamonds discovered in South Africa was found three hundred miles north of here,' he continued. 'That was long, long ago, about a hundred years. That shiny stone changed the course of history. Problem was, there weren't any other diamonds around. Geologically speaking, that stone had no right being there. Today we know an ostrich must have eaten it, walked two hundred miles, then poohed it out. That ostrich gave a lot of prospectors a mighty headache. He got them wasting their time looking in all the wrong places.'

The guide peered down at the children's contingent to see if we were suitably impressed.

I loved it. This guy was a mine of natural history know-how, like a living, walking Chappies Chewing Gum wrapper. I got to thinking about Granny with her rumbly stomach: how much worse if she had been an ostrich, her innards clacking away like castanets every time she ate lamb.

A huge ostrich rooster sauntered over to our tour. He

peered down at us from across the fence, head on one side, as we digested all this information. Then suddenly his neck unfurled in a cobra strike; I felt a nudge in my hand. In a flash, my watch had gone. He'd snapped it up and snaffled it down as if it were some pesky living thing: a gnat, say, or a dragonfly. I saw little shivers as it passed down his long, long neck.

I was inconsolable, abruptly cut adrift.

The man wrapped an arm around my shoulder and beckoned the others towards a small museum in a corner of the farm. 'The ostrich,' he said when we got there, 'is a formidable omnivore. That means an animal which eats anything. Most of all it likes shiny things. As this young lad found out when he lost his watch back there. There's just about nothing an ostrich won't eat.' He turned and winked confidingly in our parents' direction: 'Maybe your mom wishes you were more like little ostriches that just eat what's put in front of them.'

I wasn't in the mood for jokes.

Then the man began passing around objects retrieved from the stomachs of old ostriches. Spark plugs, sticks, metal ash trays, sheep bones, soda cans, baling wire, a high-heeled shoe, copper piping, the shiny skeleton of a kitten. Watery-eyed, I ran my fingers over them. Their edges and ridges were all rubbed off. Every object felt as sleek as the skimming stones I collected along river beds, smoothed and tumbled by time.

Our guide finally began to register the level of my distress.

'OK. Let's say you haven't lost your watch; let's say that ostrich is just looking after it for a while.'

He made it sound like a pawn shop, like the one where Gaffy had left his walking stick and his teeth when he had run out of cash.

The man was talking down to me. I was beginning to lose my cool.

'OK, then. When can I come and fetch it?'

He paused. He reached down for a black, sharp-handled

comb protruding from a sock. He ran his thumbnail up and down it, then passed it through his hair.

'You must understand, my boy. An ostrich can live a long, long time. Sometimes as long as a man. You might have to come back in thirty years.'

Thirty years! I did some instant arithmetic. OK, I knew how long one school day felt: a school day was endless. There were eighty school days in a school term and one hundred and twenty terms in thirty years . . .

That night I went to bed with nothing left to wind. In six hours, I knew, deep in that big bird's tummy, the ticking would stop for good.

I lay there, wide awake, trying to wrap my mind round so much time. When you're eight, an ostrich is one-hundred-feet high. And thirty years lies as far ahead as the Stone Age lies behind.

Chapter Two

The ostrich seems, at first, deficient in those romantic qualities that humans – from Icarus to John Keats – have typically sought from birds. In two million years this goofy gargantuan hasn't learned to fly or sing. Nature has left it glued to the ground, no better off than us. Its musical talents are crude: it can barely muster a croak. Yet the ostrich has feathered our dreams more luxuriantly than any other bird – as the plume passions of Tutankhamun, the Roman emperors, the Black Prince, Napoleon, the *Folies Bergère*, Marlene Dietrich, Queen Victoria and Elton John all testify. For millennia, we've borrowed ostrich glamour and used it to signal sexual and imperial power, seductive spectacle, hyperbole, escape.

Great thinkers, from Aristotle to the eighteenth-century French biologist, Georges-Louis Leclerc, have pitted their wits against the ostrich and struggled to make sense of it. Some concluded that this flightless, songless, egg-laying leviathan was one of nature's freak-shows, a cross between a mammal and a bird. When Linnaeus classified our planet's avifauna in 1758, he memorialized this creature's oddity. He noted how at a distance desert voyagers readily confused ostriches and camels. And so he gave this bird the ambiguous scientific name that it still bears today: *Struthio camelus* – the sparrow-camel.

The one thing everybody knows about ostriches is their dubious psychology. The ostrich position: this creature's most widely recognized service to humanity. What other life form embodies so lucidly the follies – and temptations – of denial? For centuries, satirists have paid homage to ostrich idiocy whenever they needed to mock the politicians of the day. Big butt in the air, head buried in the sand.

As a boy, I knew, from simple experience, that no ostrich behaved like that. Sure, it was a gawky, boneheaded creature. But the closest any ostrich came to going underground was its imitation bush trick. I had seen it in the veld. When danger threatened, the ostrich hen would often sit dead-still to avoid detection, flattening her endless neck like a garden hose against the earth. That way she could pull off a pretty competent illusion. A flattened ostrich blends easily into the dry Karoo bushes which, for most of the year, are greyish humps of dead-looking sticks. As I child, I could almost picture a bushy-looking ostrich being nibbled by a half-blind goat.

The ostrich has been in denial for nearly 2,000 years. Ever since the world's first natural historian, Pliny the Elder, saddled the bird with its reputation for head-burying. Pliny, it seems, had something of a subterranean fixation. On observing that swallows disappeared each autumn, he surmised that they didn't fly away at all, but buried themselves in mud and spent the winter underground. Pliny was a charming writer, but as a scientist he leaned towards fantasy. '*Semper aliquid novi Africam adferre,*' he wrote most memorably. 'Africa always brings us something new.' But in the case of the African ostrich, not quite as novel as he thought.

My understanding of ostriches would have remained extremely limited if it hadn't been for Dad. He used to drive my brother Andy and me deep into the Karoo scrub desert where the big birds lived. Dad himself had zero interest in birds. Plants were his passion. Generally speaking, he mistrusted anything that moved. That included winged creatures and people who were always pulling up their roots. He believed in staying put. He was a one job for life, one town, one marriage kind of guy.

For more than forty years, he worked for a tiny, provincial newspaper, the *Eastern Province Herald*. Every Wednesday morning for four decades, *Herald* readers woke to Dad's gardening column, which he called 'Growing Things'. He never signed his name to the column: it was always 'By Babiana', his *nom de flora*, borrowed from a tiny plant endemic to our area. Babiana is a ground orchid, a crawler, easily overlooked until the spring rains fall. Then suddenly it's there, breaking through the crusted earth in brief bouquets of smoky blue. The name suited Dad. By nature, he hugged the ground, belonging where he was in a deep-rooted, unobtrusive way. In all his deepest sentiments, he was a local man.

It was 'Growing Things' that first took me into ostrich country. Dad was always on the lookout for the little known wonders of desert plants. He'd never been to university, lacked any scientific training. But over a lifetime he used his camera, his car and his natural curiosity to turn himself into an amateur botanist. He believed you had a moral obligation to know the place you lived in, preferably in Latin.

As we travelled across the Karoo, he'd make jottings in his notebook while mumbling Latin plant names to himself. Those names still tinkle through my head like the childhood tunes my sisters stroked from the piano. *Euphorbia decepta, Hermannia desertorum, Aloe microstigma, Kedrostis africana.* I, too, spent long, hot days learning Latin names. But only the names of birds. If I remembered plant names it was an accident; plants held no interest for me at all.

At age eleven, I began to keep a diary called 'Flying Things'. For five years I filled it with looping observations on every bird I saw, named in English and veld Latin. I included careful notes on ostriches, though strictly speaking they weren't flying things at all.

This bird diary was my way of manoeuvring some space, my attempt to escape from beneath my father's shadow and all that overhanging foliage. This involved one of those contrapuntal movements at which children excel. I studied Dad carefully and made it my mission to become his opposite. He knew everything about roots, so I became obsessed with flight. He held the ground, so I took to the air.

I became a fledgling ornithologist. During childhood and adolescence every other calling seemed unimaginably dull. I loved things with wings, things that came and went, had the power to vanish and reappear. Like Oudtshoorn's ostrich museum, birds spoke to me of far-off places. They offered me an alternative – an otherworldly world.

Becoming a writer was an accidental spin-off of my fidelity to birds. At fifteen, I ventured into print for the first time with a small excerpt from 'Flying Things'. *The Ostrich*, the official journal of the South African Ornithological Society, published my sighting of a migrant whose waywardness was scientifically interesting. My report described a rare wanderer I'd encountered along the coast near Port Elizabeth – a European Oystercatcher which didn't belong in Africa. Gale-force winds had blown it off-course, down from the Northern Hemisphere. For me, that lost migrant trailed oceanic worlds of fantasy.

Chapter Three

Birds in general – and ostriches in particular – held me spellbound long before I started 'Flying Things'. My fascination began with Gaffy and Granny, those ancient, scattered Scots whose stories and accents marked them as strangers in our midst. The first bird I ever knew was Gaffy's best friend. I met it before I could walk. This bird couldn't fly. Not because, like an ostrich, it was too fat for its wings, but because there were bars all around it. It lived in a cage and its name was Prince Charming.

Charming was Gaffy's grey parrot. Charming had opposite eyes. One blue, one yellow. When he watched me he threw his head to one side and gave me his mad eye, his lemony one.

We spent a lot of time together, Charming, Gaffy and I. We babysat each other out on the veranda: Charming trapped in his cage, Gaffy a captive of age and me too small to run away, crawling and toddling between the veranda's four walls.

Prince Charming talked a lot of old garbage and spilled his food, just like Gaffy did. The two of them were a mess. I had to crawl through clouds of falling seed and feathers and the porridge bombs that Gaffy dropped. But I could hear that Gaffy and Charming had their own way of talking, that the old man had found a home in the voices of birds.

I could also hear that he understood very little else. When Mom or Granny or any of my sisters came out and attempted to chat, Gaffy soon gobbledygooked them into defeat. But if the Prince had anything to say, anything at all, Gaffy was all ears. Their stoep talk went on all day, back and forth, back and forth, soaring above my head. Who knows what they nattered on about: the neighbours' stinky geese, the soaring price of chew tobacco, liquorice and sunflower seeds? The heat, the Cuban missile crisis?

Mostly, it was love. Gaffy whispered and crooned and chuckled and snogged the air; Prince did the same right back. I loved to listen to their sing-song stuff, their crackerjack passion, these special voices they kept back for each other. That's when I knew this fierce old bony man once had a softer side.

They talked love, but also violence. Often, they screamed blue murder.

In my mind, it always starts the same.

Gaffy is slumped in a saggy heap in his white wicker chair. From the floor, all I see are seven stiff legs towering up. Four chair legs, two slippered legs paler than the chair, and beside them one thick brown cane. The cane disappears at the top into a huge ram's horn, as knotty and yellow as the fingers that grip it like a vine. Sometimes, from where I lie, it's hard to tell where the old ram stops and the old man begins.

Then, all of a sudden, the tapping starts up. It sends tremors across the cement: thumpity, thump, thump, thump. Then a voice begins to follow the tapping. It's a bleating, woolly voice, deep and quavery.

'I'm a murderer I am, a murderer twice over.' Thumpity, thump, thump, thump, goes the ram's-horn cane. Prince Charming supplies the chorus: 'I'm a murderer I am, a murderer twice over.' Just in case one man's guilt isn't enough. Gaffy mutters his crimes, Prince Charming screams them. The Prince doesn't just repeat the words, his voice is hoarse with remorse; he puts in for his friend a whole lot of extra pain.

Every time this happens, I shiver and scramble away. There's sadness on the stoep. But mainly, it's fear I feel. I skitter past the forest of legs. I always head for the veranda edge, where it tips onto the lawn. I duck behind the giant vat

17

of scarlet geraniums until everything quietens down. The veranda's Red Cobra Shine usually doesn't bother me. But now the stoep is streaming in the sun and my hands and knees are polished full of blood.

Sometimes, when I'm lucky, Granny comes out and scolds them both. One day when I'm a little older I ask her why they say these things: 'Don't you mind them. They're just a pair of gabbers. Leave them to their blathering. It's gibberish to you and me.'

I like her voice, she talks to me as if I'm there. But still I'm none the wiser. And Gaffy and his feathery echo continue to cry blue murder in the scarlet air.

Gaffy's closest friends were the three Russians. None of the rest of us ever saw them, but most days they paid him a visit. Every morning Mom and Granny would try to spoon Gaffy some porridge. But he would lash out at them and their spoon. 'Away with yer, away with yer. Yer nothing but a pack of auld wimmin. Look at all these Russians here. They're starving, starving, starving. Not a crust between them.'

Charming would take up the cry. 'Starving, starving, starving. Not a crust between them.'

So that was the only way the women could get Gaffy fed: by first feeding all the darn Russians, spooning porridge into the empty air.

Back then, I had no idea who Russians were or where they came from. I thought they were a special kind of ghost that only did daytime visits. But now I wonder: what dreams or waves of memory carried these Russians to our African shores? Why did the old man wish to save them from starvation? Were they hauntings passed on to him by his father, who had fought in the Crimean War?

Granny hated all Russians. She hated Peter the most. The other two sometimes came, sometimes didn't, but Peter was there every day. He was a tall man: Gaffy always looked up to him when they spoke. But Granny spat out his name. Peter the Communist, she called him. That wasn't a word I knew either. I thought she was calling him Peter the Commonest, because he was always hanging around.

Peter, two more Russians and Prince Charming: that gave the old man quite a gang. It seemed to me, down on the floor, that the only time he ever talked nicely was to live parrots and dead Russians. For the rest, he just babbled and snapped.

Prince bothered me quite a bit. At least he lived in a cage. But Peter the Commonest was on the loose: a hungry man and hungry men, everyone knew, could move like the wind when they wanted. I was afraid of his invisible speed.

That's when I found Philip the Protector. He was a boy a bit bigger than me. He had crinkly black hair, a smile and strong hands. He was someone to talk to on the veranda who knew all about Commonests and birds. He talked nicely and watched over me when I was frightened of sneak attacks. For years it was just Philip and me holding back the Russian hordes.

Mom didn't like Philip at first. She said the house was already too crowded with people: I shouldn't be making more up. But then she saw I went nowhere without him; when I was worried or sad he was there. So she said he could stay. Once she even left him a bowl of pudding – stewed guavas and custard – near the door. He told me he loved it. But Mom said she wouldn't do it again. She thought the red termites that swarmed on the veranda had carried the whole lot away.

I was born in 1954. Gaffy, wheezing in the room next door, had been around since 1865. I was in my teens before I could find him on a map of time: he left the womb the same month that across the Atlantic General Lee was surrendering at Appomattox, bringing the American Civil War to a close.

But I didn't know that back then. History was a mystery still – my world was small and I couldn't string that many years together. Yet I could see already from my veranda perch that time could make a person very, very old until he was just a ghostly shuffle bumping against the dark.

When Gaffy was younger and a bit more mobile – in his late

eighties, say – he used to walk five blocks to pick my sister Marion up from school. One day, as they were tottering back, a driver stopped, offering them a ride. 'How far do you go?' he asked. 'I'm from the nineteenth century,' Gaffy replied, like he was giving an address.

One thin bedroom wall sheltered me from deep Victorian times. For years I was haunted by whooshing dreams of being sucked right through that wall and landing in a world so long ago I couldn't scramble back. All of us, each generation, lived out of kilter with our peers, sucked back behind the times. The past was everywhere; it was the present that seemed remote. Growing up, I never felt like a contemporary of my contemporaries.

Even Granny wasn't really a granny in the normal sense. Part of her remained, well into her seventies, a little girl who performed the way any daughter does who stays at home too long, sharing her father's roof.

Sometimes for a dare, Andy and I tiptoed down the passage to the dim edge of Gaffy's room. I always kept one hand locked in my brother's and clutched the door jamb with the other – in case of sudden whooshing. We never went inside: we just peered at all his ancient stuff. It was always hard to see. The curtains were heavy and pulled tight against the African light. His room smelled of leather books, eiderdowns, must, snuff, pipes, lavender, chamber pots and illness. We just stood and watched him as his yellow walrus moustache wandered across the pillow while he dozed. Beneath his gooseneck lamp, his eyes stayed closed in sleep or death – we were always guessing which.

Then he would sense strangers, non-Russians, and make a noise, a coughing, snorting sort of cry for help. We were small, so we ran away.

Gaffy took a special pride in birthdays, mostly his own. At ninety-three he still demanded the correct number of candles. The big marmalade cake Granny built for him wasn't big enough. Dad – whose Irish father had been a fireman –

was horror-struck at the idea of a ninety-three-candle con-struction. He knew a hazard when he saw one. Couldn't the old man just make do with one candle for each decade perhaps?

But Gaffy insisted and won: 'None of you daft buggers are going to take away my years.' So the big cake got even bigger. But his pipe and all those years on earth had robbed him of his breath. The candles flickered on and on; he blew and blew, in his spittly way, but couldn't puff them out. By the time he got the final candle the cake was polished thick with wax and so gob-spattered it didn't look tasty at all.

Gaffy was supposed to live to be one hundred. At least that was his plan. But at ninety-five his interest in life and his mind began to wander. Then the committee at the bowling club had a bright idea. Gaffy was crazy about lawn bowls; he'd played into his eighties. So the Walmer Bowling Club promised him a party when he scored one hundred. Suddenly life had meaning again: he was living for a goal.

After that, every Saturday morning he appeared resplen-dent, as if today might be the day. Soft brown bowling shoes for treading on the lawns, blinding white flannel trousers and a starched shirt beneath a creamy blazer with a maroon stripe threading through it. He hid his liver-spotted head beneath a gauzy bowling hat, flat and white, from which protruded the only unorthodox touch: a single, blue-grey parrot feather.

So Gaffy kept living and counting, counting and then living some more. He wanted to live not so that he could have extra years but in order to have fewer. He just wanted everything out the way that stood between him and one hundred. Then in his ninety-ninth year he got sick. And sicker.

Mom was a tough woman, as strong as she was short. But she had a softer side. Gaffy, she saw, was slipping fast. So she called the bowling club. Couldn't they give him his celebration now; just pretend a bit, lift him over the hump of one hundred?

Prince Charming and the Russians raised no objection. But the bowling club sure did. They sounded scandalized. As if to say that stealing time was as bad as cheating on the final green.

So Gaffy never got his party. Just a funeral when, at ninety-nine and three-quarters, he gave up the ghost for good. Pneumonia carried him away and with him the Russians too. But Charming stuck around; he was made of sterner stuff.

I noticed something in those final years. The more Gaffy aged, the more he repeated himself. Like his joke about Biggar being smaller. I noticed too that the parrot never missed a chance to repeat his repetitions, even after Gaffy died.

Guests would come round for tea. Granny would be arranging doilies while I passed around her home-made ginger biscuits. Suddenly, Gaffy would blare out from beyond the grave. 'I'm a murderer, I am, a murderer twice over.' Then a pause, and a repetition for emphasis. 'I'm a murderer, I am, a murderer twice over.'

Prince Charming had his brogue just right: he rolled each murderous 'r' in guilt and pain. Gaffy's body had gone missing, but the Prince wasn't going to let his voice or his memory die.

Granny's eyes would flash behind her silver spectacles. She would bustle onto the veranda and give the parrot a dressing down.

'Have you no heart, Prince Charming? Can't you give the poor blighter some rest now he's left us for the grave?'

Charming always looked sorry for himself. As if he were the victim of some malign ventriloquist. He would duck his head, twisting this way and that. Then he would give Granny his nice eye, the blue one and say something she liked. Usually, a bit of Robbie Burns.

But as soon as she was gone a while, he was back to his murderous ways. The things Charming said left me with a frightened fascination: who had Gaffy killed and when? I asked, but nobody would say.

***

One day I awoke to find the cage empty. For the first time since I was born the veranda was dead-still. Prince Charming had passed away and taken Gaffy with him. For a second time, Gaffy had vanished for the grave.

Dad wrapped an arm around my shoulder. 'We found Charming early this morning, my boy, lying in his seed. Both eyes shut, legs in the air. He probably died of that special sickness parrots always get.'

Dad showed me the name in a big book and repeated it. 'Psittacosis' – parrot fever. He knew how I loved words. So we made a game of it – pssity, pssity, bang bang, dead goes the parrot – saying it over and over again, the way Charming would have if he'd been alive.

I went to bed that night with that word sitting in my head. Psittacosis. Psittacosis. I worked it into a ditty, like a rhyme from Mother Goose. I still didn't know quite how to feel. There'd been a death in the family. OK, just a small one, a small parroty death. But Gaffy's voice, which had survived long past one hundred now, was gone, gone for good. A bit of my heart was glad; I didn't feel as sad as I knew I should.

I was dozing off that night when my eldest sister crept into the room. 'Psst,' she whispered. 'You know pssity, pssity, that thing Dad told you about? It's not true. I know that for a fact. Early this morning, before the sun was up, Granny went to Charming's cage and strangled him. Tore off his neck.'

Chapter Four

So Granny throttled Gaffy's parrot, but she kept her mavis alive. The mavis was our mystery bird the whole time we were growing up. Every so often we heard its song but no-one ever saw it.

The mavis came out when Granny baked. First, she closed the kitchen door. Then she began her stirring, stirring, stirring, mixing the flour and sugar and butter in with singing and humming and whistling. She always started with 'My Bonnie Lies Over the Ocean'. But after a few tunes her singing tailed away and another sound began. A fluttery whistle shooting up and down like a poltergeist on a flute.

I can still smell that otherworldly song: I can smell it loud and clear. It carries on its breath the scent of ginger biscuits, vanilla fudge and volcanic vats of guava jelly and mulberry jam from fallen fruit we'd gathered in the yard.

The mavis, she said, was a Scottish bird. More than that we didn't know. I asked her to draw a picture once. Was it pink or orange? A sea-deep green, perhaps? No, she wasn't sure she'd ever seen the bird though it whistled through her head.

But she remembered exactly when she'd heard it. The first day of school and every day thereafter.

Granny always coughed when she told a story, even the shortest one. Then she'd take off her small round glasses and lay them on the tartan rug – Clan Ranald – across her lap.

'Scotland is a dark, wet place. The winters are long and weary. The school gates were miles from our back door. So when I started for school in the morning it was black and misty. And when I walked back it was blacker still. But there was a bird that sang in the hedgerows – Mam said it was a mavis. It had a mighty cheerful song that came to me through the mist.'

It was a blue bird I decided next time I heard it in her whistle. The notes it sang had the same far-off colour that I found in Granny's eyes.

Down there at the end of Africa, we knew nothing about winter or snow. Snow was just a book word that fell softly from nowhere, making little sense. The only time we ever saw it was at Christmas, the hottest part of the year. Then it drifted down on cards from the north bearing greetings from relatives we never knew. Lots of the cards were the same. A small bird with a red breast on a spade; red berries on some prickly bush; thick carpets of a word called snow. The robin and the snow were pretty, magic things other people had made up. You never saw them until Christmas, when they fell like Santa from the hot December sky.

I asked Granny if she remembered snow. 'Snow,' she grimaced, 'snow is a terrible thing.' There was nothing more to be said.

Many years later – after Gaffy and Granny and Dad had all died – Mom told me what little she knew. Granny was twelve when she left Scotland in 1910 with Gaffy, her mother, two sisters and one brother. The week before they'd caught the boat to Africa, they'd put all their worldly goods up for auction. But a blizzard had blown day after day and no-one had come to the sale. 'We had a few nice things,' Granny recalled, 'but they all went for a farthing.' Snow had done them in.

So Granny brought almost nothing with her to Africa: just a child's suitcase, her accent, snow-poor parents and a pocketful of song.

In the seventy-five years that followed, her accent didn't budge an inch. It was strongest when she was reciting poetry:

she loved whistling, but loved ballads, too, especially Robbie Burns. On 25 January each year, she'd remind us that the great man had been born. She'd give us a recital as we sat around in our bathing suits treating our jellyfish stings. January was hot as hell, fine weather for the beach, but it was risky swimming: the south-easter blew shoals of jellyfish and bluebottles shorewards from way out at sea.

So we sat quietly treating our injuries and eating cold salads, while Granny reeled off her poems: 'O, wert thou in the cauld blast/On yonder lea, on yonder lea.'

I was already a bird and wildlife fanatic. I had a better grip on the animals of the world than I did on the darker regions of Granny's accent. So the first time she announced that the next poem was 'To a Moose' pictures raced through my mind: giant antlers beside a giant lake in a giant green forest – a message from America.

But Burns, I soon learned, knew nothing about mooses. He was inspired by a creature altogether more humble. Thanks to Granny – a stickler for hygiene – moose-traps littered our hoose. There was one little grey number she could never quite catch. She talked to him in the kitchen at night: 'Come out here, yer timerous beastie.' She called him Skip-the-Grave.

One evening, as she sat darning grey socks after dinner, I asked her: 'Granny, do you ever dream of visiting Scotland? Would you like to see it again?'

'The auld country? Och, no. I could na be bothered.' She paused and raised her eyes, then let them fall again. 'Mind, maybe just the once. To hear the mavis sing.'

Then her voice tightened, sounding strict the way it could. 'But that's a daft thought. No, really, the truth be told I could na be bothered.'

She – we – didn't have the money. That's why she ruled it out. I knew even then – in the strange way of a child – she was afraid she'd let something slip. She wouldn't want to sound like a dreamer after things she could never have.

26

We were all taught that – we got it from her, I suppose, and she got it from the people behind her. Don't let your mind wander off into dreaming. If you want something you can't afford, cut out the wanting. Desire is the root of all damage. It's a selfish and a wicked and a fearful thing.

Granny had some very strong views. Among other things, about the English. When *their* royal family visited South Africa, she made sure no newspapers entered our house. 'The English? Nothing but trouble.' She made them sound like snow.

It was hard, sometimes, to know just who we were. Officially, all of us, our whole family, were English South Africans. The choices were clear-cut. If you weren't black or coloured or Indian, you had to be white. White came with two choices: English or Afrikaans. They called you by what you spoke. All the boys at my school were English – including the Jews, the Hungarians and the Portuguese. The same with our family: even Granny was English, though she refused point blank to write it on a form.

So I was born an English South African into a family of fierce Scottish separatists. It was our job to dislike the English, so I knew something strange was going on. If I was English it had to be make-believe, or someone was having me on.

Our house was heavy with Scotland – except for the mavis song, that was a window of light. Most of the time, Granny and I kept up a warlike truce. I was, she told me, disobedient, argumentative. 'This boy never stops. This child is asking, just asking, for a leathering. Do you always have to be so otherwise? You're the giddy limit, you are.'

It was always Mom who did the beating, with Granny goading her on. More an apple-boxing than a leathering. Mom bought apples in big wooden crates; it was cheaper that way, and it also gave her planks to hit me with. On my bad days, Mom would hold a box down with one foot, me down with one hand, rip off the planks, and break them over me, one by one. Then she and Granny would lock me in a bedroom for the afternoon. Sheelagh, my kind sister, would come and rescue me just before Dad came home for dinner. He stayed out of the punishment end of things; he didn't really approve. Granny shook her head. He was, she always said, too soft on the young ones for their own good.

It was through those long, locked-up afternoons that I learned the hidden power of song. I knew if I cried or vanished into silence, something in me would die. There were a lot of us in the house, maybe I'd be forgotten. So I sang – hymns, psalms and anthems, mostly – a one-child protest movement. Palestrina, Vaughan Williams, Purcell and bits of Bach; The *Te Deum*, The *Magnificat*, 'Rock of Ages', 'Jerusalem the Golden', all at the top of my voice. Singing seemed the safest way of reminding them you were there. And no-one could say you were answering back: the tunes all came from the choir I sang in at the church.

When Granny went on the warpath, I took revenge by stealth and indirection. I knew you couldn't win head-on. So I turned the bathroom taps on her, tight as I could; that was her weak point, her arthritic wrists.

'Can't help it, Granny, I'm a growing boy. I'll try better next time, I promise.' Next time: an extra twist.

She hated it when I sang during punishment. To give her credit, she did approve of my whistling. 'This boy,' she would say with just a hint of pride, 'this boy can hold a tune.'

Granny was good at some things. Like baking and bottling. I see her with rows and rows of green-tinted bottles. Even when empty they seem to be full of the sea. Alongside them, neat rows of silver screw-on caps rimmed with brick-coloured rubber washers. And piles of fruit, cut and peeled, ready for drowning in sugar. Bottling was Granny's way of helping feed us all; it was also, I came to learn, her way of showing us how to live. If we felt angry, hurt or confused, she had a ready solution. 'Just bottle it. Where would we be if everybody spoke their mind?' And so we all mastered, in our way, the special art of bottling.

Granny could knit up a fury. She knew how to knit at you, without even catching your eye. Clickety, click CLICK CLICK when someone mentioned that Sheelagh had a boyfriend and that boyfriend – clickety, click CLICK, CLICK, CLICK, CLICK – owned a yellow scooter.

That was our house. Most times no-one would say a word. But you would hear a thundering silence as the orchestra of disapproval tuned its instruments. Gaffy spluttering into his liquid foods – soup or porridge, mostly – when somebody answered back; the accusatory clattering of Granny's knitting; Dad's strategic vanishing acts as Mom crashed food onto the plates; kids galumphing in a huff up and down the passage.

Our bodies spoke for us: Granny's spoke eczema, sciatica and rheumatism; Dad had a wide vocabulary of heartburn and stomach cramps; Mom was bilingual in dizzy spells and surging blood pressure; Andy perfected vocal bilious attacks; Gaffy was fluent in every ailment under the African sun. These mute disturbances erupted everywhere. Small wonder that when, as a super-spiritual teenager, I felt the need for a religious epiphany and chose the beautiful babbling of glossolalia. Speaking in tongues without saying a word.

Was this, too, why Granny chose – without ever speaking her mind – the song of that unknown bird to say so many things?

Granny never made it back to Scotland. I was in my mid-twenties, already living in America, when she died. Mom wrote to us all explaining. It had been a bad and painful death. One cancer, then another. Granny had long since stopped her whistling. She just wheezed towards the end: her wheezing became the surest sign of life.

Mom lay night after night, month after month on a mattress in the passage by Granny's door. Half-awake, dozing on and off, but mostly just listening: for any change of breath, for the beginnings of the noise of death.

When Mom wrote to us after Granny was gone, she added a note for my sister in England. 'Sheelagh, I've been wondering, could you send me a picture of a mavis?' She asked it out of the blue.

Sheelagh was dubious. She'd lived for twenty years in an English country village and knew British birds pretty well. The bird books weren't any help.

She replied: 'There's no such creature. Granny's mind must have been running away with her. You know how it is when you're a kid.'

So we let the mavis drop.

We all agreed Mom needed a breather. The year Granny died, my brother had entered a spiral of schizophrenia. Now Granny was dead and Andy was in a mental home. Her whole life Mom had tended to people much older or much younger than herself, all in the family: spoon-feeding, sponging, dosing and dressing them. Infants, children, the unbalanced, the dying, the infirm. She dreamed, she once told me quietly, of a day when she'd live in her own house as nobody's mother or daughter.

Now she had, and needed, a rare break. She spoke fondly of seeing her two English grandchildren and travelling to Scotland as well. So at sixty-three she flew in a plane for the first time and went overseas with my father. I travelled from America to meet them at Mallaig on Scotland's west coast, where Sheelagh had booked us a cottage for two weeks.

For most of those weeks we were prisoners: of wild rain, high winds, smur and stormy family memories. Then, one Monday, the ghosts of mist wandered elsewhere, leaving behind them a crystal day. We decided, on the spur of the moment, to sail to the Hebridean island of Eigg. It was a couple of hours across. When we got there, Mom shooed us ahead. She had a gammy knee, didn't want to go far, preferred to wander alone. We – Sheelagh, her husband, her kids, my lover Anne and I – headed off with Dad for the peak.

When we saw Mom again, later that day, she looked radiant. It was May. She had seen her first vale of bluebells and had met a lad in the lane.

He introduced himself as the farrier's son. 'Lifted his cap. So polite.' Then he walked with her to a barn and at sixty-three, for the first time, she saw a horse shod.

Coming back, she'd heard some singing in the hedgerow. She asked the lad what that could be. 'That,' he said, 'that would be the mavis. They have a nest around here, I believe.'

He had to go. But she lingered awhile to listen. Peered deep, but couldn't see.

Some years later, Anne and I moved from New York to London where we lived for a couple of years. I spent as much time as I could in the Reading Room at the British Museum: it became my favourite place to write, to read, to be. I loved the sinking leather chairs and the rows of worn, green-leather desks arranged in the circular room like spokes of a giant's wheel. I was free to disappear into my reading, then emerge again, looking up to discover, along the spokes, rows and rows of other readers, all finding and losing themselves in books.

I loved, most of all, to lean back and gaze overhead while turning a phrase or a thought in my mind. I'd never written in a room like that, beneath a hundred-feet-high blue dome. It was like writing inside an enormous indigo egg.

The room answered to both parts of me – the writer, the child-naturalist. I loved keeping the company of books and book people beneath this sky-high dome, curving blue and away. Looking up from the page I half expected to see a cloud scud by or a skein of geese labouring south, high and fast, looking down on all these readers with a migrant's eye.

One morning there, I got thinking back to that bright, clear day on Eigg. And thinking, too, of Granny's mavis, her skylight on the past. Despite her all-screening severity, what memories had she allowed to fly in through that tiny window of song?

I decided to try once more to track her mavis down. This place, with its strange blue indoor-outdoor feel, seemed as good a place as any to start looking for a bird. So I called up a barrow full of books. I didn't have much luck at first. Then, in an ancient volume of Encyclopedia Britannica I found it. The entry came with a thin-lined sketch of a spotty-breasted bird with a snail wedged in its beak. The entry read: 'Song Thrush. *Turdus musicus*. Fifteenth Century Colloq. Obsolete.'

That confirmed everything I'd ever felt about our family: that we lived way behind the times. The living obsolete.

I went back that evening to the flat Anne and I were renting in North London, on a terrace in Islington, opposite Highbury Fields. I was planning to drop a note to my mother. She'd be interested, I knew. *Turdus musicus*: the name sounded just right.

It was a late summer's evening by the time I reached home. Anne was out tending her roses in the mellow, yellowing light. A robin redbreast kept her company as it usually did when she dug or pruned or weeded.

I wandered off for a twilight stroll across the fields. They say there are ley-lines beneath those fields, which on an evening like that, I didn't doubt. It must have been ten, ten-thirty: I was still charmed by this druidic northern light that lingered and lingered some more. In Africa, day broke and night fell, a world without half-measures. As a child, twilight was a far-off, fairy-book word that had no weight at all.

I could hear all around me the thud of boots on leather as kids kicked a soccer ball about. Amber shadows and little twinkling voices, running in hot pursuit. I loved the generosity of this half-light that let children play on into night.

Then a small black lad with a dancing step pranced through the defence to score. The ball flew through the keeper's spreadeagled hands and across the field, disturbing two birds as it went. The birds glided a short way towards me, then settled again. They ran along the ground, I noticed, in short bursts. After each run, they'd stop and bend an ear to the ground, listening for underground sounds. Straight off, I recognized them as the bird I'd seen in the book.

I waited and watched. Eventually, one of the pair flew into the oak corridor lining the path. I couldn't see it any more, but I heard, all of a sudden, a beautiful, tumbling, other-worldly song. All those months of strolling across these fields, I must have heard or half-heard it without hearing. Now I heard and knew exactly what it was. The mavis: a small bird-word for a very old song.

The amateur naturalist in me marked it down: *Turdus musicus*. But that didn't tell me much. I was left with two birds that I couldn't quite turn into one. This plump speckled creature very much alive in a North London tree; and another bird, so familiar yet so various, that I'd pictured in a hundred shapes, but always through a bouquet of kitchen smells – baking and bottling. What I saw was a song thrush. But what I heard was a mavis – a bird that couldn't, no matter how hard I tried, ever be seen at all.

The book said the mavis was 'obsolete'. Perhaps so. But that word still sang in the minds of farriers' sons. And it echoed through our space-and-time-bent family, down there at the bottom of the map where Africa runs out – the giddy limit of the Celtic fringe.

Chapter Five

Every family has its movers and its stickers: those who dream of staying home and those who dream of nothing but departures, for whom hope means somewhere else. Gaffy and Granny moved; Dad and Mom, both children of immigrants, stayed faithful to the same town for half a century. But from an early age, my parents' rootedness and my discomfort with the world around me made me want to stretch my wings and take flight.

I envied the visiting birds that congregated near the lighthouse ten miles from where we lived. The lighthouse stood on the tip of a jagged, wind-swept promontory which pushed into the Indian Ocean. That slab of rock was the last landfall before Antarctica. Strange seafaring birds often paused there, dazed, storm-shocked or enfeebled by long flight. The lighthouse was famous for its terns – which looked like gulls, but were smaller and more fluent on the wing. They flocked around the lighthouse, resting and refuelling, in great numbers and variety: including my favourite species, that marathon traveller, the Arctic tern.

A group of local birders sometimes gathered at the lighthouse to band migrants. After dark, I'd help them stretch the black mist-nets, thin as spiderwebs, across the rocks. I was too young to do the ringing myself but I loved to watch the adults work. They caught the terns, then weighed and banded them, before letting each one go.

One night, an Arctic tern crashed into a net close by. The

lighthouse beam swung round just then and I caught a flash of silver. The bird wore a tiny band around one ankle. I called a lady who removed the tern gently from the net, strand by strand. Then she wrote down the details on the ring, while I held that world-wide wanderer in my hands. I tried to think where the bird had been, but the places that it knew defeated my efforts at imagining. Yet there it was, hot and pumping in my palms. A few minutes later, I gently uncupped my hands and felt the tern take off with a sudden surge of purpose before I lost it to the windy dark.

The ring details we'd recorded were sent off for inspection. Somebody had banded the bird, we learned, three months before in Iceland. I was young enough to take it personally: as a sort of message in a bottle.

I found a book in the local library that let me follow the travels of the terns. I learned that they nested in the Arctic Circle, then migrated past where we lived to the Antarctic at the bottom of the earth. Back and forth the terns went, every six months, clocking 20,000 miles annually. All their lives, these birds pursue the sun from pole to pole. So that of all the creatures which share our planet, the Arctic tern comes closest, by living on the move, to staying permanently in the light.

I bought a map of the globe and traced onto it the tern's flight path. I followed the bird with a pen, stitching up the world with a long thin yellow line. Then I pinned the tern chart to the ceiling above my bed. Alongside it I placed a map of Iceland, marking with a red star the spot where someone had held my bird. The last things I saw each night were the tern map and the map of Iceland. I fell asleep to the shadow cries of migrant birds, arrivals and departures, ocean-hoppers that came, but never stayed.

Bird stories made my small world bigger, but they could also terrify. When I was nine or ten, I shared a desk in Miss Shaftsbury's nature study class with a boy who boasted an ostrich scar. When Miss Shaftsbury was busy drawing pistils and stamens on the board, Jinky would pull his shirt up and flash his wound at me.

Sometimes, for a dare, Karoo farm boys would do what Jinky had done: play chicken with an ostrich, try to see who could get closest to the nest. And risk getting kicked and clawed by the male ostrich's eighteen-inch front talon. The other risk was getting sat on by an infinitely patient, three-hundred-pound bird. If you lay flat on the ground so the ostrich couldn't kick you, that's how it would punish you instead: sit on you until your ribs and lungs were crushed. If you were lucky enough to wriggle free and run that just meant the forty-five mph ostrich could pursue you and start kicking you again.

Jinky's wound came swooping down from his left shoulder. It turned across his chest and stomach and died above the groin. It had a pinkish ridge and thirty little tracks where the stitches had all been. The scar looked like the railway line that crawled up Africa: Cape to Cairo, page four of our school atlas.

I loved the way Jinky's body told a tale. You only had to watch him soaping his sewn up chest and stomach in the showers after gym, and it all came flooding back. Sometimes he let us finger it. His wound looked best in summer when it puckered in the heat. It was sort of frightening, but we all wished we had one too. A scar was a brilliant thing to have, it made him the kind of boy every other boy dreamed of having on his side whenever there were playground fights. Hey, he'd fought an angry ostrich barehanded and come away OK.

If a new boy joined our class, we'd ask Jinky to repeat his story. He'd grunt and flick back his blond mop of hair. Then, without further encouragement, up his shirt would go like a curtain before a show.

Often, while he explained how to survive an ostrich fight, Jinky would pull at the edges of his wound, like he was trying to open it up for us to see inside. I watched a movie like that once at Rocco Reinhardt's house. Rocco's father played a whole reel backwards while we laughed and screamed. An

Indian had slashed a cowboy with his knife. Rocco's dad just flicked a lever and the cowboy's hole opened and closed, opened and closed, as if he were breathing through his side. Jinky, I thought, would have craved a lever just like that.

Each time, the story he told came out differently. Once, the ostrich had caught him because he'd tripped in an aardvark burrow; another time, it was a honey badger's fault. Often, Jinky's story didn't have burrows in it at all. Sometimes, the ostrich chasing him was half-lame, at other times half-blind. Once or twice, it turned out to have been a two-eyed rapid runner.

I noticed – we all noticed – these inconsistencies. Funny though, we never tried to catch him out. We loved the way his story changed and grew. One thing that kept on growing was Jinky's ostrich – in size and evilness. If dinosaurs were still around, his memory would, I'm sure, have started growing spikes and scales.

Years later, in high school, I spent a weekend under our mulberry tree lost at sea in *Moby Dick*. When I came to Queequeg he made instant sense. It was Jinky. He'd leaped from our world into a book. There he was: his story-telling body, his exquisite scrawl of pain.

Chapter Six

The ostrich is a violent bird, but it was the hoopoe I feared the most. When I was nine, it haunted me, flying slowly through my dreams. It had a flappy, ghostly flight. The lights would go out and there it was, a bird of total terror, waiting in my head.

By day, the hoopoe looked innocent, no bigger than nine inches and brightly coloured: cinnamon, black and white. It wore an Indian crest of feathers that popped up when it called. This gave the bird a startled look, as if it hadn't meant to speak.

The year our Hoopoe Club was founded, I used to watch a pair of them from the safety of my bedroom window. They'd pace up and down our lawn, beaks at the ready. That's what makes a hoopoe a hoopoe: the long, thin, curvy bill – all the better for pulling out worms. I grew obsessed with the way these birds plunged their beaks into the ground, tugging and slurping up earthworms – for breakfast, lunch and dinner. It was a horrifying sight. I've never wanted anything more than I wanted not to turn into a hoopoe that year.

Miss Shaftsbury founded the Hoopoe Club when I was in Standard Two – the American Fourth Grade. She taught us all of our classes. She had a puppety walk and a nose as sharp as Pinocchio's. Miss Shaftsbury couldn't teach without marching back and forth across the room, her legs and arms flung high, as if someone up above were tugging at her strings.

She wore a green, felt hat with speckled pheasant feathers

poking out the top. It perched at crazy angles on her head and often slid off as she stormed about. Her big, dark dresses hung like curtains and made us cough because they swished dust up from the floor.

When Miss Shaftsbury gave her anti-hoopoe demonstration – in the middle of a history class, geography or nature study – we always knew she'd caught someone in the act.

'Class Two A, what do hoopoes do? Wilson?'

'They look for worms, Miss.'

'Exactly, Wilson. Wilson, I'm afraid you are a member! Boys, boys, boys. Now tell me, does this look nice?'

Then Miss Shaftsbury would set off on one of her long marches, giving a lively approximation of a bogey hunt. She'd crook a forefinger at the knuckle and pretend the upper half was stuffed right up her nose. She'd grind and rotate her finger to capture the awful ugliness, chanting all the time: 'Yuk, yuk, yuk.' Up and down she paced, up and down, grinding and marching and shouting 'Yuk, Wilson, yuk.'

'And who do we have to keep Wilson company in the Hoopoe Club today?'

She'd stop and squint at the left-hand corner of the board. Club membership got updated every day. There were two lists: Hoopoe Club A (the diggers), and Hoopoe Club B (the diggers and eaters). I very badly didn't want to belong to either club.

Every year, a pair of hoopoes built a stinky nest in the corner of our roof. They shared the gutter with two starlings who bred at the other end. I lived in dread of turning into a human hoopoe, but Dad hated the starlings the most. They raided our mulberry trees and dribbled purple droppings all down the front of our white house. Dad liked to keep up appearances. He said the starlings make our house look tie-dyed, the kind of place only hippies would want to live in.

Mr Hoopoe shared Dad's dismay. His call always sounded to me like an accusation. Morning and evening, he'd perch on the gutter corner, tuck his beak into his chest and pop up his disapproving crest. Then he'd train one eye on the starlings' trail of purple droppings, the other eye on me and shout for all to hear: 'Who pooh? Who pooh? Who pooh?'

That year in class, whenever I wasn't writing with my hands or sticking them in the air to answer Miss Shaftsbury's questions, I was very careful to sit on them. I hid them in my trouser pockets and gripped the flannel tight inside. Then I tucked them beneath my thighs just in case they tried to wander. That's where my hands spent most of that long year. One day I showed them to Sheelagh, my middle sister. She looked at her hands then looked at mine again. She was worried. She said my hands were flatter than the human average.

The hoopoes were part of a bigger problem: the problem of 'wandering hands'. That seemed to be Miss Shaftsbury's biggest worry in life – the things that happen when your hands begin to wander.

When I turned eleven, Miss Shaftsbury's warnings came flooding back. I had entered that blurry age where I could feel something stirring down there, a tingly something I didn't understand. My voice had begun to crack, new parts were sprouting hair. Miss Shaftsbury's fears returned to me when I discovered sex for the first time.

My first sexual experience was a wildlife affair. It involved ostriches and a pack of jackals. I knew absolutely nothing about sex at the time, though I knew an awful lot about jackals. I could distinguish the tracks of a silver jackal from the more common black-backed kind; I could also tell from the tone of a mother jackal's call whether she had cubs.

I was ill with glandular fever at the time. As a treat, when we were sick, Mom usually let us spend the day in Granny's big, comfy bed. One morning, when Mom was gone, I discovered the key to Granny's wardrobe and opened up that dark, illicit space. Inside, I found all sorts of things: a brandy bottle tucked way in the back; books chewed by fish moths; rows of old lady clothes; wrinkled photographs of men in uniform with big smiles and frightened eyes. Then my hand, running along the hangers in the dark, felt feathers. I gripped and pulled. Out came the ostrich boa that Granny wore to funerals – soft and gorgeous, inky black. I loved the way it snaked through my fingers as I pulled. I tucked it round and round my neck, so warm that the rest of me suddenly felt cold. I angled the wardrobe mirror so I could watch myself all fancy-looking, then tumbled into bed.

The boa shimmered a glossy blue-black in the mirror. It felt right, it felt wrong – it felt like me.

But my body was still shivering, feverish and chilly. So I pulled up Granny's huge kaross, a Xhosa duvet made from ten jackal skins sewn head to toe in two rows of five. At the top, a pack of gouged-out jackal eyes stared into my face.

Was it the fur and feathers, so warm, so dreamy to the touch? Or was it just the thrill of doing wrong and being eye-balled by the dead? When it came to coping with the predators that prowled in Granny's bed, even Little Red Riding Hood was in better shape than me.

When I look back on it, it seems an awkward place for sexual memory to start: somewhere between necrophilia, bestiality and cabaret. First I got excited, then wet, exhausted and utterly confused. I'd managed to escape the Hoopoe Club. But somehow I couldn't stop the wandering in my hands, their desire – despite my iron will – to explore Down Under, to go places they'd never been.

Chapter Seven

Books were northern creatures that seemed to wing their way towards us from as far off as any migrating bird. I could never find the world around me in the words I read. Until, one day when I'd just turned eleven – shortly after my initiation into sex – Dad handed me a book. It was different from all the rest. Purest magic, it changed the way I saw.

I opened the leathery green cover. Inside I found a painting of a sombre, flabby-looking man. He didn't look very promising. Almost bald, owly glasses, a wide-lapelled suit and a tie tied so tight that it made his fleshy neck look fleshier. He looked like a headmaster or one of Dad's dull friends from the mayoral office. His name was Albert Jackson. But as I read, I fell in love with the boy behind the man.

I read Albert Jackson's *Trader on the Veld* so often that sometimes it felt as if I'd dreamed it on my own. I never knew a book could be crammed with so many things, so many places that I knew. As I turned the pages, they all came tumbling out: ostriches, merino sheep, mimosa thorn trees, the Karoo, our town of Port Elizabeth and the Feather Market Hall where I often went with Dad to listen to Gilbert and Sullivan, cello concerts and Christmas oratorios. I was startled to find that hall inside a book. It was a huge, old, ghosted place that always made me feel too young, too small. From Dad's stories and the photos on the walls, I knew that long ago our Feather Market Hall had been a hectic place where crowds of feather buyers from around the world waved and shouted at auctioneers; where merchants and brokers roared, clutching their cables from London and New York as they traded in ostrich plumes. Sometimes when the concerts got boring, I'd stare at the ceiling and picture the hall like it used to be, filled with feather mountains.

Albert Jackson's life held me spellbound – and not just because he wrote about the Feather Market Hall. He was someone who had lived in our town, but came from far away. He'd swapped countries as a boy and, in *Trader on the Veld*, turned two worlds into one story: our desert world on the edge of Africa and the cold north, where books and maps and Gaffy and Granny and migrant birds all came from.

I traced Albert to his village on one of the myriad maps I used to decorate my bedroom walls. Hohensalza was its name: a village in Poland, though then it was called East Prussia. Albert was born there in 1873, eight years after Gaffy. As I hid in Albert's shivery Prussian schoolroom, I could hear Gaffy gasping in the heat next door.

Albert came from snow. He remembered cold, mysterious things I'd never seen and battled to imagine: fur coats, sugar beet and icy fields. Prussia never got hot. When the temperature tipped eighty it was such a miracle that Albert's school shut down for the day. They called the holiday a 'Beneficium Caloris'.

One day, out of the blue, his parents told him they were sending him to Africa. 'The Antisemitic troubles had begun to show themselves,' the adult Albert explained in his low-key way. I now see that as a child I underlined 'Antisemitic' with a question mark pencilled next to it. In the book, Albert never spoke of those things again.

Next he knew, this boy about my age found himself on a mail ship steaming towards an uncle in Port Elizabeth. When he arrived in 1888, Albert had just turned fifteen. The town was bursting with ostrich and wool merchants: the plume boom had begun. Fresh off the boat, Albert saw the newly erected, sandstone Feather Market Hall as something magnificent, a soaring expression of possibility. He met other immigrants, including many Jews, who viewed the South African interior as a place of sudden promise. Word was spreading across Europe about the diamond-diggings in Kimberley, the gold recently discovered near Johannesburg and the flourishing ostrich trade.

Albert soon left coastal Port Elizabeth for the infernal hinterland. Another Prussian Jew, Sigismund Hochschild, had promised him work at his remote trading post. So Albert trekked 800 miles north across the Karoo: beyond Oudtshoorn, beyond Kimberley, all the way to the brink of the Kalahari Desert. The further he travelled north and west, the more the heat rose, the dust thickened, the rainfall sank and the human population seemed to evaporate. Finally, he reached Hochschild's trading post. It lay somewhere between Prieska and Putzonderwater – which means, in Dutch, 'Well Without Water'. Out there on the Victorian frontier, high hopes mostly ran dry.

Albert's new home bordered on the Richtersveld, a moonscape notorious in South Africa to this day because most of the names begin or end in hell. Rainfall averages four inches annually. The mercury squats for months in the nineties, the hundreds and beyond. Here, his Prussian classmates would have been on permanent vacation. Hell: the ultimate Beneficium Caloris.

Two aspects of Albert's story really caught my imagination. One involved sheep, the other ostriches. To supplement his wretched income, Albert became an expert at biting off the balls of sheep. This proved to be a talent worth cultivating: on the immense farms around there sheep castrators were in short supply. As Albert quietly observed, 'Using one's teeth was considered the healthiest method.'

He acquired a reputation for being skilful at the job. Over time, he bit off the testicles of thousands of sheep. He was careful not to lose or swallow the balls – it was important to save them for the farmers' wives. Fried sheep-testicles were a much fancied breakfast delicacy.

It sounded like tough work. I knew that sheep were foolish

animals, but were they foolish enough to give up their balls without a fuss? I had no idea what balls were for. They didn't seem as immediately useful to me as other sticking out bits of my anatomy, like legs and arms. All the same, I had some sense that it might be painful to say goodbye to them. Still, on balance, I sympathized more with Albert than with the wounded sheep.

Albert had ambitions. He knew a dead-end job when he saw one. So after a few years, he left the trading post and turned his thoughts to ostriches. The Victorian vogue for voluptuous, plumed hats had almost reached its peak. Across the hinterland, ostrich had become a byword for quick wealth. The kiss of foreign fashion had turned this toad-ugly bird into a prince, royalty of the veld.

Albert wanted to cash in on the craze. But he was still in his late teens and too poor to buy a farm. Besides, he'd suffered a nasty financial setback. Like many folk in the desert hinterland, he followed the practice of cutting all his bank notes in half before sending them to the bank. The idea was to foil brigands between Putzonderwater and the distant coast. He would wait until he'd heard by wagon mail that his Port Elizabeth bank had received his first pile of severed notes, before dispatching the missing halves. The bank employed somebody to tape the notes together. However, on one such occasion, misfortune struck. The desert journey proved so protracted that in the months between the arrival of Albert's first pile and the second, the bank collapsed, taking literally half Albert's money with it. The other half, still labouring by wagon across the Karoo, was worthless long before it arrived.

But ostriches seemed to offer Albert a genuine chance for a fresh start. So he pushed farther north by oxwagon – into the depths of the Kalahari where he'd heard that wild ostriches thronged. Albert couldn't afford to buy birds and land, but maybe, he figured, he could shoot his way into profiting from the plume boom.

He lived off springbuck too: frisky, lyre-horned antelope so prolific that, some years, they massed in locust numbers before migrating across the Kalahari and Karoo. These travelling buck, or *trekbokke* as they were known, marched by the million inexorably across the desert. Nineteenth-century witnesses reported unbroken herds a 150 miles long and 20 miles wide searching for grass and water. It could take a herd four days to pass. The migrating springbuck left behind them a land so ravaged that it appeared to have been scorched by fire. Travellers reported seeing lions swept to their death, unable to escape the tumbling tidal wave of antelope. Some years, the herds pushed all the way west to the Atlantic desert coast, where the migrant impulse drove tens of drowning thousands out to sea.

Albert Jackson shot springbuck, ate the venison and sold the skins to bookbinders. The white, tan and almond coats made exquisite covers which were cheaper than calf leather. Albert profited from the Kalahari's abundant jackals too, curing the skins and sewing them into karosses, like the one on Granny's bed.

But mainly Albert dreamed of giant, money-spinning birds. With them in mind, he erected a tin shack in the heart of the Kalahari. 'Nothing', he recalls, 'in sight but sand.' Sand and ostriches, shimmering on the skyline like figments of wealth in a prospector's fantasy.

Unfortunately for Albert, he set up camp too far east and some years too soon to reap the full benefits of ostrich hunting. In the coming decades, alluvial diamonds would be discovered along the Atlantic's Skeleton Coast. Humans seldom ventured into that formidable terrain. But those who did made a second profitable discovery – that the local ostriches sometimes swallowed diamonds as a digestive aid among their daily dose of stones. This news meant that feather-hunting and diamond-prospecting could become a single enterprise. The Skeleton Coast lured a new wave of hopefuls who dreamed of shooting their way to a treasure trove buried in some ostrich gut. Sometimes these hunters struck it lucky. Was there ever a more precious creature than the Skeleton Coast ostrich which, in addition to a lustrous feather-cloak, coughed up fifty-three jewels from its diamond-bloated maw?

Albert was in the wrong place and the wrong time to cash in on that particular bonanza. But he had his fair share of fortune. His luck turned with his discovery that the San, the so-called Bushmen, were ancient ostrich hunters far more adept than himself. The word went out that Albert wanted ostrich plumes and soon these Kalahari nomads were bringing them in for barter.

Albert's brief rendition of the San ostrich hunt was for me a marvel. Nothing he wrote – not even his sheep-biting saga – gripped my childhood imagination quite so powerfully. The San are maestros of mimicry. They weave the voices and body talk of desert creatures, from the Kalahari lion to the scorpion, in and out of their fireside performances. But the ostrich hunt involves a death-dealing mimicry of a different order. Each hunter cloaks himself in an ostrich hide and, under cover of his plumes, infiltrates a flock. With an arm or a stick inserted up the neck he bobs his head like the ostriches around him. He pecks at shrubs, snaps at flies on his ostrich body and imitates the prancing gait of the primordial birds around him. Slowly, as he wins the group's trust, he edges ever closer. Then pulls out a bow concealed between his human and his ostrich skins and twangs poisoned arrows into the choicest birds. Such mimicry is not without its perils. It can become too convincing for the hunter's good. Sometimes, a breeding rooster will kick one of these human ostriches to death, believing that his territory has been invaded by a rival male.

A few years after reading *Trader in the Veld*, I began, with Dad and my brother Andy, to search for San paintings in inland caves. Once we came upon an ostrich hunt sketched in black, white and ochre on a wall. Six plump ostriches: one human-legged, with two hands and a tiny bow and arrow protruding from his chest. That painted figure played on my mind for years. I came to see him as Mercury, messenger of the gods, returning in centaur form. The painting also flashed back to me the powerful sensation of first mounting an ostrich and riding it away; how the warm wings felt as they closed around my thighs, until below the waist I had become all feathers and strong bird.

Ostriches were the closest the nomadic San came to owning stock. They depended on these multi-purpose creatures for their livelihood. The dinosaur birds provided roaming hunters with meat, eggs, hides, crockery and jewelry. The women turned the thick shell-shards into necklaces, earrings and ankle-bands.

The San relied on ostriches for the only kitchenware they knew. Unlike the indigenes of the American Southwest, they lived in a world lacking mud and clay. Pottery was unknown. But each ostrich egg, corked with beeswax or grass, could store three gallons of water. The San buried these stoppered eggs full of water for the endless droughts. Sometimes, a trekking San woman would sling a dozen water-filled eggs in a grass bag over her back.

When the San discovered an ostrich nest – which could contain fifteen or twenty eggs – they normally left one or two, so the bird would keep on laying like any barnyard hen. Nest-raiding was a breakneck art. One slip and the raiders could be kicked to death. The rewards, however, were high: gallons of instant protein and a whole new crockery set, as precious as any Wedgwood.

The San lived off other game, but none of it enjoyed the ostrich's versatility. Nor could any other creature inspire these gifted illusionists to such heights of metamorphosis. Their other desert prey were four-legged ungulates: sabre-horned gemsbuck, springbuck, giraffe and eland the magnitude of oxen. But only the erect, two-legged ostrich shared something like its hunters' human shape and posture.

I found it impossible, as a child, to read Albert's brief sketch of a San ostrich hunt without sharing his astonishment. The San's pantomime was good news for his feather business, but in their skilful hunting that's not all he saw. Albert watched these little men turn themselves into birds and was amazed: 'The Bushman's spreading of his wings,' he exclaimed, 'is a work of art.'

Albert's fascination with San ostrich mimicry seems to contain a hint of something else. A thread of fellow-feeling linking this Jewish wanderer to these feathered nomads and a bird with fallen wings. I now hear in his account of humans turning themselves into flightless birds a melancholy note: some recognition of the limits of human escape, something of Icarus perhaps.

Albert Jackson eventually left the desert world of the San and free-range ostriches. He settled in Port Elizabeth, where he became one of our town's most celebrated sons. Chairman of the School Board, the Agricultural Society, the Thrift Committee ... Someone with a municipal imagination, someone my father – an inveterate joiner of local charitable, historical, musical, photographic and botanical societies – was proud to know and wanted me to admire.

But that person didn't interest me. It was the desert adventurer who cast a spell. The roaming immigrant boy who drew a magic line between the bird mimics of the Kalahari, strutting in their ostrich skins, and the grand ladies of Paris, London and New York promenading their lavish plumes. The feather trail he followed made the world seem big and small. For the first time I saw how, when put inside a book, the ordinary things in life – like ostriches – could suddenly seem wild and strange.

Part Two

Chapter Eight

O ur early passions place enormous pressure on reality. But
in the Karoo, this feeling grew for me especially intense.
The scrub desert stretched across the horizon of my childhood as a landscape where truth flickered elusively. The
Karoo was vast and empty-looking – spooky, sometimes – but
I knew it wasn't as barren as it appeared. The desert's natural
life, like its human history was full of hidden, deceptive things.

The ostrich, for one. A hulking bird that could vanish
miraculously by turning itself into a bush. So many other
desert life forms proved equally adept at pretence, at lying
low, at keeping up appearances. In the Karoo, looking like
death could become a way of life. My childhood obsession
with ornithology led me to the scientific term for this deep
camouflage: cryptic colouration. The phrase still has, for me,
a certain sad beauty to it. To take on the colours of the crypt,
the tomb, is to learn through hiding how life shades into
death.

The desert shimmered with illusion. The chameleon, like
the ostrich, seemed to dream of turning into a plant.
Sometimes chameleons wandered from the veld into our
backyard. It must have taken them the better part of a lifetime
to scale our wall; they moved with a patience that was almost
geological. They progressed so tediously and blended so
perfectly they were almost impossible to spot. The
chameleon's whole metabolism seemed organized to resist
the principle of progress. The creature rocked backwards and

forwards, as if debating with itself the merits of true movement. Then finally it would lift one hand and leave it groping in the air, like a drunk half-hoping someone would close his fingers round a drink.

These bug-eyed, four-legged twigs had one advantage over ostriches when it came to playing dead: polychrome disguise. I'd pick up a chameleon and move it from a green branch to a black one or from a yellow leaf to a white flower. Then I'd wait for the skin to melt slowly into its new surroundings. I never tired of watching them change colour as they travelled.

Because the Karoo was so brutally exposed, self-revelation could be costly. I noticed that not just with the creatures, but with the people too. They didn't talk much, were slow to open up. To draw attention to yourself was to ask for trouble, even the plants knew that. Like those succulents called Lithops that made themselves invisible by imitating stones.

These living stones had the gift of hiding in plain sight. It was my father who pointed them out to me. This plump family of succulents came in many kinds. None had stems, they all lay low, hugging the ground in little clusters. Where the stones where white, the stone-mimics wore white too; where the rocks got darker, we found the darker types. Some had grey-green skins, rusted and chipped like weathered rock. One of these mimics the Afrikaners called *volstruistoon*. And it was true: it looked as hard and knobbly as an ostrich toe.

Sometimes, wandering across the desert plains, I'd step on a clump of those pebble-copying plants and feel them give slightly underfoot. And I'd realize that the world beneath me wasn't solid stone, wasn't all that steady.

Only botanists and spring rains could penetrate the stone-mimics' disguise. After a rare storm, they'd send out frilly, canary-yellow flowers, much bigger than themselves. These floral stones always startled me, the way they split open into sudden colour. That was the surest sign of water's power in the Karoo: it could persuade even the rocks to break into bloom.

At night, before I drifted into sleep, I had migration dreams in which I turned into a bird. But the birds around me were dreaming of turning into bushes, and the chameleons of turning into twigs. The plants, too, were dreaming downwards, living enviously among stones.

Looking at the life forms all around me, I became fascinated by disguise. Trusting your eyes didn't do you much good in a place where camouflage went this deep. So long before I understood South Africa's stony politics, the Karoo taught me that things weren't always what they seemed.

Chapter Nine

Igot to know the Karoo in the 1960s, more than half a century after the ostrich boom. Chimeras rippled through this desert world – not just natural ones, but man-made illusions as well. Like the feather palaces that reared up out of nowhere. Dad was driving us through a dust-storm towards Oudtshoorn the first time I saw a feather palace: suddenly, it was there, appearing to have been conjured from pure air. It looked way too big, too fancy to be anybody's home. I stared with a child's amazement at the fantasia of turrets, spikes, columns and twirly gables looming through the dust. I loved the way the roofscape punched holes in the big sky. I'd never seen anything so alien, so magical, so grand.

Dad slowed down and told us the story of the feather palaces. How the ostrich barons had erected them during the height of the feather craze. How the barons had had so much money they'd run out of ways of spending it, so they'd started erecting rival palaces, each one bigger and fancier than the last.

Feather palace: even the phrase seemed to have tumbled from the clouds. Palace wasn't a word that fitted the Karoo. It didn't belong with mimosa thorns, goats, ostriches, drought and sun-scrunched faces. Palace had a greener feel, spoke to me of velvety lands, full of princes and princesses, far away and long ago. The word carried a story-book sound to my childhood ears, an echo of make-believe.

The feather palace ahead of us looked almost edible, as if it belonged to the counter of a giant's confectionery. It was built from huge sandstone slabs, the colour and grainy texture of biscuits. In the late afternoon sun, they gleamed an appetizing yellow. The biscuit-cake boasted a frosting of icing-sugar turrets and frilly, white touches like the paper doilies Mom sometimes used to decorate her cakes. It looked exactly like the kind of delicacy an adoring mother might conjure for a birthday treat.

Oudtshoorn's turn-of-the-century ostrich barons and baronesses were the faux aristocrats of the veld. Nouveaux riches, they made big money fast and wanted to make a big statement with equal speed. Their palaces appeared in a very short time. The first to go up, The Towers, was built in 1903; the last two, Greylands and Pinehurst, in 1911. All nine were the handiwork of two architects: a British settler, Charles Bullock, and a Dutch immigrant who bore the fine name Johannes Egbertus Vixseboxse. Each palace rested on a financial foundation of feathers. And each stood as a reminder to neighbours and passersby that the owners' ostrich wealth bound them to a finer world than the Karoo: a world of salons, promenades, balls and lustrous garden parties where flair, sensuality, fine breeding and profligacy ruled.

I'm holding in my hands a photograph, dated 1887. It shows three ladies chatting at a London garden party. An insectivorous tropical bird teeters on one lady's hat brim, peering over the edge, as if it has spied a worm crawling across her vast monobosom. The lady is engaged in pleasantries with a second grandee who has an entire fox twisted around her hat, biting its own tail. Behind them stands a third figure, partly obscured, wearing what appears to be an arboretum. A stuffed robin crowns the mass of vegetation (moss, satin pansies, cabbage roses) that adorns her head. The robin's beak hangs wide open, frozen in twilight song.

In a second photo, a seagull wing angles across a woman's head, suggesting that the bird crash-landed in her formidable hairdo, mistaking it, perhaps, for a nest or a garbage heap, and that the gull managed to extricate itself only by sacrificing a wing. Sometimes, in her quest for elegance, a woman would complete her outfit by balancing a slaughtered screech owl on her head. An owl in a third fashion photo from the period stares with glass-eyed ferocity at the matron opposite, as if it has smelled a rat. These late Victorian ladies were the original deadheads.

The 1880s and 90s saw the dead come into vogue – most conspicuously, dead feathered things. Humans have long borrowed flamboyance from birds. But such borrowings had never entailed the level of mass slaughter that the closing years of the nineteenth century saw. In England, France and America, the craze for hunting sports was coupled to a rise in the prestige of taxidermy as an art. Stuffed creatures suddenly became de rigueur, appearing as adornments on pub and living rooms walls, on mantelpieces, in hotel lobbies and banks' foyers. This mania for zoological decoration spread to women's hats, until millinery threatened to become an offshoot of taxidermy. These weren't just fussy hats, they were mobile museums.

The vogue for dead animals didn't stop at birds. Suffocated butterflies, reptile skins and fish scales complemented the bigger, stuffable things. A salon of posh hats could boast almost as much wildlife as a square mile of English countryside. Hats grew taller to support all the bric-a-brac. Not just piles of bird remains, but violets and roses and bluebells too, wired bows of lace and velvet, bronze buckles and steel ones, scads of jewelery and frothy veils of tulle, net and gauze. Trimmings seems too frail a word for such voluptuousness. Hat-crowns often rose to extraordinary heights, as popular designs of the time suggest – like the 'sugarloaf' and 'three storeys and a basement'.

More than a hundred years on, it is hard for us to picture a time when to appear hatless in public constituted a breach

of taste scarcely less acute than appearing with
It is even harder to picture the murderous
borne in the name of beauty by late Victoria
necks.

In the quest for extravagance and upward lift, the ostrich feather had no rivals. A prime plume could tower twenty-two inches above the head, while smaller ostrich feathers added foamy volume. The giant bird's feathers had been used for adornment since the Roman empire, but in the 1880s they became stylish as never before. The stage was set for the world's first ostrich boom.

Even after the century turned and the stiff corpses of Victorian taxidermy became passé, ostrich feathers stayed in vogue. Cascading things came in: crêpe de Chine, satin, chiffon, lace, tulle, chenille and wilting feathers, as *belle-époque* fashions grew frothier. Ostrich plumes again had no equal, this time in evoking flutter, bobbing and flouncing with every dip of the hatted head.

The Colonial Ostrich Feather Company on London's Oxford Street prided itself on being 'the originators of Direct Supply from Bird to Buyer'. By 1910, the company was promoting forty different styles of hats with ostrich trim – like 'dainty Marie Antoinette ostrich ruffles to fasten at the neck with satin ribbons'. Among Colonial Ostrich's many rivals for the brisk trade in plumed hats, ostrich stoles and swirling eighty-inch boas, were two Long Island based enterprises: Pan-American Ostrich and the African-American Ostrich Corporation.

Hat brims grew more and more voluminous, spilling the bric-a-brac of imperial trade. By 1913, some hats had reached two yards in circumference, requiring homicidal eighteen-inch hat pins to prevent them flapping away. By 1913, a single top-notch ostrich plume fetched twelve pounds, roughly the cost of the four-week sea voyage from England to South Africa. By 1913, only gold, diamonds and wool were more pivotal to South Africa's economy than the nation's one million ostriches. By 1913, foreign fashion consumed 100,000 tons of Karoo feathers annually. By then, ostrich ranching was making people richer faster than any other kind of farming anywhere in the world.

Chapter Ten

It is fair to say that in the 1860s no Lithuanian Jew was dreaming of a career in ostriches. Or of starting life anew at the bottom of Africa. Especially not the Karoo: a quarter of a million arid square miles where rain and the sighting of another human were memorable events.

But in 1867 a Khoikhoi child's discovery of a glistening pebble in the South African hinterland began to change all that. A local trader, testing the pebble on his storefront window, found that it cut glass. In the great diamond-rush that followed, the colony drew prospectors from around the globe. Migrant mining camps – Cawood's Hope, Delport's Hope, Good Hope, Last Hope – sprang up near where the Hope Diamond had been found. Kimberley and the Cape Colony were suddenly names that spelled hope in foreign dreams.

Diamonds brought the first wave of Jewish settlers to South Africa. Some made fortunes so vast that Sir Ernest Oppenheimer, the wealthiest magnate of them all, declared: 'Jews *are* diamonds.' Soon Jews would be ostrich feathers too.

At the time, ostriches seemed headed for extinction: plume-hunters were slaughtering them right across their range. The giant birds didn't exactly aid their own survival. When panicked they run at great velocity but also typically in a circle, which rather defeats any advantage they gain from speed. Their natural enemies – lions, cheetah, African hunting dogs – know this and try to cut them off across the

61

diameter. (Some biologists have speculated that ostriches fraternize with zebra and gazelles because, when a predator is spotted, the ungulates help the birds run in a straight line.) This weakness for circular escape gave colonial hunters ample pot shots. They would fire away while their quarry swung round and round them like painted ostriches bobbing on a fairground carousel.

In 1869, just two years after the discovery of diamonds, an inventive Scotsman called Arthur Douglass radically improved the ostrich's chances of survival. He did so by perfecting, on his Cape farm, the world's first ostrich incubator. He called it the Eclipse. Unlike most of his fellow frontiersmen, Douglass recognized that if you clipped an ostrich instead of putting a bullet in its head, you could turn the bird into a renewable resource. Every nine months, like clockwork, it would reward you with a harvest of exquisite feathers. Soon, armed with an Eclipse, a captive flock and pruning shears, any indigent immigrant could dream of making a fortune from ostriches.

The grand era of ostrich feather fashion – from 1881 to World War One – coincided with the high age of Jewish immigration. By the 1860s, South Africa boasted a total of just one rabbi. The place had been virtually untouched by the emigration of German Jews in the first half of the nineteenth century. There was nothing to entice them: no diamonds, no gold, no ostrich trade and little they would have recognized as culture. Even in the feather age, Jewish immigrants to South Africa weren't as diverse as those drawn to America. Almost without exception, they came from a single region: the *shtetls* of Lithuania.

These Litvaks, as they were known, were frontiersfolk already, used to living on the edge. But the frontier they inhabited was a crowded place: the Pale of Settlement along Russia's western limit. The Pale dated back to the late eighteenth century, when Catherine the Great seized a large slice of Poland and with it 400,000 Jews. Catherine – and the Tsars who followed her – barred Jews from settling freely in

Russia, confining them to the Pale. By the end of the nineteenth century, that narrow corridor held three-and-a-half million Jews, twenty times the number spread across the rest of Russia's immensity.

Under Tsarist tyranny, Jews suffered double taxation, forced conscription and were barred from owning farmland. Military 'recruiters' invaded villages, kidnapping young boys. Pogrom followed pogrom. After Alexander II's assassination in 1881, these assaults reach a new pitch of viciousness. That year, anti-Semites attacked 265 *shtetls* – Jewish villages and small towns – across a swathe of southern Russia. Within months, the Tsarist government issued relocation decrees, uprooting Jews by the hundreds of thousand and packing them into cities. There, most languished in terror and joblessness.

The Pale Jews knew little enough about America. But South Africa must have seemed galaxies away. Rumours began to circulate about a place deep in the African desert where a person could grow rich herding huge flightless birds. Some Lithuanian refugees fell captive to this dream. They became a new kind of argonaut, risking everything in their search, not for the golden fleece, but for almost equally mythical gigantic golden geese.

Before chancing their luck on the gruelling voyage from the Pale to the Karoo, what could these Jews have known of ostriches? Certainly, no *shtetl*-dweller is likely to have seen an ostrich in the flesh. The ostrich must have appeared to them as a creature of the mind, a dreambird, weighing in the scales of reality not much more than a unicorn.

Perhaps some stranger passed through the villages bearing an ostrich plume. But a large feather is still just a feather: frail evidence for the existence of a money-spinning bird eight-feet tall and weighing as much as two local men. A feather could be a hoax. After all, European explorers used to return from Greenland's seas brandishing the narwhal's corkscrew tusk as proof of the unicorn's materiality.

Jewish refugees who fled to late-Victorian South Africa usually followed a set course. From Lithuania to the Russian port of Libau, then on to England where they were housed at the London Jews' Temporary Shelter. There they awaited documents that would grant them entry to the Cape, then still a British colony. Finally, at Southampton, the gangplank closed behind them and they set sail for Africa's farthest extremity.

Many of those who boarded were, like Albert Jackson, children travelling alone. One woman, fearing separation from her five progeny in a land of strangers and strange tongues, took the precaution of sewing squares of her dress material onto the clothes of each daughter and son. That way, she prayed, the family bonds would be visible to all.

On arriving in South Africa, many Litvaks clung to Cape Town, the only city of any consequence. Others headed north for the mining madness of Kimberley and, after 1886, Johannesburg, where gold had been discovered. Some bolder families trekked to Oudtshoorn, hazarding the Karoo's extremities – like the furnace summer that consumed most of the spring and autumn too. But in the midst of this sprawling scrub desert, the Jewish newcomers also found new liberties. At last, they were free to own land, work at their chosen occupations and worship unmolested. Word spread that this ostrich oasis offered religious sanctuary. Soon Oudtshoorn had acquired a new name – *Yerushalayim shel d'rom Afrika*, the Jerusalem of Africa.

Has there ever been a Promised Land that wasn't brutally cleared of its inhabitants to make it more mythically promising? The Jews were refugees. But they were also – like all South Africa's Europeans – invaders too.

Since the eighteenth century, white settlers had fought episodic wars against the Nguni in the lush lands to the east of the Karoo. The spoils were those frontier fundamentals: grazing rights, cattle, water, land. But the late-nineteenth-century rush of immigrants from Europe, including

Lithuania, coincided with a sudden change in the scale and urgency of British designs on South Africa. The discovery of the world's richest gold and diamond fields was transforming the region into prime imperial real estate. Hope was twinned with greed.

The mines sucked in poor immigrants from around the world. But those same mines became sinkholes for African aspirations, soon turning Africans into involuntary migrants in their own land. The colonial magnates started to demand armies of cheap labour for their diggings. So the authorities built those armies by spreading poverty, levering African farmers off their land with taxes, wars and seizures. The newly dispossessed began trailing back and forth between mining misery and their shrinking lands. 'Migrant labourers' seems a rough euphemism for people so cynically uprooted and driven into lives of restless indigence.

The Karoo itself possessed neither mineral wealth nor fertile grazing: it was too parched to sustain many people. But when nineteenth-century Jews and Afrikaners both started dreaming of it as their Promised Land, people had been living there for at least 20,000 years. The Karoo belonged first to the San, roving hunter-gatherers whose claim on the land colonials and non-nomadic Africans could readily discount. Kraals (corrals), fenced property, branding and personal livestock were all alien to San notions of belonging. Over the millennia, they had learned to live lightly within the limits of a dry, fragile land that punished the profligate. They had found a way to dwell in movement, respecting the desert's slender margin of survival by following the seasons and wild herds. But to the settlers, the San were drifters without a claim. A herdless people, they lost out to pastoralists competing for their terrain.

The advancing whites and their flocks denuded the Karoo of game – the antelope, zebra, giraffe and ostriches on which the San's survival depended. The whites erected fences, interrupting the free flow of migrating animals and the San who followed them. These nomads, in turn, approached the settlers' livestock as they would any herds of game, shooting them when hungry with bows and poisoned arrows. During the eighteenth and nineteenth centuries, *trekboers* and Brits slaughtered the San relentlessly, treating them as little more than vermin. So by the time the Lithuanian Jews arrived, the Karoo's first inhabitants were virtually extinct.

The Khoikhoi, the other people indigenous to the area, fared little better. Pastoralists themselves, they had no answer to the Europeans with their horses and advanced technologies of decimation. Most ended up working as servants and farm labourers for the victors in the land wars: Khoikhoi culture vanished beneath a history of conquest and assimilation. But to this day, most of the Karoo's inhabitants are Afrikaans-speaking mixed-race coloureds who trace their ancestry back to the Khoikhoi, the San, the Dutch, the Huguenots, the Xhosa and the British, as well as to slaves from the East Indies and the coasts of West and East Africa.

Chapter Eleven

Ihave on my desk before me a bureaucrat's list of fifty-one Oudtshoorn Jews who, between 1883 and 1890, became naturalized. In official memory, no women are listed: they remain invisibly in tow behind their fathers, husbands, brothers and uncles. Of those fifty-one new male citizens, thirty-six gave the identical profession of 'feather buyer'. For these refugees, owning land and ostriches was a pervasive fantasy. But in the 1880s they were still too poor: they had first to find some other foothold in this strange, overlit, arid land. Most took up feather buying.

'Feather buyer': it sounds professional, respectable. One envisages a merchant and a sprawling warehouse, a background din of money being made, of bidders and auctioneers. But in those early days, a feather buyer was really a feather walker. That's what his job required: walking. Then walking some more. Across the immense scrub desert, up the mountains, down the other side and back again. The Afrikaners referred to these tireless newcomers as *loper-Jode*, foot-slogging Jews.

Through his labours, the foot-slogging Jew bequeathed a neologism to the Yiddish language. *Shmoyzer* – a transliteration from the local Dutch word *smous* – the term for travelling peddler. The *smous* or *shmoyzer* schlepped his way from one remote Afrikaans farm to the next. He traded in much more than feathers, carrying a leather bag of goods for barter slung over his buckled back. In that dusty wilderness, money possessed an uncertain reality, but goods were goods. The *smous* and *boer* often swapped them directly without need for cash.

The novice 'feather buyer' was little more than a wandering shopkeeper. He made ends meet by trading combs, brushes, scissors, mirrors, pots, pans, caster-oil, chew-tobacco, snuff, pumpkins, brandy, salt and buckets. But all the time he kept one eye on his plume-dreams. From children and coloured labourers he'd buy cut-price feathers that had fallen off a transport wagon or blown across the farm. These modest pickings the *smous* would carefully store in a separate leather bag.

In the absence of real roads, the feather buyer followed the dry river beds which offered at least a semblance of a route through a landscape that must have seemed disorientingly featureless. But even the river beds were rugged going. An almost infinite variety of thorn-clad bushes slashed at the *smous*'s clothes. Rocks slit his feet. Sand, endless sand, seeped into his shoes. And the African sun bore down on him with unfamiliar hostility, adding its heaviness to his bag.

As soon as he could he bought a donkey. Later, he'd trade the donkey for a horse and cart. Strictly speaking, by then he was a *smous* no more. With a horse and cart, he'd graduated into a *tokher* – still a roving, but no longer a foot-slogging, Jew.

By early Edwardian times, some Oudtshoorn Jews had made enough money to purchase their own ostriches and join the ranks of the fashion farmers. No-one made the ascent from *shtetl* to *smous* to ostrich baron more spectacularly than Max Rose.

In 1890, nine Rose brothers and sisters emigrated from the *shtetl* of Shavel, all heading for new worlds. They fanned out across the globe: Baltimore, New York, the English home counties, Cape Town and Oudtshoorn. Max's parents sent him to join an uncle in South Africa; the boy reached the Karoo when he was just sixteen. Even before he boarded ship, he'd probably heard rumour of the lucrative dinosaur birds from letters received in Lithuania. Whatever his expectations, within a few short years of landing at the Cape, he'd become the world's wealthiest fashion farmer.

On arrival, Rose bought his leather bag and set off, with all the other *smouse*, on the weekly trek across the Karoo. But he was too ambitious to linger at that level. Rose arm-twisted a more established immigrant into becoming his business partner. Together they built a rickety store alongside a mission station, in the middle of the mapless boondocks. For two years, Max ran the store. But bartering pots and pans for pumpkins and eggs couldn't hold him for long. He was impatient to get his hands on ostriches, which he saw as living gold. Lacking the capital to buy land, he rented some acreage and ran a small flock of cut-rate birds on it.

After a few seasons of plume profits, Rose had saved enough money to buy his first ostrich farm. He had just turned thirty-two. His farm was called *Weltevreden*, Dutch for 'well-satisfied'. But Rose was far from content. About the capricious cycles of fashion there was little he could do. But he could, he thought, rectify that other great source of instability – the cycles of drought that tormented the Karoo.

Rose became the first South African farmer to think in terms of irrigation. He built a skein of canals and introduced lucerne (alfalfa). Ostriches adore lucerne. In 1906, Rose had paid £18,000 for *Weltevreden*; seven years later, he got £200,000 for it. He sold the farm, but kept on buying others – more and more of them. Mostly scrappy-looking scrub-desert lots. But the mix of ostriches, irrigation and lucerne soon transformed them into the most profitable farmland in the world.

Rose knew at gut-level the meaning of land-hunger. Back in the Pale of Settlement, the Russian authorities had barred Jewish families from owning farms. But two decades after trading a claustral *shtetl* for the Jerusalem of Africa, Max Rose had risen to become one of the Karoo's largest landowners and the world's undisputed ostrich king.

Resourcefulness evidently ran in the family: three of his brothers also became millionaires. But they didn't try to make their millions off something as obvious as ostriches. Max's brothers, Barney and Albert, hatched a more offbeat scheme involving locusts – the curse of the Karoo. The insects rolled across the skies in huge, Biblical thunderclouds. In an hour or less, a farmer could be ruined. But the Rose brothers believed that one nation's curse could be alchemized into another's blessing. All it took was a little creativity. So they decided to get into the dehydrated locust export business. Their target market: English chicken farmers.

The Rose brothers' first shipload of dead locusts hadn't been properly dried and somewhere off the coast of West Africa, the cargo started to stink. By the time they got to England, the insects were positively inedible. However, no Rose ever admitted quick defeat. More locusts were caught, dried and crated; a second shipload set sail. This time, the English chickens got to dine on Karoo locusts. But most of the chickens promptly died: the locusts had been killed with arsenic.

Barney and Albert abandoned their locust dreams and emigrated to England. There they founded one of the country's largest market-gardening businesses. They did finally make their millions, but only by turning their talents to a life form as prosaic as the vegetable.

Max Rose was worth, in today's money, around three hundred million dollars. He became *the* living authority on ostriches, a self-taught agricultural ornithologist. Rose was said to recognize – by body talk, plume pedigree and temperament – every individual among the tens of thousands of ostriches he owned.

But his vocation also required him to become an urbane cosmopolitan. He had to master – and, more importantly, anticipate – the vagaries of high fashion. He learned to mingle with millinery mavens and couturiers in the salons of Paris, London, New York and Vienna. He would spend one month with his primordial birds in the Karoo, the next month consorting with Parisian popinjays. That's how he split his life:

between his ugly-mugged, blue-blooded birds and Europe's often equally unlovely blue-blooded aristocracy.

Despite his abundant farms, Rose chose to keep no home. He prefered to rent a room in a hotel, as if at heart he were always ready to pick up and move again. He lived simply, but at a furious pace; his only hobby his violin. Lights out by eight p.m., rising four hours later: his working day began at midnight.

Rose died in 1951, aged seventy-eight. He remained a bachelor all those years, wedded only to his ostriches.

Chapter Twelve

Oudtshoorn's ostrich elite – whether Jews, Afrikaners or Scots – were typically pious people who came from simple backgrounds. In this, they hardly differed from their desert neighbours who farmed tobacco and sheep. But rubbing shoulders with the sophisticates of European haute couture, whom they hosted on their Oudtshoorn farms, the ostrich barons began to hunger for some swank themselves. And so the palace idea caught on.

The feather palace walls were typically built from local sandstone, cut and dressed by immigrant Scottish masons. Karoo sandstone was cheap but hardly prosaic. The architects, Bullock and Vixseboxse, turned the ochre stone to brilliant advantage, responding, like their contemporaries, California's Mission Revival architects, to desert textures and light. The Karoo sun gilded the sandstone palaces, giving them a royal gleam. Visitors remarked how the sandstone and light called to mind Oudtshoorn's fantasy twin, Jerusalem. And so these rough-hewn walls supported not just the palaces but the town's necromantic allegory. Here, in the Jerusalem of Africa, sand, like ostriches, could be turned to gold.

The *Gormenghast* roofscapes of the palaces that have survived seem to mock Oudtshoorn's tight-wrapped Calvinism and the encircling landscape's dour aridity. Some stand in solitary splendour on isolated farms; others stand in town, intimidating the box houses that surround them. The typical feather palace is a grab-bag of allusions: the ostrich barons and their architects mastered the art of the magnificent mis-match. Uniformity of style was beside the point. Everything, it seems, was deemed potentially appropriate so long as it had once – somewhere, some time – evoked opulence.

Baroque parapets, pyramidal turrets, gazebos and Spanish arches mingle with neo-Cape Dutch gables, cast-iron porticoes, an iron lace tympanum, red Belgian fish-scale tiling and odd borrowings from the dreamlife of a Byzantine potentate. In some palaces, faux Romanesque columns poke through a wide colonial veranda. Iron trimmings in an art-nouveau idiom – tulips or fleur-de-lis – usually frame the veranda rim. (These are often scrambled with classical designs, like honeysuckle and acanthus.) Ornate barge-boarding on the rooftops, teak balustrades on the stoep, triangular bay windows, stained-glass mullioned windows and generous genuflections in the direction of Victorian Gothic all add to the atmosphere of promiscuous fantasmagoria.

Inside, the rooms are darkish, as dark as anything in the fiercely overlit Karoo. The architects' attempts to filter out the sun suggest a touch of cultural cringe: as if light itself were philistine and sophistication could only flourish in a European gloom.

Few local materials were used: sandstone, yellowwood beams, stinkwood for chairs. For the rest, the decor is a medley of Europe, the British Empire and North America. Art-nouveau brasswork embellishes Burmese teak doors. An English Adams fireplace with an Indian rosewood frame dominates a living room stuffed with Persian carpets, satin-wood furniture, French chandeliers and ponderous Viennese curtaining. A Swiss music box squats on a hand-carved German dresser.

The stucco cornices and dados were made from com-pressed papier mâché. The Belgian stained-glass windows – a palace signature – were set in copper not in lead. Beneath them, art-nouveau tulip lamps from cranberry glass cast pools of pinkish gloom. French mirrors flicker in the hallways and bedrooms; brass beds peer from behind folds of Irish lace.

Blue and white delft tiles decorate some palace kitchen floors, Italian marble graces others. Like all imported materials, the marble was shipped from Europe to the Cape coast, then hauled by oxwagon over the formidable Outeniqua Mountains and into the Karoo.

Inter-palace rivalries soon flared between the ostrich barons. Which baron had the tallest tower? Who could boast the biggest bath? The palace on the farm *Welgeluk* triumphed in the bathroom contest, with a personally commissioned lion-footed tub that held 1,300 litres of water, enough to keep a small family submerged.

The barons did what the desert rich do everywhere, from Arizona and Southern California to Mexico, Iraq and Saudi Arabia. They spelled out their wealth in water and in lawns. It was the obvious way to flash their opulence. When nothing is more priceless than rain, tinkling water and the sheen of well-fed grass become trademark ways to announce that you've moved beyond reach of scarcity. Desert money is a universal currency: it is always blue and green.

So each palace had its emerald spread. Peacocks and ostriches paraded there together – dreambirds of foreign and local royalty. Beyond the palace limits sprawled the parched thorn desert, beyond that, the jawline of the Swartberg Mountains, and beyond that, more desert again.

I discovered the feather palaces in the 1960s, a brutally conservative decade in South Africa – doubly so in a town like Oudtshoorn. By that stage, an aura of scandal had attached itself to them. There was an Afrikaans phrase which fixed that sense of outrage in my mind. '*Broekie*-lace' – panty lace, a reference to the delicate filigree of ironwork that decorated the palace turrets, rooftops, verandas, gates and fences. The ironwork did have exactly that embroidered look. But in Sixties' South Africa, the very word *broekie* had an illicit ring. What kind of person would decorate their mansion to look like ladies' underwear? In an era of Calvinist repression, the palaces hung with *broekie*-lace warned against the dangers of godless minds and wandering hands.

My palace visits loom in childhood memory as redemptive things. One visit, in particular. I must have been twelve or thirteen at the time, when I travelled to Oudtshoorn on a school brass-band tour of the dry hinterland. It was a unpromising enterprise. We played dust-bowl parks in Afrikaner-dominated dust-bowl dorps – Jansenville, Willowmore, Oudtshoorn – wending our way from one sad town square to the next. During the long bus trips, I'd tune in to creaking iron barriers beside the road and listen to them absorb the day's furnace fury.

A cranky Yorkshireman – whom we called Mr Music – ran the band with the brutal nostalgia of a frustrated immigrant. He wanted us to look and play like the great British bands of yore. So he fitted us with woollen uniforms made specially in Leeds: stiff navy trousers, a heavy scarlet tunic, blue-black epaulettes and a leaden bus conductor's cap for warming up the head. Ideal plumage for Blackpool Pier, less so for the Karoo.

As a bandsman, I had a weakness for fainting, sometimes denting my E-flat saxhorn in the fall. On this trip to Oudtshoorn, it happens again: my body buckles beneath the mind- and metal-bending heat. One moment, I'm scanning the thin crowd of sun-ruined faces, pumping my valves, giving Dvořák my best. Next thing, I feel the desert gather in my head, my brain boil over, the scene sway and liquefy. Then I hit the dirt, adding an unscripted cymbal crash to the *New World* symphony.

When I come round, someone has dragged me to the side. The band plays on while I stagger off in search of shade. Released from the band, I don't want to go back, and something in me keeps walking through the clenched streets of this town. I pass a copper monument of cannons, wagons and men twisted together in pain: a memorial to the fallen of the Anglo-Boer War. That's seventy years ago, but in a place like Oudtshoorn the wounds of history are barely cauterized.

Every few years a plague of flightless locusts – red hoppers – descends on the Karoo. *Rooi baatjies*, the farmers still call them, redcoats, commemorating, even now, the pestilential British scourge.

I attract some dubious looks as I sway down Oudtshoorn's streets. My scarlet tunic, my sweaty pallor, my glinting silver buttons: exactly the kind of Brit whom Boer snipers used to pick off easily against the stark, dun-coloured veld. I must look like a straggler from some long lost regiment, emerging from a Swartberg Mountain cave to the belated news that the Boer forces have surrendered.

I pass two derelicts sucking rotgut brandy on a culvert. They stare at me then at each other with an air of disbelief.

'What the fuck is that?'

'That's a spook, man. *Nagspook op dagdiens.*' Nightghost on dayduty.

I continue twitching down the road like some phantom limb of history.

Six tanks rumble past, followed by jeeps and armoured cars – down from the massive infantry base angled on the hill. All the soldiers are tanned to the colour of their fatigues, so it's hard to tell where the uniform ends and the man begins. Too many soldiers here, too many churches as well. Oudtshoorn seems overrun with moral and military police. It's palpable in the streets: the disapproval, the paranoia, the air of imminent brutality.

Then I stumble upon a camel-coloured palace that I've never been inside. A fringe of delicately flowered iron-railings separates the palace from the street. It's open to the public so I duck up the stairs and through the doors. Crossing the palace threshold, I feel a rush of sudden cool. The walls are thick, the ceilings high, all outside sounds obscured. Pure silence, except for one wobbly fan writhing rhythmically.

It's a relief to be inside, alone. My sun-tightened pupils start to open in the amber gloom. As I move from room to room, I find myself surrounded by cocoons of luxuriance: yellow velvet couches, loose folds of lace slung past pillowy beds, stained-glass windows whorled with carmine and indigo. Here the world seems sensual and curved. The rooms reverberate with the soft rustlings of the past. They stir something in my awkward, changing body, stranded between the shadowlands of childhood and an adolescent's stark sexuality.

From a boudoir tallboy I pick up a vanity mirror set in silver and mother-of-pearl. It sprouts, from the top, a spray of diminutive white ostrich feathers. The mirror startles me with an accidental glimpse of my scarlet-tunicked self. I look like a bit of history myself – a museum exhibit that has wandered from its plinth.

How many mirrors there are. In our family, mirrors smack of self-indulgence and decadence. I'm not used to them, especially such operatic ones. They make the rooms – and the past they represent – seem even bigger. But through the looking-glass it's not just the past I see. This bolthole of a world feels like the future too. It gives me an unexpected rush of hope, glimpses of another way of living where the senses aren't smothered with reprimand and fear. A place where flights of fancy are free to flex their wings.

I'm loathe to leave this quirky palace. It seems to conspire with me against the brutality, the piety, the blankness of the town outside. But I need to find the band.

As I leave, I spot a blue porcelain jar resting on a foyer table. It's the shape and size of an ostrich egg but it doubles as the world. A trail of white porcelain honeysuckle wanders through the continents engraved on it. The egg-globe is hinged at the middle: it's obviously a biscuit jar. I open it, using the handle – a carved figurine of a child. I hold him carefully between my fingers, this three-inch boy in yellow knee-length trousers, perched atop an ostrich egg, the world spread beneath his feet.

Chapter Thirteen

During the feather-palace era, South Africa was desperate to hold on to its global domination in the field of ostriches. But by 1911, California breeders were importing the big birds hand over fist. So that year, a cabal of South African politicians and ostrich buffs met and hatched a covert plot. Their plan: to foil the upstart Americans in the coming feather wars.

What the country needed, the clandestine gathering agreed, was a dreambird so magnificent it would blow the competition away. So on 31 July, 1911 a government-bankrolled expedition set sail secretly from Cape Town for the Sahara. Their brief: to track down an elusive, almost mythological creature called the Barbary ostrich and bring it back alive. For ten months, the men would labour across oceans, rivers and deserts in pursuit of the perfect ostrich. Their venture became a sort of ornithological, El Dorado quest with a plotline that could easily have been lifted from an H. Rider Haggard novel.

The Americans were a problem. But so was what we now call genetic drift. South Africa's finest ostriches had sprung from a happy genetic accident. In the 1870s a Karoo farmer had crossbred some local birds with four ostriches smuggled into the country from somewhere in North Africa. Their off-spring boasted unimaginably opulent plumes. Those four legendary birds became known as the Barbaries. But after forty years, the Barbaries' descendants were getting dangerously inbred. Clearly, what Karoo ostriches needed to crush the American competition was a fresh infusion of Barbary blood.

The clandestine scheme to build an *uber*-ostrich in South Africa hinged on two words: double floss. This was the trade name in fashion circles for the immaculate plumes associated with the Barbary mix. Dense, springy, curly feathers with an exquisite gloss, they fetched fourteen times the standard price. In *belle-époque* Paris and Edwardian London, couturiers went to sleep dreaming double floss.

The South Africans chose thirty-year-old Russell Thornton to lead their covert operation. He had proved his mettle fighting for the British in the Anglo-Boer War. Two other ostrich hunters were to accompany him: Dick Bowker, a farmer, and Frank Smith, a twenty-two-year-old feather whizz.

But first Thornton needed some clue as to the Barbary's whereabouts. All he had to go on was a vague memory and a dream. Old-timers recalled that the original Barbaries had been shipped during the 1870s to Port Elizabeth from Marseilles. But before that? Some folk thought the birds derived from Morocco, others thought from Libya, others still, Algiers. The ostriches themselves could have been captured anywhere in the Sahara, an area as vast as the United States.

The British government rallied their consuls to the cause of Thornton's feather quest. Wherever ostriches wandered wild – Kenya, Nigeria, Algeria, Morocco, Somalia, the Levant, French West Africa – the local consul received directives to buy ostrich plumes and ship them to Thornton at his agricultural college in the Karoo.

Parcel after parcel arrived. All duds. Finally, a bag of plumes arrived from Tripoli. Superb – clearly Barbaries. But the British consul in Tripoli knew nothing of their origins except that Arab traders had bought them from a caravan crossing the French Sudan.

Armed with this scanty information, Thornton and his men sailed for North Africa. They left secretly. If news of the scheme spread to America, they risked setting off an international ostrich chase. It was a matter of national urgency that Thornton and his men find the lost Barbary birds first. The government also feared a tax-payers' revolt if it became known that public money was being lavished on a trans-Saharan ostrich hunt.

When Thornton vanished from his job, his family announced that he'd gone to England 'to look at cattle'. But the rumour-mill started rumbling. A Cape newspaper claimed that Thornton's men had instructions to capture a hundred Barbary ostriches and slit the throats of any others they could find – to prevent rival nations from adding Barbaries to their breeding stock.

One Karoo farmer protested, in an irate letter to *The Cape Times*, that the expedition was an insult to all South Africans: 'a way of telling the world our ostriches aren't good enough'. Besides, he said, the Barbary bird was apocryphal: 'It exists only in the imagination of Mr Thornton and his government.'

The journey from Cape Town to Southampton took the Trans-Saharan Ostrich Expedition seven weeks. In London, they were outfitted by Messrs Fortnum and Mason of Piccadilly and picked up a translator, an English sergeant-major seasoned in West Africa. Thornton travelled briefly to Paris. There he met clandestinely with a man named only as Hassin, a wealthy Jewish-Arab trader intimate with the North African feather scene. 'Hassin,' Thornton confided to his diary, 'proved most useful.'

On 20 September, the Barbary mission sailed south, sliding down the western bulge of Africa: past Grand Canary, Dakar, Sierra Leone, Monravia, Accra and Lagos. On dropping anchor in Forcadas Harbour, at the mouth of the Niger, the men changed from an ocean-going vessel to a river steamer and began their 500 mile passage upstream.

Thornton kept a meticulous record of the expedition's every phase. His diary echoes at times with the brooding tone of *Heart of Darkness*, Joseph Conrad's colonial classic which had appeared just ten years before. Like Conrad's Congo River, Thornton's Niger menaces and fascinates. The diary reveals a man by turns alarmed and charmed by the seamless forest and the watery silences enveloping him. Thornton marvels at the river pilot's skill as he charts a faultless course through channels, creeks, snags and overhangs.

At Baro, 500 miles inland, further river travel proved impossible. The members of the expedition disembarked, smartened up and over a five-course dinner assessed the local administration. (Thornton's view: 'Met Resident, not much of a chap.') Next day they left by rail for the ancient walled town of Zaria. The journey led them through hilly country, thinly populated but teeming with game. At Zaria's crumbling portals the railway ran out. From there they'd have to proceed on foot.

Meanwhile, back in South Africa, a scandal had erupted. Thornton's brother, Ernest, had resigned mysteriously from his job as a government agricultural officer. A newspaper report suggested that Ernest had defected to the Americans. This rumour gave rise to a fable of two brothers, one noble, the other treacherous; one risking his life for his country in the Saharan wastes, the other selling his soul and the nation's ostrich secrets to the Americans.

Ernest later cleared his name. He did cross the Atlantic but only as a South African spy. A predatory California ostrich syndicate had headhunted him, promising him a lucrative job for life. But Ernest turned them down: American birds, he wrote, were junk. However, he was awestruck by the newly erected Roosevelt Dam and by the 200-mile strip of irrigated alfalfa (every ostrich's favourite food) which he witnessed in Arizona. If the Yanks got their hands on some Barbaries, Ernest reported back, they could become the greatest ostrich power the world had ever known.

This news added urgency to his brother's expedition. Russell Thornton, by this stage, had reached Zaria, on the lip of the Sahara. There he recruited 107 Hausa porters. He loaded them with supplies and silver, which he'd been warned was the only acceptable coinage in the French Sudan. Then the convoy began their trudge on foot into the desert.

After some skirmishes with Tuareg raiders, the expedition reached the ancient Islamic city of Kano in northern Nigeria. Caravans bearing plumes to Europe had passed through this city for centuries. Having won over the local emir, Thornton began to scrutinize every passing camel-borne plume for a hint of Barbary pedigree. It was microscopic, melancholy work. Most of what he saw was ragged stuff, grim parodies of the feather he cradled in his dreams.

By day, vultures ringed the camp kitchen; by night, hyenas howled and guffawed. There was also the minor problem of bald ostriches. A photograph glued into Thornton's diary illustrates his quandary. A tall Hausa, with the erect bearing of an owner, stands beside an ostrich stripped to its birthday suit. The bird looks like no known creature: it most closely resembles a 350-lb. broiler, a foretaste of the fantasy life of Frank Purdue.

These featherless giants, Thornton discovered, were part of the Hausa's ancient ostrich culture, hitherto little known to Europeans. The Hausa had never bred ostriches. But for centuries they'd captured wild birds for their plumes. Thornton noted in his diary that 'one Hausa ostrich hunter employs 300 men to hunt the birds for him'. Instead of clipping the feathers so they could be harvested repeatedly, the Hausa pulled them out by their roots. They then massaged the bald ostriches with a balm that doubled as a disinfectant and a sunscreen. Thornton was aghast: the plumes that grew back from the damaged follicles were scruffy, crooked things.

After weeks of checking every Kano feather-caravan, Thornton and his men encountered a small parcel of paradisal plumes. The Tuaregs who sold the feathers said they had bought them on the far side of Timbuktu. To get there would take the expedition into treacherous terrain. Taking up the chase, the men were soon sinking knee-deep into the Sahara and the quicksands of colonial politics. Their Barbary ostriches, it turned out, lived across the border: they weren't British as the men had prayed, but French.

Thornton's party set off for Zinder, the French Sudan's colonial capital. There they sought permission to hunt ostriches. Slowly, the maw of French bureaucracy digested their request. Six weeks later, a decision: permission refused. Under no circumstances was any ostrich to leave French territory. The French had long fantasized about turning Algiers into the next Oudtshoorn – epicentre of the fashion world's feather dreams.

So the thwarted Thornton cabled Pretoria: what was to be done? More weeks went by. No reply. The expedition was sinking beneath the weight of two national bureaucracies and the harmattan's silting sands. The Saharan winds blew month after month, making movement impossible. Fevers struck and sunstroke, in the unforgiving, unforgivable heat.

Thornton's diary offers glimpses of the men's misery:

2 November: 'The harmattan blows every day from about eight a.m. to five p.m., covering the world in a haze.'

8 November: 'Harmattan bad this morning . . . The sun was up for an hour before one could see where it was; and yet, a cloudless sky. This is a rotten country in some ways.'

9 November: 'Nothing doing, waiting for that cable.'

10 November: 'Nothing doing, waiting for cable.'

11 November: 'Nothing doing.'

On 6 December, the men's spirits lifted. After a six-week delay, a cable from Pretoria. Permission to spend £7,000 buying birds. Despite the French ban, Thornton was to bring back 150 Barbary ostriches. By any means possible.

However, if French legionnaires caught them red-handed abducting ostriches, Thornton and his men would have to fend for themselves in prison. Pretoria made it clear that it would profess ignorance of the expedition. The South African cabinet doubted whether diplomatic relations with France could survive a public admission of state-sponsored ostrich smuggling.

So the men were on their own. But the desert march to

Timbuktu proved far from solitary, with sporadic attacks by Tuareg horsemen and suspicious French legionnaires shadowing them everywhere. Worse still, the delays had allowed the Americans to get wind of the Barbary scheme. Soon American spies were in hot pursuit. California's leading ostrich syndicate had bankrolled Thornton's pursuers and given them instructions to buy whatever ostriches the expert South Africans were buying.

In an effort to shake their pursuers, Thornton's party split into three, heading east, west and north. But the Americans split up too. So Thornton tried a different ploy. He went on a shopping frenzy, paying local ostrich hunters to capture junk birds. The Americans followed suit. They bought totally trashy ostriches on the assumption that the Karoo men had hit genetic paydirt. Then the Americans and their pseudo-Barbaries headed as fast as possible for the coast.

Through all this, the harmattan and the heat seldom eased. Thornton's diary records the expedition's continuing torment:

23 December: 'The men's faces – Hausas, Tuaregs, Asbonen and Arabs – are hidden except for the eyes. This is easily understood owing to the terrible dust-laden harmattan, a dust so fine that you cannot feel it, and yet people and everything become grey when exposed to it . . . Impossible to describe this desert waste of huge granite boulders and sand, this terrible and perpetual wind.'

25 December: 'Christmas Day. Hard to believe in this howling wilderness.'

29 January: 'Very hot, sky like brass.'

20 February: 'Harmattan has not allowed the sun out, wind very heavy . . . 116 degrees in the shade.'

The expedition eventually tracked down and bought 156 Barbary birds – courtesy of the local emir's ostrich hunters. But having found the ostriches, Thornton still had to keep them captive and escort them out of the Sahara.

The expedition couldn't possibly shoo 156 ostriches across that vast empire of sand. The birds would vanish in an instant.

And ostriches were way too cumbersome to be carried on camel-back. So the resourceful Thornton had to improvise. Procuring some palm leaf stems, he had them woven into twenty pens, each light enough for four men to carry. Then he squeezed eight Barbary birds into each eight-by-eight-foot pen. Four bearers supported each mobile cage. In this manner, Thornton frog-marched his 156 ostriches across the Sahara. His diary has a photo illustrating the effect: twenty multi-headed, multi-legged pantomime creatures trapped in twenty outsize laundry baskets.

The desert had no fencing wood. So at each overnight stop, the porters were reduced to digging six-feet-deep pits and persuading the birds to jump in. Thornton's ostrich squadrons lurched towards Kano and the railhead. From there, the port of Lagos – where the S.S. *Ethiope* awaited them – lay another 800 miles. And from Lagos, another 5,000 miles to the Karoo.

On reaching Kano, Thornton was felled by malaria and sunstroke. He had to send his men and ostriches ahead by riverboat and train, while he remained behind. His diary records his feverish misery.

24 March: 'History of a dog day . . . Sweating from every pore, lying down trying to read, too hot, keep washing myself at intervals, nerves terribly on edge, tea four p.m., terrible thirst. Thank goodness everything must come to an end, only a few hours more of sun. Must complete this tonight. Too hot at present, perspiration from my arm saturating paper.'

6 April: 'Hot as Hades.'

11 April: 'Heat terrific, can't stick this much longer.'

22 April: 'Hottest night I ever spent in my life . . . I must get out of this, wires pouring in, feel too rotten to rewrite them, but got them off somehow.'

24 April: 'Head buzzes like a swarm of bees . . . infernal heat.'

On 30 April, 1912, Thornton rejoined his men in Lagos. They crated their ostriches and hoisted them onto the S.S. *Ethiope,* before setting sail for Cape Town. The sea voyage was awful. Soon the party had two invalids: the still ailing Thornton and Jack Bowker who wrecked his back falling down a coaling hatch. The *Ethiope*, a cargo vessel, had no provision for passengers. To add to the men's misery, the ocean heaved massively and the desert-loving ostriches proved to be amateur sailors.

Frank Smith noted in his report that 'with the rolling of the ship, the ostriches would get turned upside down inside their boxes and start kicking and struggling, and if not released might die. This meant that the members of the party got very little rest, for, at any hour of the day or night, the warning kicking and struggling might be heard. This would necessitate one of the party going down to the hold, knocking the box apart, getting the bird the right way up, and nailing the box together again.'

The expedition's stock of Guinea corn ran out. The men were reduced to chopping several tons of onions a day in an effort to keep their priceless ostriches happy and alive. This became their routine: shovelling mountains of ostrich crap overboard and chopping onions. The men wept much of the way home.

On 25 May, 1912, first Table Mountain, then Cape Town harbour angled into view. The media were waiting. They mobbed the 134 Barbaries that had made it all the way. From Cape Town, the ostriches travelled by train the final 400 miles across the Karoo. Perhaps it was the sight of decent desert again or the thrill of dust in the nostrils after all those weeks at sea, but on reaching their destination the ostriches kicked open their carriages and stampeded for liberty. A commando had to gallop across the Karoo flats in hot pursuit. By dusk, all but three of the Barbaries had been recaptured and corralled for posterity.

The Trans-Saharan Ostrich Expedition endured eight months of desert and two months at sea in pursuit of the ultimate ostrich. With characteristic precision, Thornton noted that the venture had cost the South African government £7,722, nineteen shillings and sixpence. But the hardship and expense seemed cheap at the price. 'Our endeavours,' Thornton exclaimed, 'have made the ostrich industry safe for all time.'

On his return, Thornton became something of a celebrity. Frank Smith was appointed to the world's only tenure-track lectureship in ostriches. At the Karoo college where he taught, Smith set in motion a breeding plan to create double floss ostriches more resplendent than any the world had ever seen. Paris was soon buzzing with the news. But Smith's work would take time. And neither he nor Thornton had any idea that time wasn't on their side.

Chapter Fourteen

At what point does optimism turn into hubris? When the rich start lighting their cigars with five-pound notes? When ostrich barons bathe in brandy? Such were their rumoured activities in Oudtshoorn, 1913, the year after the Trans-Saharan Expedition's return.

Fine plumes now fetched £500 a pound. As feather prices shot through the ceiling, land prices went soaring after them. Top ostriches became as hot as prime real estate. Some barons took the slumlord route: they realized they could make huge profits in the rental market. The owner of Cetewayo (a prize ostrich named after a famous Zulu chief) refused an offer of £1,000 for him. Instead, the bird's wings were rented for plucking on an annual basis to the highest bidder.

It was easy for the barons to forget they were merely fashion farmers. They talked of the 'feather industry': a comforting phrase that gave their line of work a ring of solidity. But in haute couture sudden change is the only certainty. Oudtshoorn's farmers had hitched their wagons to a shooting star and had no idea where it would fall.

The 1914 Paris season brought intimations of bad news. Feather merchants, returning from overseas, reported that demand was down. It had in fact been halved. Everybody agreed this was just a hiccough. Indeed, the slump prompted a surge of new investment. Imagine the profits, people said, when plumes bounce back again. Fresh hopefuls kept moving into town, among them, a New York delicatessen owner called Dan Wilk. From across the Atlantic, he'd heard about the quick money to be made from ostriches. So in 1914 Wilk sold his midtown Manhattan business, emigrated to Oudtshoorn, and sank all his deli money into ostrich stock.

On 28 June that year, a Bosnian gunman shot Archduke Ferdinand, the Austrian heir-presumptive, in a Sarajevo street. Europe plunged into war. Shipping lines from Europe to the Cape were severed. And, as Oudtshoorn soon discovered, calamity drove fashion far from most Europeans' minds.

The war, people insisted, would be a short one. Three months, perhaps four. Six at most. Then the feather trade would flourish again: Europe's fashion-starved modistes would surely prove more ravenous than ever for the Karoo's exquisite plumes.

But the prophecies proved ill-founded. The war dragged on. The ostrich barons' problems went well beyond interrupted shipping links. As ever greater numbers of women entered the war, so even their civilian clothes became more practical, more austere. The world of tumbling hats prettified with feathery filigree lay at the furthest imaginable remove from a world in uniform. Women adopted a low-key look – money was tighter now. But the changes in style also had an ethical dimension: amidst the human slaughter, frippery appeared too frivolous. British royalty used their influence to oppose flamboyant wartime dress. Their measures included banning ostrich plumes at court.

Oudtshoorn's barons lamented the way that many of their finest markets – Paris, Berlin, St Petersburg and Vienna – had become inaccessible. The interruption, they convinced themselves, was only temporary. But the barons couldn't envisage the long-term effects that post-war changes in the European map would have on the Karoo. Ostrich plumes were an aristocratic look in origin – even when popularized for the middle and lower classes, their inspiration remained blue-blooded. In quick succession during World War One, Europe lost most of its powerful aristocracies, as the Austro-Hungarian, Hapsburg, Prussian and Russian empires all fell. Never again would fantasies of aristocratic elegance carry the same chic authority. The Europe of 1914 had disappeared for good.

Even in America, where people were little touched by the shortages or moral climate of war, the aura of plumes evaporated. When affluent and middle class women went shopping in New York, Boston, San Francisco and Philadelphia, feathered hats, cloaks and boas now seldom featured on their lists. Fashion tastes had changed for reasons more complex than wartime austerity. The First World War may have knocked the ostrich boom on the head, but it was Henry Ford and Coco Chanel who together buried it.

During the Edwardian heyday of the ostrich business, Oudtshoorn's barons became big car buyers. It was the swank thing to do. Roaring around the Karoo in one of Ford's new-fangled contraptions, the ostrich moguls advertised their affluence: the automobile was a sort of feather palace on wheels. Little did they know they were buying into calamity; that the automobile would threaten their livelihood as dramatically as the war. The Model T destroyed the horse-drawn carriage. It killed off the ostrich too.

When the first Model T appeared in 1908 it was a gleaming black novelty – a luxury, still moderately expensive. That year, Ford sold 10,000. But once he'd introduced assembly-line production, Ford – and his rivals – kept driving down the cost. By the time the final Model Ts rolled out in 1927, fifteen million Americans had bought one of his cars. The elite fantasy of car ownership had become a common dream.

Henry Ford fostered a new culture of mobility. People didn't just want automobiles: they expected more from space and time, began to fetishize the wings of speed. Voluptuous *belle-époque* fashion now felt immobilizing, especially inside a car. Feathered hats proved hopelessly unwieldy. The pricey plumes got crushed in covered vehicles, while in roofless ones, the wind turned bulky headgear into parachutes and shredded delicate arrangements. Hurtling along at twenty mph, women found their boas mutating into boa constrictors and abandoned them to avoid elegant strangulation.

The automobile changed dramatically the lines and mood of millinery. Hats didn't just change, they shrank. They became tighter and trimmer, shaped for a faster life. With the turn to a sleeker silhouette, pillboxes and cloches became de rigueur.

Women were on the move in other decisive ways. During World War One, many had joined the military and auxiliary corps or taken jobs, in unprecedented numbers, as postwomen, bus conductors, tram drivers, at munitions factories and on farms. Women's enhanced mobility – together with wartime shortages – gave fashion a pragmatic turn. The new look was spare: less decorative, less crimping. Neither wartime sobriety nor these expansions in physical and professional liberty favoured feathered hats.

Curvy corpulence and frou-frou became demode. The fashionable silhouette was now flat and square. No bust, no hips, no waist, tight hats. Not a look to warm the hearts of desert farmers stuck with thousands of ostriches. The picture, however, wasn't solid gloom. In 1922, a ray of hope broke from an unexpected place: Tutankhamun's tomb. Howard Carter surfaced from the crypt bearing news of, among other things, a three-thousand-year-old ivory-handled ostrich-feather fan. King Tut and Egyptian styles quickly blew into vogue. Fashion-conscious women promenaded in neo-Egyptian gear and rushed to buy their ersatz pharaonic ostrich fans.

Oudtshoorn greeted the news with jubilation. Especially when Egyptologists announced that, in King Tut's time, the ostrich feather had served as a symbol of justice. Most bird species produce lopsided plumes, more heavily weighted on one side of the quill than on the other. But the ancient Egyptians noticed that an ostrich quill perfectly bisects the barbs on either side. And so they seized upon it as a symbol for even-handedness. Ordinarily, justice wasn't a pressing concern in colonial South Africa. But when it took the form of a pharaoh's feathered blessing, it had to be taken seriously. Ostriches, this proved, were indispensable to civilization.

The Egyptian craze soon fizzled out, taking the fan fad with it. From here on the hat was going to make or break the bird. And on that front the news stayed grim.

Within a year of Carter's emergence from Tut's tomb, the first cloche appeared in Paris. By 1926 it reigned supreme. The helmet-shape suggested the continuing imprint of the war, girls borrowing their looks from soldier-boys. Hats styled after bells or helmets weren't the only fashionable modes: the Twenties saw the toque, turban, beret, pillbox, flower pot and faux-aviatrix leather bonnet all come into vogue. None of them had brims worth speaking of: which meant less landing room for birds and feathers.

Coco Chanel became the prime agent and apotheosis of the streamlined look. The image jibed with her figure and her origins. An illegitimate child, born in a poorhouse and raised in an orphanage, she brought to the beau monde a maverick disdain for allusions to aristocratic anything. The simple elegance she promoted affected classlessness. The 'poor look' she made famous was, of course, a look of pricey austerity – what the couturier, Paul Poiret, called 'poverty de luxe'.

Apart perhaps from Henry Ford, Chanel did more than anyone to ensure that there was no rush, post-war, back to ostrich feathers. Her rise sealed the grand divorce between taxidermy and millinery that the war and the Model T began. She scorned the Byzantine confections that women balanced on their heads – not least bird parts and plumes. 'How,' Chanel asked witheringly, 'could a brain function normally under all that?'

In 1914, ostrich feather prices slumped. By the following year they had gone into free fall. Each year thereafter, they lost more of the little value they retained, until even the finest

plumes were virtually unsaleable. The golden gosling h
fledged into a feather-duster bird.

Less than two years after returning from his epic trans-
Saharan quest, Thornton was fighting Germans in trench
warfare in France. By then, double floss and Barbary birds
had become an irrelevance – yesterday's fantasy. One can only
guess at Thornton's sense of futility, his anger, his disappoint-
ment at being betrayed by history and duped by ill-timed
dreams. The ostrich debacle broke his life in two. But with the
help of a determined amnesia, he learned to start again,
devoting his energies to cattle husbandry in various British
colonies for which he earned an OBE. He didn't talk about
his ostrich past. And on his deathbed, he asked that his
unpublished expedition diary be burned.

Karoo farmers had long been at the mercy of two fickle
forces: haute couture and drought. In 1916, they struck simultaneously. Demand for feathers dried up as the Karoo entered
the longest drought in memory. As the rains failed and the
feather trade failed to revive, many Oudtshoorn inhabitants
joined the trail of dust bowl migrants heading for the cities.
Among them, hundreds of Lithuanian Jews. Oudtshoorn's
desert diaspora suffered a second scattering: many sank to a
level of *shtetl* poverty they thought they'd left behind. The
Jerusalem of Africa was turning into a town of curdled
dreams.

Morris Lipschitz had the resources to last longer than most.
He'd amassed an empire of thirty-four ostrich farms. His
vision of the future had recently made headlines across the
country's newspapers. Lipschitz had foreseen 200 miles of
unbroken ostrich farms, stretching from Oudtshoorn all the
way past Port Elizabeth. Two years after his pronouncement,
Lipschitz became just another millionaire reduced to soup-
kitchen mendicant.

Ladies clad in foreign silk joined the queue for handouts.
The luckier men found work on road-gangs. In all, 1,000
ostrich-owning families lost their farms. Many thousands

more – ostrich hands, feather sorters, merchants and speculators – were driven into poverty and out of the Karoo. Coloured and black tenant families – who had never been allowed a stake in the ostrich bounty – now left the land in droves. The most destitute of the destitute, they were vulnerable, as ever, to the white farmers' fortunes and whims.

Among those leaving town were the stonemasons and iron-mongers who had finessed Oudtshoorn's palaces and churches. They fled to Cape Town, Johannesburg and Port Elizabeth. As a child, I grew up surrounded by these artisans' post-palace handiwork. When I trotted down Port Elizabeth's Cape Road, I used to click a stick across the decorated iron fences that fronted even the simplest houses. That's what the iron workers turned their hand to when the feather boom expired. Compared to the exquisite filigree of palace panty-lace, the designs seemed modest and crude: depression-era ghosts of a vanished opulence.

One ostrich merchant framed two cheques as a record of the speed with which he had been ruined. The first, a 1914 cheque for £100,000, his bank had honoured. The second, dated a year later for £1, had been refused.

When his bank failed to bail him out, a farmer called Fourie ambled into his ostrich paddock, shot some birds, then put a bullet through his head. His was the first of a run of suicides.

Karoo farmers shot their ostriches by the thousand or, to save on bullets, simply chased them into the veld. When the government realized that 50,000 ostriches were being slaughtered or abandoned every year, a commission was set up to devise a money-saving scheme. Why not turn all those worthless ostriches into something truly practical? A blue-print appeared to build two ostrich soap factories, one in Mossel Bay, the other in Port Elizabeth. The dreambird had fallen as far as it could go: the paragon of Parisian finery was to be boiled down into a vat of soap.

One day the local newspaper, the *Oudtshoorn Courant*, quietly removed the ostrich plume that had always graced its masthead. The editors didn't explain their decision. They didn't need to. Everybody understood what lay behind it: the anger and the shame.

Even the Oliviers, the richest of the Afrikaner ostrich moguls, joined the procession of bankruptcies. A few years before, they'd tried to uplift a neighbouring hamlet by building an exquisite sandstone Dutch Reformed Church. The Oliviers had insisted that the church be erected some distance from the settlement to allow for the community expansion that the feather boom would bring. The hamlet's original name was Armoede: 'poverty' in Afrikaans. But the Oliviers had felt that Armoede needed a more upbeat name. So, henceforth it was to be called Volmoed, 'full of courage'.

After the crash, the Oliviers were forced to sell The Towers, their Gothic feather palace. The hamlet they'd renamed reverted to a condition better expressed by its old name of 'poverty'. To this day, the villagers grumble that the place of worship the Oliviers built for them is too long a trek from home. The church stands there still, marooned in the middle of the veld, a solitary monument to an outsize dream.

But Max Rose refused to abandon his ostrich reverie. He kept insisting that feathers couldn't possibly stay out of vogue for long: they were a feminine necessity. He blew his last £200,000 on ostrich feathers which he baled and placed in storage waiting for prices to bounce back. In the 1920s, Rose led the government's effort to revive the trade. Envoys were sent to bribe the biggest French fashion houses and to Milan to proselytize for plumes. Both ventures failed.

The British royals repealed their wartime ban on feathers and gave the stricken barons some gallant pro-plume publicity – notably the Prince of Wales on his visit to Oudtshoorn in 1926. But fashion had moved beyond reach of royal influence. In the age of the flivver and the flapper, Rose faced a daunting array of obstacles: the automobile, aristocratic decline, mass-manufactured clothing and women's emancipation. In the end it proved to be no contest. The world's ostrich king wasn't just battling some quirk of fashion. His adversary was nothing less than modernity itself.

Rose crashed badly. He had further, after all, than anyone to fall. Over the ensuing decades, he clawed his way back to wealth by building a lucerne (alfalfa) empire. However, long after all his neighbours had slaughtered their ostriches, Rose still maintained a flock. By 1940, only 9,000 of the Karoo's one million ostriches remained and Rose owned half of them.

Why did he remain so bonded to ostriches? Was it immigrant optimism or immigrant nostalgia for the bird that had lifted him out of *shtetl* poverty? To his death, Rose believed that the ostrich had a future, that the past could be revived.

After the crash, the feather palaces took on an elegiac air. Whole palaces – some no more than five or six years old – changed hands for what it had cost to import just one of their teak doors. Others were abandoned and slid towards ruin, among them, the aptly named Foster's Folly, a strange pseudo-Tudor-Bethan fantasy. Foster himself slunk out of town. But not before staging, in impeccable detail, his own funeral.

The Oliviers' Towers held on for a while. I remember ogling them as a child in the mid-Sixties shortly before they fell. (Some say they were pushed; others say they were already collapsing beneath the weight of their own decay.) On out-lying farms, palaces like Welgeluk gained new occupants: puff-adders, rats, scorpions and silting sand.

Of all the poems I had to learn by heart at school, 'Ozymandias' touched me most. It made immediate sense as a story about the Karoo. The huge, half-buried statue jutting out the desert; the broken grandeur of the past. And, clearest of all, Shelley's instinct in his closing lines for spectacular calamity:

Round the decay
Of that colossal wreck, boundless and bare
The lone and level sands stretch far away.

Part Three

Chapter Fifteen

In 1980, at the age of twenty-five, I emigrated to America. My grandparents had left Scotland and Ireland early this century, arriving in South Africa at the height of the feather boom. Now, two generations later, the grandchildren of those immigrants had scattered across four continents: two of us settling in Africa, one each in Europe, Australia and North America.

Politics played a hand in my departure, as it did for so many departing South Africans of my generation. I left clandestinely in response to an apartheid army call-up. I entered an exile of sorts, though I had always felt, from early childhood, that my destiny lay overseas, that emotionally I would have to leave.

Like everyone who travels towards a new life in a land they've never seen, I wondered how much of me would survive the crossing, how translatable I would be. No migrant ever knows how much they're going to need or want their past. A few things, though, I recognized as excess baggage, things that would surely prove worthless in America. Somewhere mid-Atlantic I mentally dumped my expertise in African birds and my degree in African languages and watched them hit the ocean far below. For the rest, I guessed, I'd have to wait and see.

I had already done a lot of dumping, starting years before. The novelist Nadine Gordimer has spoken of the moment in early adulthood when she went 'falling, falling through the

South African way of life'. I experienced that trapdoor sensation at college, as I discovered the full enormities of apartheid and felt assumptions of normality slide from beneath my feet. A world that had seemed to possess an ordinary stability became foundationless.

The Karoo scrub desert had always held for me the emotional density of a child's first landscape. All childhoods are provincial: they start from me, from us, from here. In the absence of a social analysis, where we are becomes the centre of everything. My boyhood and adolescent passions had flowed straight from that centre: my desert rovings and the un-wavering knowledge that I possessed a calling – ornithology.

But after my fall into politics, the landscape around me seemed illusory, distorted by an unethical geography. I lost all interest in Oudtshoorn, the ostrich world and birds. The Karoo became code for a long hallucination, a mirage-thin dream – like the shimmery haze above a tarmac that skews your vision, rippling through everything. Emotionally, that world, that time of life, sank from sight. For many years before leaving South Africa, I avoided travelling through the sparse interior. Driving between Port Elizabeth and Cape Town as I often did, I always opted for the coastal route.

So before migrating to America, I'd already folded child-hood and adolescence carefully away. I'd placed them in a box, tied the string and dropped them down a chute marked Forgotten Things. I found myself living almost beyond reach of memory.

Every migration is an opportunity and a kind of death. The new world may be rich and strange, but you're somehow weightless in it. I moved through my first two American years – spent in Iowa – with a certain spectral insubstantiality. I had such a shallow purchase on the place and the place on me; every day, I felt the force of my absence from its past. In Iowa I lived as an extraterrestrial, an 'immigrant alien' in the full sense of the phrase. I probably won't ever feel so otherworldly again, this side of the grave.

There's a burial ritual in certain West African cultures that has long haunted me. It's called the crossing fee. The mourners place a sacrificial bird on the dead person's grave. Like the obolus left for Charon, the bird guarantees that the boatman who links past and future, this world and the next, will ferry the departed spirit across the waters to the other side. The bird must die: no journey is made for free.

But it's not just our final passage that demands a crossing fee. Every migrant knows the sensation of arriving in some kind of afterlife. It's a disembodied feeling: your solid self lies buried in the place that you've abandoned, that gave you the ballast of a past.

After crossing the Atlantic, it took me two years to find my way to New York City. I became a convert, an instant cosmopolitan. I loved the company I found: crowds of weightless people who'd made the journey from some other side. The freedom to be weightless here gave us all, I felt, en masse, a paradoxical solidity. I hung out with former misfits – foreigners and Americans – who'd grown up at an angle to places that had made them strange. Struggling people, many of them, yet at liberty to forget the places, the people they needed to forget. Here, for the first time in America, I didn't lack a history because almost everyone I knew lived past-free.

I was still uncomfortable with the idea of a permanent address. I wasn't ready to belong, I just wanted a place to be. Unlike towns, provincial cities, suburbs and nation-states, New York didn't demand that you jump through hoops of conformity. Not insisting that you belong was the city's way of ensuring that people like me did. A stray spirit among stray spirits, I'd arrived in a place where restlessness could be a home. Maeve Brennan – that Irish immigrant to New York (and *New Yorker* writer) – described this sensation perfectly. Hers was a city, she once remarked, peopled by 'travellers in residence'.

So New York became a counterweight to my Iowa immateriality. But it also served as a perfect antidote to all the one-mistake towns I'd ever known in South Africa. Places where eccentricity, flair, experiment – any defections from the norm – were punishable offences. Here, at last, I felt free to live in a community where defections were the norm.

I acquired a doctorate in literature and watched myself, with a certain immigrant irony, metamorphose into a professor. South Africa still haunted me as a shadowland, but as a place composed purely of politics. For twelve years, the anti-apartheid cause became my passion, my revenge against an injustice and an illusion. This obsession stood at the heart of it all: my teaching, my journalism, my scholarship, my political and private life.

My appreciation of the bird world had long since been bankrupted by politics. Nature shrank: it seemed unnatural. At college in South Africa, I'd whittled it down to a line from a Bertoldt Brecht poem that I'd hung above my bed: 'To speak of trees is treason.' Brecht's six words were a note to myself and to my father behind me, still writing his gardening column and putting me through college on the proceeds of 'Growing Things'. Now in New York, I shared the sentiments of that ur-New Yorker, Woody Allen: 'Nature and I are two.' I never went anywhere where I risked getting sand inside my shoes.

So I settled happily among people for whom ostriches roamed only on the Discovery Channel or in the menagerie of the mind. I had made a double crossing – first into politics and, later, into America. On the far side of both those journeys, I never thought I'd hear from ostriches again.

Chapter Sixteen

I had been away from South Africa twelve years. My lover Anne and I were living temporarily in London at the time when, late one winter's night, I was woken by the phone. Through a haze of leftover sleep I was listening to my brother's voice: 'Dad has had a cerebral haemorrhage.' He'd returned home from reviewing a play in the Feather Market Hall and collapsed. Andy had picked him up off the cork-tiled bathroom floor and carried him to bed. 'It was strange,' my brother said. 'He felt light for a father.'

An hour later – three a.m. – it was Anne's mother on the phone: 'Your father has vanished.' Lost in storm-struck mountains south of Oudtshoorn where he'd gone hiking with his grandson. By the time morning broke, this was our tally: two fathers gone – one dead, the other disappeared.

I stood on the balcony of the flat listening to the huge city stir. Blurry sounds, except for the pulsing wail of somebody else's ambulance. I felt suddenly estranged from the streets beneath me in a very foreign dawn.

Mom called. 'Don't come to the funeral, Rob. It's so expensive. I can manage. I'm coping, honest.' She said this in a voice thinned by distance and pain. Our family's way: always this awkwardness around giving voice to hope, only our most trivial wants getting spoken in the broad daylight of desire.

'I'll fly out today.' When next we talked, I was about to board the plane. 'I hope you don't mind,' Mom said, 'but I've pencilled you in as chief pallbearer.' By then, Anne's father had been found, huddled in a cave.

I flew south, falling through the accelerated seasons, the twelve hours that turn winter into summer. Two days later, I was standing in a dark suit at the mouth of a church, sweating and shaking hands with mourners. Mom had worried that the pews would be empty. Her fears proved needless – locally, Dad was too well-known for that.

A smattering of black teachers and principals arrived to pay their respects, people whose schools had benefited from the Christmas Cheer Fund which Dad ran for thirty years. But, mostly, the half-remembered faces that filed past me came from the white community, from the infinity of clubs that Dad had joined. The Male Voice Choir, the Oratorio Society, the Amateur Musical and Dramatic Society, the Gilbert and Sullivan Society, the Shakespearean Society, the Mountain Club, the Wildlife Society, the Photographic Society, the Bowling Club, the 1820 Settlers' Society, the Walkers' Club, the Horticultural Society, the Dendrological Society, the Bonsai Society, the Dahlia Club, the Wild Flower Society . . . I forget the rest. As the mourners passed, I gripped hand after hand. Their fingers, root-gnarled with age, felt almost botanical.

Belonging was Dad's *métier*. Sometimes I thought he couldn't stand to hear of any club without becoming a member straightaway. Yet from where I stood he appeared opaque. He'd always seemed to me someone who went public to stay hidden; a man who lacked the gift – or the luxury perhaps – of knowing how to be known. If questioned about his past, he shrugged it off as 'so much ancient history'.

For the next ten days, we helped Mom sift through my father's accumulated papers, clothes and photographs. Most of it would have to go – she and Andy would be moving into a little flat. 'Take anything you want,' she said to her five children before we scattered again to our corners of the earth. I took very little; I believed in travelling light on principle. But I pocketed the photo Mom had found of me teetering on ostrichback the day I lost my watch. Also, Albert Jackson's book, a pile of my father's 'Growing Things', and a thin green paperback, called the *Ostrich Feather Ready Reckoner,* that I discovered buried amidst his underwear. Enough.

Soon, I was travelling north again. For the first hour I stared out the window blankly, as we overflew the drought-encrusted, ostrich-flecked Karoo.

Chapter Seventeen

At the time, the events didn't seem connected in the least. But something in me must have stirred. Eighteen months after my father's funeral, I decided to travel to San Diego to cover the American Ostrich Association's annual convention for a magazine – not the sort of assignment I normally undertook. This was the first I'd heard of Americans and ostriches. A bemused Texan friend had sent me an article from the *Dallas Morning News* trumpeting the ostrich as a brand-new bonanza bird: 'You can eat them, you can pluck them, you can turn them into leather. Could this be our new golden goose?' My curiosity was aroused.

When you travel to a major ostrich convention for the first time, it's hard to know what to expect. How would 1,500 ostrich professionals behave? On the first morning, I found myself sitting behind a potted palm in the lobby of a San Diego hotel, listening to a delegate's voice talking to a cell phone: 'Thanks for the tip, Jack. I'm tellin' ya, Jack, I'll be callin' my egg-broker right away.' Cradling my coffee, I watched the big-buckled, big-hatted crowd troop into the cavernous hall and wait for the proceedings to begin. Most delegates, I noticed, sported satin Rode Walker jackets, ranch name and ostrich logo monogrammed on the back. The jacket that seduced me most was worn by a guy from Texas Thunderbird Ostrich Ranch. It would have done any biker proud. Shimmery silver, except for two black condor wings stretched across the back, shoulder to shoulder, as if in heraldic compensation for the ostrich's incapacity to fly.

All I knew about America's newfound romance with ostriches was what the *News* had revealed. I flicked through the piece again. The name Max Rose came back to me: the man who'd always sworn there'd be an ostrich renaissance. But the resurrected phoenix depicted by the Dallas paper wasn't a bird Rose would have recognized. Nobody was talking feminine hats and boas; now they wanted to turn ostriches into manly hunks of steak. If a century ago the buzz was all ostrich à la mode, the *fin-de-millenium* dream was ostrich à la carte.

Over the next few days I would discover that the big-bird craze sweeping the American southwest was an unexpected spin-off of the anti-apartheid movement. In the mid-Eighties, American college students had erected Soweto-style shanties, shackled themselves to lecture halls, starved themselves in headline-grabbing hunger strikes. I remembered that time intimately: I'd gotten involved in the protests on our New York campus and covered the events for magazines. In 1986, US congress finally relented, slapping sanctions on South Africa, including a ban on imported ostrich skins.

Shudders shook the world of Western wear. For twenty years, ostrich-hide cowboy boots had proved highly lucrative, fetching $500 to $1,500 a pair. Overnight, Congress had declared off-limits the world's only serious source of ostrich hides.

By 1987, desperate American entrepreneurs had begun scouring local zoos, parks and monasteries – wherever they could find pockets of the primordial birds. Speculators snapped up every ostrich in sight. Within two years, prices had gone fabulous: $80,000 for a single breeder pair. The ostrich was indisputably hot. And so the American Ostrich Association was born. Now the AOA's 3,000 members were hellbent on assimilating the ostrich to the American Dream. Could Western ranchers coax this behemoth broiler onto the suburban family dinner table?

The first morning of the convention, I seated myself in a

corner of San Diego's Golden Hall, from where I listened to a stream of venture capitalists, converted cattlemen and chefs. A meat expert explained that the big bird was perfect eating – low cholesterol and free-range. He pointed out all the succulent bits on a giant ostrich projected overhead, and taught us 'which muscle groups to serve friends you're trying to impress'.

Down at floor level, ostrich footwear proved de rigueur. There must have been 400 pairs of 'full quill' ostrich boots present in the room. The boots had turned out in solidarity with the cause, but also as a flashy display of class. They all bore that prized knobbly look, the myriad eruptions where the bird's feathers have been pulled. This gives ostrich leather the Vesuvial texture of pubescent skin. Pricey pimples, though.

I was sitting beside a burly, broad-browed guy from the AOA's Arizona chapter, who clapped and cheered all morning with the metronomic energy of an applause machine. He sported a carmine Rode Walker jacket, chocolate ostrich boots, black jeans and a T-shirt bearing the image of a punk-haired yellow chick, sketched in the manner of Dr Seuss. The chick – in the final stages of busting out of an oversized egg – has an air of bug-eyed astonishment, as if dazzled by all the light and fuss. Beneath this nativity scene, wrapped around the rancher's stomach, rolled the words: 'Ostrich. Filet of the Future.'

Our keynote speaker, Dr Jim Braun, was a motivational professional with a self-declared expertise in ensuring that dreams become realities. Dr Braun hailed from Waco, Texas. He had written books – big sellers, he said, in Japan – on the goal-setting business, the inspiration business, the attitude business and the business of hope. He also owned ostriches.

Dr Braun preached the gospel of possibility in its purest form. 'Remember, your goal-setting mechanism and your unconscious mind magnetize whatever you want to make happen. You magnetize the condition you seek.' His words seemed spoken not by the distant, stick-human on the stage, but by the giant simulacrum that stretched out its arms across the video screen, embracing the future grainily.

This video man had a rangy look and an off-centre smile. His suit dangled from a bony body that exuded a lean kind of energy. His full, silver hair was meticulously tamed, in contrast to the erratic pleats, pits and twists of his steeply angled face. We were looking at Samuel Beckett reincarnated as televangelist.

Exhortation was his expertise. Dr Braun's voice sounded throaty with promise as it called for faith in cadences that swooped and fell. This good-news salesman spoke the body talk of the revival tent: enraptured eyes, rocking hips, wide, imploring arms, a face luminous with desire.

'I want to share this with you . . .' Dr Braun revealed his vision: 100,000 ostrich farms stretching across America. He paused to correct his tie and soak up all the clapping. Then he continued to unveil the future. 'Thank you. The ostrich will make a positive impact on our economy unlike any other new industry that's happened in the last ten, twenty, thirty years.' His eyes narrowed. On the road ahead, he could see a multi-billion-dollar industry that would reinvigorate the American economy with two million ostrich-related jobs. That's what he called his 'worst-case scenario', his 'minimum goal'.

Dr Braun then clarified his terminology, explaining in the process how collectively we would bring his vision to fruition. First, we needed to set three types of goals. A 'dream goal', a 'realistic goal', and a 'minimum goal'. 'We generally reach our goals so close it's almost scary, it's like a deja vu when we get to that year, it's as though we lived it all before.' To believe was to achieve, to prophesy to insure. Dr Braun was an impassioned exorcist, deadset on driving from his ostrich rancher congregation every incubus of doubt.

Our leader paused to reprove some errant strands of hair scattered by the fervour of his delivery. Then he moved towards his finale, tightening his eyes and gripping his forehead with one hand. 'You can't teach an ostrich to fly. But you can succeed and find success for whatever heights you choose. The road is open, the ladder's up and the sky's the limit. Whatever you vividly imagine, ardently desire, sincerely believe and enthusiastically act upon must and will come to pass.'

His eyes reopened. A handkerchief appeared. Dr Braun adjusted his heavy-rimmed spectacles and scanned the hall with his video gaze, as if daring anyone to doubt that he has closed for good the gap between hope and destiny.

The crowd was high on the pure hydrogen of hype. 'Yeah,' one rancher bellowed, rising and pumping his right fist in the air. 'Let's get this baby off the ground.'

I watched the ostrich, like a wayward blimp, float higher and higher until I'd lost it to the stratosphere.

I found myself in the unfamiliar situation of remembering too much. To admit memory was to entertain the sacrilege of doubt. In the desert world I'd once known, people had drummed into them from birth stories about the profligate palaces, squandrous luxuries and hubris that had cleared the way for the great ostrich crash. Palace ruins still dotted the Karoo – moral beacons, pointers to a ghostly history that still possessed a present force. In San Diego, I felt as if I'd stumbled on a world where memory hadn't been invented yet, where the future could be inhabited so sanguinely that it doubled as the past.

Later that day, I accosted Dr Braun at the cappucino cart. I asked him if he knew about his dreambird's checkered ancestry. Bankruptcies, suicides, that sort of thing. The doctor frowned and gave his polystyrene cup a brutal stir. Then shrugged: 'No need to talk about that here,' he said. 'That's ancient history.'

I retired to my room early for the evening, feeling the need to decompress. I lay back and flipped the pages of the *Ostrich Feather Ready Reckoner* I'd inherited from Dad. Year after year, at the turn of the century, a new *Reckoner* would appear every week, listing the going prices for sixty varieties of ostrich plume. Back then, feathers weren't simply feathers. They were abundantly divisible to the discriminating eye – the way camels are to Berbers, who are said to recognize one hundred types. But that fine-meshed way of seeing ostriches died with the desire: when the fashion turned, it took the language with it. All that remained were sixty discriminations reduced to a flat memory on the page.

I ran my finger down the columns, checking the going rate for the week in question – 7–14 March, 1913. Extra Super Primes were fetching £100 a pound, roughly $10,000 today. The list of feather types looked strangely colonial now, like an irrepressible irruption of the mania for racial classifying: Special Long Blacks, Long Good Blacks, Long Fair Blacks, Long Drabby Blacks, Medium Blacks, Short Blacks, Wiry Blacks, Super Whites, Good Whites, Narrow Whites, Third Class Whites, Broken Whites . . .

My *Reckoner* was in shabby shape. Nibbled, dog-eared, green cover thumbed thin by some forgotten feather broker, sweating over this week's dip in the price of Narrow Whites. Inside the cover, Dad had tucked a yellowing article that sketched the history of the Feather Market Hall. Around World War One, I learned, plume prices had become so fickle that the town fathers decided that the building required more stable forms of sustenance. So they added a concert organ, a stage, and, in the basement, a dungeon where prisoners could be held.

Musicians performed at the Feather Market at their peril: the hall was a graveyard for voice and lungs. When the feather sorters plumped the plumes to flattering effect, mite hordes, dust and tiny hooked barbules flew out, spreading all kinds of pulmonary distress. At night, when the sorters had all disappeared, it was the soloists' turn to suck in those clouds of menacing particles.

The Feather Market became my second home. I was forever accompanying my father there when he reviewed concerts for the *Herald*. But by the time I knew every splinter, creak and cavity in the Feather Market's time-scuffed floor, the dungeon and the plume trade had long since disappeared. This immense, grey, Victorian edifice became a way for me to measure space and time. It always felt far too vast: evacuated, somehow, even when concert-goers filled it. The hall had been meant for bigger things than Port Elizabeth's Gilbert and Sullivan Society. From its heyday, all that remained were the shell of the building and the appalling marketplace accoustics. Dad was forever griping about the dreadful echoing.

If I closed my eyes here in my San Diego hotel, I could still catch snatches of the contrapuntal music of the past. Ostrich merchants and mezzo-sopranos emitting their rival yodellings. And, in answer, from beneath the feather mountains, the strangled bellowings of the prisoners below.

Chapter Eighteen

When I see the snaking neck of an ostrich, I can't just see an eight-foot dollar sign. But as it happens, I'm a fan of the meat. Over a lifetime, I've probably munched my way through the better part of an ostrich, or at least all the relevant bits. Ostrich liver pâté, ostrich neck soup, sliced ostrich stomach à la ox tongue and the like. I did my gourmandizing in the Karoo. But now, I learned, some elite American restaurants – like Huntington's in Dallas – had started offering such innovative entrees as ostrich tenderloin with a raspberry chambord demi-glace. This was all part of a gastronomic tradition reaching back to the Roman Emperor Heliogabalus, who once served 600 ostrich brains at a banquet. (These were presumably appetizers: the thinking bit of this bird fits snugly into a teaspoon.)

On the Saturday night in San Diego, I joined a mass test-tasting of 'the filet of the future'. It was a gala event: eighty gaming tables stretching across one side of the hall, while, at the stage end, a rollicking auction got underway. In the middle, ostrich was served. It proved succulent – the way ostrich is meant to be. Somebody announced that 700 lb. of ostrich meat would be consumed at the event. But with breeder prices soaring, I wondered how this could be. Even if we ate only the impotent and infertile, 700 lb. of ostrich gotta be costing somebody a whack. I tried to do the arithmetic: fifty dollars a steak? Were they serving us road-kills or what? I broached the subject with one of my dinner companions, a seasoned California breeder. 'Well,' he said, 'put it this way. With prices so high, we can only afford to eat our mistakes.'

If the dining held a few surprises, the trade fair proved a revelation – an emporium of ostrich gadgetry. I was awed by the humungous womb of an incubator called MOM – the Mechanical Ostrich Mother. MOM was the unrecognizable great-granddaughter of the Eclipse which that Karoo Scot, Arthur Douglass, had invented in 1869, helping set in motion the first great ostrich boom.

Past the serried ranks of Mechanical Ostrich Mothers, I came face to face with the ultimate ostrich trailer. The salesman, Frank Hague, caught me ogling his Turnbow Vision 2000. I was standing well back, trying to scan the whole trailer, end to end. Where I'm from, you just round up your ostriches and bang them in the back of your Toyota. The trucks are a familiar sight in the Karoo, belching smoke and clattering down some dirt road on the way to the slaughterhouse, the crowded birds peering over the top like a convocation of periscopes.

But if anything justified ostrich millennarianism, the Turnbow Vision 2000 was it. Frank Hague, a muscular, black pony-tailed, six-feet-four-inch Oklahoman gave me the low-down on the trailer. 'Each bird has its own individual rubberized and double-padded compartment.' Each compartment comes cushioned with red leather and is 'specially equipped for on-route snacks'.

And the price? 'Twenty-eight five,' Frank replied in a casual, loamy voice. 'Matter of fact, a gentleman was over here a few minutes ago, and he bought five.' I did a brisk calculation: a cool 140 grand. 'Yup,' Frank concluded, with a flick of his ponytail, 'you're looking at the Cadillac of Ratite Hauling.'

'Ratite' was the buzz word of the day. It popped up everywhere: ratite haulers, ratite managers, ratite railing, a Louisiana ostrich ranch called the Ratite Riviera. I hadn't heard the word in decades. Not since my ornithological heyday. Ratite is Linnean Latin for the genus of flightless birds –

ostriches, Australian emus and South American rheas. (Not everyone agreed that the effort to commercialize this bit of ornithological jargon was a good idea. A chef complained to me that he could maybe sell ostrich steaks but he sure couldn't sell ratite steaks, well-done, medium or rare. 'In a restaurant, rat anything sounds bad.')

Down the aisle from Frank Hague's Turnbow Vision 2000, a perky young salesman for HITSS – Head in the Sand Software – was trying to assess my level. Would I need Head in the Sand Basic Program, Basic Program Plus, or the Complete Program, all available in MacIntosh, MS-DOS and Windows? Ostrich software appeared to be a highly competitive field. Over the course of the morning, I had tested Ost-tech, OstrichComp, the Complete Ratite Manager, Birdtrak Systems and Ostrack (Ostrack 3.0 now available).

After weighing up my computer options, I decided on Head in the Sand. I'd soon buried myself deep in the software, setting up an egg diary and a deworming schedule for my fantasy flock. Then this guy, short and fortyish, sidled up to the terminal next door. He stuck out a hand and squinted at my name tag: 'New York, New York'. 'So,' he said, looking doubtful, 'how many do you have on the ground?' There was something man to man about the way he said it, like a general or a little boy sizing up an adversary's troops. But I knew he was talking about ostriches. 'On the ground': it struck me as a peculiar formulation, an odd way to count birds that are solidly, irredeemably pedestrian. Some flightless species, like penguins, at least enjoy an aquatic option. But if you're an ostrich either you're on the ground or you're on the ground.

His phrase remained a puzzle, but I thought little more of it until the following night. It was Saturday evening and the American Ostrich Association had laid on a five-hour Sunset Cruise of San Diego Bay. I found myself dining aboard the *Hornblower* at a table with six Texans. I chatted mainly to a young woman who ranched near New Braunfels. We got talking about ostrich orthopaedics. Ostriches, apparently, are prone to leg rotation. One or other leg begins to move around until the bird doesn't know whether it's coming or going. But a veterinarian in Florida had invented an ostrich boot that could arrest the rotation orthopaedically. The lady from New Braunfels wished the device had come sooner; she'd had a bird like that herself once which she'd kept as a house-pet. For three months, the family had heaved the ostrich up and down the stairs, until it had grown too vast to carry.

She seemed pretty au fait with the industry, so I pressed her about this 'on the ground' thing. She toyed with her tumbling black hair and smiled. It was all quite simple. Ostriches have notoriously temperamental embryos; 'They're real weak on hatchability.' But some ranchers wanted to count every fertilized egg as a full-fledged head of livestock. Perhaps, she suggested, that was because most of them could only afford a small flock, or because at $1,200 a pop, an egg was a genuine part of their investment. So in the trade, the opposite of 'on the ground' was not 'in the air' but 'in the egg'.

I was starting to get the picture. The phrase served as a reality check, separating actual ostriches from merely imminent ones. It was all part of agricultural ethics, a way of keeping charlatans and fantasists in line.

As the cruise entered its fifth hour I climbed onto the *Hornblower*'s top deck for a respite from the cigar plumes and whisky breath. I felt pleasantly adrift, looking out over so much water after hours of landlocked table talk. I stayed for a time, watching the dim hulks slumped in the naval repair yards, like iron herds of hippopotami that had heaved themselves onto the bank for the night.

The cruise had left me curious about the underbelly of the ostrich trade, the *demi-monde* of boosters and brokers, smugglers and hucksters who shadowed the regular, upstanding crowd. I'd heard bits and pieces about a black market and telemarketing scams. Certainly, some of the talk I'd heard that evening, with its blend of zealotry, prosperity and credulity, would have given heart to any 1(800) snake-oil salesman plotting a profitable ambush.

I was joined on deck by a taut, tuxedoed man in his mid-fifties; he'd visited South Africa, so we chatted about that. Then I asked him straight out about crime. 'Ostrich rustling,' he said. 'There's a real problem with rustling. We've gotta get that under control.' Successful sting operations in Florida and Texas had knocked out some of the key actors in the ostrich black market. 'I tell you what, though, there's this couple in the Oklahoma Panhandle . . .'

The Panhandle couple had noticed some folk were dreaming a little too fast, a little too far ahead. They'd also noticed that America's appetite for ostriches had far outstripped the national supply. So they devised a scheme to profit from the gap. Fifty per cent down on the value of a newborn ostrich would guarantee you a chick from next season's brood. The couple raised $1.5 million off these phantom futures, then vanished themselves, taking plenty from the bank but leaving nothing on the ground.

Back among the booths next morning, I found an expert on foiling ostrich rustlers in a microchip age. I joined the knot of bystanders watching Jean-Anne Mayhall unveil the latest weapon in the war on ostrich rustlers: the Avid Power Tracker 11 All Weather Extended Range Multi-Tag Reader, a magic wand for reading ostriches microchipped for ID. Jean-Anne expressed concern about chip migration, a burning issue in the ostrich business. If you don't put your chip in right, it will migrate all over your bird. And if it's carelessly inserted, she warned, any rustler can remove it by palpating the skin. Best way to reduce migration is by burying the chip in a muscle: 'Trust me, I know it's scary at first, but the neck is the place to go.'

'When you wave your magic wand over the ostrich,' Jean-Anne exclaimed, with a flourish towards a large hen parked nearby, 'you will see the serial number pop up.' I half expected the ugly bird to turn into a prince.

By the third day, I was struggling to maintain control over my identity. The problem started with the label pinned to my lapel. At the registration desk, I'd been handed a yellow badge announcing my name and origins. In three days I hadn't seen another 'New York, New York'. It wasn't a promising point of origin for any serious ostrich wannabe. It certainly didn't cut it with this crowd. Ranchers from Lubbock, Texas, Geronimo, Oklahoma and Bakersfield, California would approach me, squint at the label, then back off with an expression and a tone I soon came to recognize: 'New York? You *live* there?'

I got fed up with the disbelief, the sawn-off silences. It made casual talk too hard. So on my third afternoon, I whited out the York bit, and replaced it with South Africa. I hoped that way to blend in more easily. Besides, 'New South Africa' expressed something deeply felt. South Africa's first democratic elections lay a mere two months away, and I felt animated by the chances of real change down there.

But if I'd hoped to fit in anonymously, I'd sure made the wrong move. I became a magnet for everybody's queries and concerns. I soon realized that the only South Africans these guys had ever met were in the ostrich trade – egg-brokers, chick smugglers, breeders and ostrich middlemen. The questions came thick and fast. 'You've *been* to the Karoo? You *come* from around there?' 'Hey, Randy, come on over here. This guy's from the source.' 'Now tell me, sir, I've just bought a pair of bluenecks from Namibia. I'm thinking of crossing them with some regular South African rednecks? Will that give me a stronger bird?' 'You guys down there, do you give your birds kelp additives? Stuff's darn expensive. Is that real necessary?' 'Upper respiratory problems. All my birds are getting them. Some guy tells me it's the humidity. Is that right, sir? Humidity?'

I was in mortal danger of being morphed into an ostrich guru.

I was totally out of my league. But often the hardest reputation to shake is an inadvertent one. My protestations couldn't halt J. P. MacNamee's disquisition on ostrich osteoporosis. J. P. gave me the symptoms, posed the question, then waited for my prognosis. I shook my head: 'I'm sorry . . .' It was his third question; all three I'd failed to answer. He stared hard at the look of blank apology on my face. Perhaps he thought I was being miserly, deliberately holding back some profitable knowledge.

'You're a South African? Really? I don't mean to be rude, sir, but you're the first South African I've ever met who knows nothing about ostriches.'

By day four I was beginning to wonder. How much more venture capital could this bird devour? Was the ostrich heading for America's boom-bust bestiary? Alligators, chinchillas, minks, llamas, Angora rabbits, sharks, Vietnamese pot-bellied pigs, even earthworms have all enjoyed their fifteen minutes of speculative euphoria and, by now, have all entered the animal kingdom's inverse hall of fame. Sometimes a few gamblers made money early on; latecomers typically got burned. But the prospector's dream dies hard: the gut feeling that nature is seamed with lucre, that there's another super-creature out there just waiting to be revealed.

I listened, on the convention's final day, to a man proclaim that ninety per cent of every ostrich can be anatomized for gain. Meat eaten, feathers turned into showgirl plumage and dusters, hide into boots and handbags, bones into bonemeal, eggs into ornaments. Eyelashes? – paint brushes. Ostrich toe-nails? – no problem, he insisted that they make incomparable jewelry abrasives. Even ostrich eyes would prove ideal for cornea transplants.

A few ostrich sceptics were muttering – sharks, alligators – they'd seen it all before. But the ostrich revivalists countered with a precedent all their own: the turkey, too, was once an unlikely, uneaten bird. Without the risk-taking and self-belief of America's turkey pioneers, Thanksgiving could never have become the dream dinner it is today. Hubert Schmider, a portly chef from Purdue University, captured this sentiment memorably in his closing exhortation: 'You guys are missionaries, you guys are entrepreneurs, you guys are doing what your forefathers did in the Twenties for the turkey.'

Was the ostrich going to be a turkey or a dog? A chinchilla for the Nineties or (as one speaker described it) a kind of nouvelle-cuisine cow? These questions pointed me, inevitably, towards Willcox, Arizona.

Chapter Nineteen

The name Willcox was on everybody's lips – America's coming ostrich nirvana. At San Diego, the man from Global Ostrich had first briefed me on the town's virtues, waving a pamphlet that urged in travel-brochure tones: 'Treat Yourself and Your Ostrich to the Arizona Advantage'. In two brief years, Willcox had enticed some forty ranchers to migrate there with their flocks and more were on their way.

It was Charlie Biggs who first suggested I visit Willcox when I met him at the convention bar. Charlie was a dark-haired, rangy man in his late thirties with a haunted handsomeness. He wouldn't have looked out of place in a Parisian café. But his ancestry was Scottish South African: for four generations the Biggses had farmed ostriches in the Karoo. Charlie had tried to escape the Karoo and the weight of all that ostrich heritage by moving to Johannesburg and making films. But a few months before we met, his family had persuaded him to drop his film career and emigrate to Willcox. So here he was, a bohemian on hold, doing the ancestral thing. The Biggses had set up a lively two desert, transatlantic enterprise – Charlie running ostriches in Arizona, his father and brother William doing the same in Africa. William Biggs? The name rang a bell. It turned out I'd been to school with Charlie's brother 10,000 miles and a quarter of a century before.

There was something uncanny about this chance encounter in San Diego with my schoolboy past. But Charlie was offering me something different: a window on the future.

123

'Come to Willcox,' he urged. 'It's perfect, perfect for ostriches.' Charlie cocked his head: 'Seriously. Give Willcox five years. It's going to be the next Oudtshoorn. They're already calling it the Oudtshoorn of America.'

On the map, Willcox looked precariously poised on the northern extremity of the Chihuahuan Desert, a vast yellow swirl sweeping up from Mexico. The Arizona-Mexico border lies fifty miles to the south, the New Mexico border forty miles due east. My reasons for deciding to travel to Willcox were indistinct – almost as vague as my image of the place. But the New York spring was late and soggy; the winter had been long. My body felt impatient for light and space. I was also just plain curious in a disbelieving way. The notion that people anywhere would feel inspired to create a second Oudtshoorn seemed astonishing. My memories of that tight, sermonizing town persuaded me that one Oudtshoorn per planet was more than enough.

A freezing storm delayed our takeoff at La Guardia. When the plane landed in Arizona I felt myself begin to thaw – the emotional equivalent of ice melting off the wings. Driving east up the steady incline from Tucson towards Willcox, I could almost hear the senses sloughing off their urban, winter overload.

It was over twenty years since I'd last travelled through a desert. My eyes had to adjust to the enlarging clarity. New York is so densely forested with things and signs for things that you learn to screen out most of the flickerings. But on the road to Willcox I began to feel those forms of self-protective inattention drop away.

About sixty miles east of Tucson, I passed through a jumble of huge boulders called Texas Canyon. A pink billboard near the canyon's entrance took a rectangular bite out of the landscape. In exchange, I learned that a Baskin-Robbins ice-cream store lay thirty-three miles ahead. The billboard was an eyesore. But in a sense the scale felt right. I had re-entered the landscape of the long approach, where everything announces itself deliberately before inching its way towards you. The desert gives objects an adhesive quality: they attach themselves to your vision one at a time and don't let go. The world out here had the sharp-etched feel of childhood, when things named by our senses possessed an alphabetical simplicity: fence, gate, house . . . road, sun, tree.

As Willcox drew closer, I seemed to be approaching not some place entirely new, but a point on the map that memory's reach was bringing back to me. A familiar place, in some deep, forgotten sense. I found myself driving through two landscapes simultaneously: southeast Arizona and the Karoo. The visual echoes were everywhere: the bald earth, cacti and bony bushes; a certain grain to the light; the countless nuances of brown; that distant lift on the horizon where the mountains began.

Like the Oudtshoorn I recalled, this Oudtshoorn of America was surrounded by a semi-arid, walled, scrub plain. Both towns offer the traveller an apprenticeship in extremity. The climates are severe, rainfall limited in each to an identical eleven inches a year. But the enclosing mountains shield Oudtshoorn and Willcox from the full force of the brutal deserts beyond – creating, as I would come to learn, a kind of giant ostrich corral.

My sense of re-entering a place I thought I'd left behind disconcerted me. I couldn't have pictured such topographical familiarity. The look of the land brought Karoo bird names flocking back – a whole aviary of nonsense names, in Latin and English, that could mean nothing over here. I was mildly annoyed by these synapses of irrelevance. I thought I'd perfected my displacement, had jettisoned all that. But I had travelled further than I'd expected, had crossed over into the past.

Willcox was known as the Cattle Capital of America long before it aspired to become the nation's ostrich hub. As I entered town, I passed a roadsign: 'Willcox. You are Now Entering Cow Country.' The broad streets felt emptied out – way too wide for so few cars. Down these avenues, ranchers once drove immense herds in the days when Willcox shipped more cattle than any centre in America. An hour after my arrival, I heard a ping, ping, ping, then a few offtune blasts as fifty-two Southern Pacific Railroad carriages bisected town. These days, the train was little more than noise and rushing air – it didn't stop here any more.

On my third day in Willcox, a flinty man in the gun shop drew himself up with defensive pride when I asked how cattle ranching was doing in the area. 'Well, I don't know about you, sir, but I still eat beef.' The store's only other customer wore on the front of his shirt the single word 'BEEF' and on the back, 'BBQ WITH ATTITUDE'. At the Arizona Bank, around the corner on Maley Street, I got pamphleteered by the Willcox Cowbelles. The big, blowsy woman who thrust the pamphlet at me wore a message on her T-shirt: 'Save an Endangered Species: Hug a Rancher Today.' The cowbelles' handout catalogued eighty-seven beef byproducts (tennis racquet strings, dog biscuits, piano keys etc.) and contested the charge that cattle degrade the environment. A charcoal cowboy on the cover fixed me with a low-brimmed glare and the reminder: 'You Are In Beef Country.'

Grafting ostriches onto an historic cowtown would require, I guessed, a certain tact. Willcox had a raddled look – blotchy paintwork, snaggle-tooth fencing – that suggested it could benefit from the amped-up hope and cash that ostriches might bring. But any hint of the ostrich as an alternative cow would surely outrage already beleaguered cattlemen.

Willcox's ostrich immigrants had arrived from all over: South Africa, Switzerland, Colorado, Texas, Florida, Arkansas, California, Indiana, Ohio, Iowa, Nebraska, Louisiana and Utah. Most had settled northwest of town along the Fort Grant Road in a cosmopolitan patchwork of ranches and ranchettes. A realtor told me the ostrich had pushed up land prices there forty per cent in a year.

Eight miles down the Fort Grant Road, I spotted a flock of ostriches edging the horizon. Heads down and grazing, they resembled a battalion of bushes on the move, a dry-country rendition of Burnham Wood marching on Dunsinane.

Military history, as it happened, lay deep around there. From any ostrich ranch in Willcox you could see, etched against the eastern skyline, the serrations of Cochise Stronghold. Cochise – the redoubtable Chiracahua Apache chief – eluded the US Army for twelve years during the 1860s and 1870s in those rhyolite badlands. South of Willcox you pass the adobe vestiges of Fort Bowie, where federal troops advanced against Geronimo, forcing his final surrender in 1886.

If you press on past all the ostrich ranches, the road winds towards the ruins of Fort Grant where a regiment of buffalo soldiers was stationed during the Apache wars. But I wasn't going that far. I was looking for the Annie Apple sign that marked the turnoff to Pacesetter Ostrich Ranch. Right at the exit, I noticed a blond woman crossing a paddock with tiny birdlike steps, a straggle of baby ostriches tripping behind her. This was Peggy Christensen, Pacesetter's chick manager; twenty minutes later she was pied-pipering me around the outfit.

We set off towards the chick barns in an E-Z Go Golfcart commandeered from the ranch's fleet. Our wheels whirred in the soft earth of freshly graded roads. The E-Z Go and the ostriches galloping in twenty-foot strides along the fence sent up a sepia veil of dust. Through that grainy filigree, the scrub desert and the vague, looming birds appeared more remembered than seen, as if recovered from some flyblown photograph.

Pacesetter lay on an ex-lettuce farm that had gone bankrupt. 'The farms around here,' Peggy told me, 'have gone in and out of bankruptcy so many times.' Not just the farms, but the mining and milltowns too. The ostrich arrivistes of Cochise County were just the latest in a long line of prospectors. Over breakfast that morning, I'd scanned a ghost map of Arizona, a map that charted all the towns that had disappeared; a map of prospects past that helped you go places that no longer existed. Cochise is strewn with more ghost and semi-ghost towns than any county in the state, towns like Grand Central, Contention City, Hilltop, Courtland, Charleston, Dos Cabezas, Hamburg, Middlemarch, Paradise and Total Wreck.

Peggy had a haunted look that one could easily ascribe to this local sediment of failure. But it was a look that after just a short while in Willcox, I had come to associate with people who worked with infant ostriches. The day before, a neighbouring rancher had woken to find $20,000 worth of dead chicks. With its big dipper rides through mystery ailments and mass mortalities, ostrich chick management is a volatile profession.

We drove to the far end of the 320-acre ranch to meet Peggy's newest charges. When Peggy climbed out, the chicks swarmed all over her, wheezing neediness, clearly imprinted on their foster mom. A wrap of freckly spines cloaked their hen-shaped bodies, suggesting the offspring of a hedgehog and a bantam. Behind us, an ostrich raised its tail and launched some titanic ablutions. I'd forgotten what an ostrich load sounds like when it hits the deck. Chicken shit it aint.

While Peggy and I talked about the prospects for the farm, a large strutty bird on stacked heels sashayed up to the fence. He was flushed with the ardent pink blush that tints neck and legs as the breeding impulse quickens. That coral lipstick smile, that black velvet cape, those terrific legs . . . I found myself fixed by the huge, deliquescent gaze of a Zsa Zsa Gabor, Queen of the Desert. His unblinking eyes peered at me from beneath the awnings of two-inch lashes, tartily lathered with green eyeshadow – the effect, Peggy told me, not of nature's coquetry, but of burying his head in pulverized alfalfa.

Over by the colony pens, we noticed some hens nestling into the mesquite when another rooster thundered along the wire in a high freak of testosterone. His neck swelled like an enormous hiking sock. Without opening his beak, he emitted a gravely roar – Boo-oo-oo – the sort of sound I imagine wild men release on woods weekends with Iron John. I'd always loved that about ostriches. Real switchers: so butch, so femme.

Later that afternoon, as Peggy and I are parting on the ranch-house patio, a roadrunner leaps out of nowhere and speeds across the farm. It seems to have shot straight out the living-room TV which has been squawking all day through an open window. The roadrunner, Peggy explains, has built its nest in one of her potted shrubs. But even when I get to know it well, the roadrunner appears less an authentic piece of desert ornithology than an escapee cartoon. For me, this bird will always nest on the far side of reality.

The roadrunner can reach speeds of eighteen mph, with or without Wil E. Coyote in pursuit. Quite formidable for a twenty-four-inch bird. Unlike the immigrant ostriches which have now occupied the ranch, the roadrunner isn't flightless, just a reluctant flyer. An earthling by preference not design.

Sometimes around Willcox I'd see these birds flap to the top of the nearest cactus in search of an aerial view, then hang-glide down again. But fundamentally they prefer life on the ground. They adopt an extraordinary lowslung, ducking posture when running, as if permanently alert to max. head-room signs on slick-wire fences ahead. When these flattened birds buzz by at speed, they resemble battery-powered road-kills that have bounced back to life without fully recovering their sense of vertical possibility.

The roadrunner is a cuckoo in the strictest ornithological sense of that word. But it's an eccentric cuckoo, one that builds its own nest rather than parasitizing some sparrow, robin or other host species in Old World cuckoo fashion. The roadrunner snacks on scorpions and diamond-back rattle-snakes. Rattlers – prolific in Arizona – kill more Americans each year than any animal other than *Homo sapiens*. But the roadrunner pounces on snakes happily, spreading its wings umbrella-style as a decoy and a shield. For this Warner Brothers desert cuckoo, a rattler is simply another item in the lunchbox: a peanut butter-and-jelly sandwich that just happens to have fangs.

Reptiles also play a prominent part in roadrunner love-making. To impress his date the male bird will often arrive bearing a dead lizard. A sign, biologists surmise, that he's a capable provider and not just in it for the sex. The male then mounts the female from behind, the trophy lizard gripped in his beak for the duration of their passion. Much too triumphalist for my tastes: too reminiscent of the kind of man who makes love with his stockholder's certificates firmly clenched between his teeth. (And the kind of woman who'd be impressed by that.) But who's to say, these days, what's kinky and what's not?

I waved to Peggy and wished her luck. As I drove off, a solitary cottonwood tree reared up in my mirror like an exclamation mark on the landscape's long, flat line.

Chapter Twenty

'How big can this thing get?' Gary Harguess repeated my question, narrowing his eyes and pulling hard on his cigarette. 'Imagine China . . . Imagine the horrendous amount of food the world is gonna need.'

His voice tailed away. He leaned back in his chair, feet on his desk. Gary sat there rocking for a while, crossing and recrossing his ankles, as we both tried to imagine China.

Then he pointed to the huge map of Arizona sprawling across the wall of his realtor's office. He explained how only forty per cent of the state's 113,000 square miles is open to private ownership. Indian reservations, national forest, national parks and Bureau of Land Management property make up three fifths of Arizona. Cochise County, however, is an Arizona rarity: it's mostly private land.

'I see Cochise being the biggest ostrich country in the United States. All the way down to Elfrida, down to Douglas. I'm figuring that this area right there can produce half a million ostriches.'

A dog's leg of ash hung precariously from Gary's cigarette. But he was in control: he tightened his lips, jerking his cigarette towards Cochise on the map without spilling anything.

'Come back in a few years time. I believe you'll see Cochise County covered in the next three years. Covered with ostrich.'

As a realtor, Gary's business was people moving. And nothing had shifted people Willcox's way in a while like ostriches. Even Gary himself was hungry to move out of real estate and get back full-time to the land. He had his 300 acres and his seven pairs of breeder birds. 'I wouldn't mind, a year or two from now,' he said, 'being nothing but ostrich.' Gary paused, perhaps to survey that future, as a dreamy look scrolled across his eyes.

He proved a generous conversationalist. The only thing he refused to discuss were emus, far too touchy a subject. Sporting a Beatle hairdo, the emu – the ostrich's smaller Australian cousin – had recently come into vogue. California and the Southwest were awash with emu-oil salesmen who claimed that their bird possessed a magic gland that the ostrich lacked. Aborigines – the pitch also went – had been using emu oil as a cure-all for millennia. So the emu was acquiring more of a New Age aura than the ostrich and was gaining on the ostrich among suburban breeders. For one thing, it didn't kick people to death.

'I hate to comment on emu,' Gary continued. As a realtor he had to watch his back. 'I've been caught in a lot of fire already about this emu business, so I'd prefer not to talk too much.'

His cough betrayed an edge of nervousness. 'Let's just say I'm not as enthused about the emu. The ostrich offers so many more advantages. So this emu thing . . . I just let people make their own choices. Me as a person, I wish 'em luck.' With that, he exploded into smoke-frayed laughter.

That evening, I caught up with Gary again at the Best Western Plaza Inn, where the southeast Arizona chapter of the American Ostrich Association was gathering. A friend of his buttonholed me with a story about emus and alligators.

'You heard how the alligator craze went bust? There's a lady I know in Florida who's trying to get rid of four hundred alligators. She can't pay their food bills – can't even give them away. I told her: just wait until the emu market crashes, then you can feed your alligators real cheap.'

The ostrich fraternity in Willcox was getting pretty fierce about pretenders to the throne. Everywhere I went, the attitude appeared to be the same: this is a real ranching town, we accept no lightweight substitutes. Leave the emu to California.

At one point in the evening's proceedings, a thickset rancher appeared at the back of the room. He was holding up a sign: 'You can emu-late an ostrich but you can never duplicate it.'

In southeast Arizona, the big-bird range wars were hotting up.

Chapter Twenty-one

Halfway through my stay in Willcox, I drove 170 miles north to the outskirts of Phoenix for an event I was eager to attend. Each spring, the community of Chandler in Maricopa County plays host to Arizona's annual ostrich games. So I booked into the San Marcos Hotel and, next morning, joined the crush of people streaming towards the arena.

It was nine a.m. and hot as we squeezed into the bleachers and awaited the start of the world's largest *Ben-Hur*-style ostrich tournament. Ten thousand strong, we were gathered in that desert coliseum to witness the revival of the ancient Roman sport of ostrich charioteering.

I'd attended my first ostrich derby back in Oudtshoorn, thirty years before. But I'd never witnessed ostrich racing of the *Ben-Hur* variety. Towards the end of the Roman empire, ostrich chariots became flashy conveyances for ladies of noble birth and adorned triumphal processions as a mark of imperial might. The flamboyant emperor Firmus developed a particular passion for the ostrich-drawn carriages: he believed they created an aura of soaring supremacy – no matter that the birds in question couldn't fly. Amidst the pageantry of the Roman circus, these creatures came into their own. Sometimes 1,000 luxuriously plumed ostriches were paraded through the arena. Ostrich charioteers commandeered the strongest and finest of these birds to flaunt their breakneck art.

The Chandler festival has revived the sport, drawing 200,000 visitors each spring. For the first event on that crystal morning, four chariots lined up, a single ostrich harnessed to each. The birds appeared restless, their little bum-fluff heads bouncing around at the top of weaving, serpentine necks, their huge, daffy eyes blinking expectantly. The charioteers, clad in local legionnaire style, fussed with their gear: each contestant sported a Lycra bodysuit, gladiator boots and a silken hip-length cape in silver, red or blue. The helmets – high-crested with a heavy chin-strap – blended the traditions of the Roman coliseum and the British bobby.

A bugle boy called the post; a bell rang; the stalls swung open, and they were off, beak to beak, wing to wing, thigh to thigh in a pounding flurry of dust and feathers. As they hared out the starting gates and down the first straight, the skittish birds scattered across the track, running forwards in great surging dashes, then sideways, backwards – every which way but up. One ostrich ran round and round in rings, a mark perhaps of its ancestral penchant for circular escape.

I began to appreciate the challenge of directing a speeding ostrich without bit or rein. For steerage the charioteers were armed only with brooms, which they waved to the left or right of the ostriches' eyes, in the hope of exciting some movement in the opposite direction. But these lunges had little impact on the birds' waywardness and none whatsoever on their awesome powers of acceleration. Dust devils didn't help, whipping eddies of grit into the riders' eyes and enveloping one charioteer in his cape as he hurtled round the hairpin bend. As the chariots clattered past the post, the triumphant legionnaire leaped out to applause and to the amplified ovation of the compère, a man who was all stomach and Stetson.

Awaiting the next round of races, I wandered through the crowd to the booth of the Arizona Ostrich-Emu Association. A young rancher, hat to boots in seamless black, was cranking up his pitch before a cluster of the curious. He was on about the 'ostrich advantage'. A guy toddled over from the Dog on a Stick. 'Hell,' he said contentedly, through a mouth full of sausage, 'I'm floatin' in hot dogs.' He didn't look a likely candidate for alternative cuisine. But his eyes lit up at the words 'ostrich filet'. He fixed the speaker with a dubious stare. Then he shifted his gaze to the ostrich thundering across a demo video. 'You mean we're gonna eat that critter? That's one shit ugly bird.'

The rancher warmed to the challenge. 'Eat 'em? Sure folks eat 'em. Back there in Europe,' he said, flinging an arm in a vaguely eastward direction, 'back there in Europe they can't get enough of 'em. Hardly eat nothin' else.'

I hung around a while and listened to his pitch. Why we should eat more ostrich, because its red, beef-like flesh was lean and had all the dietary pluses of turkey. The rancher assured us that the American Heart Association has just given the ostrich its stamp of approval.

As an ex-cattleman himself, he explained, there was something in it for the ranchers too. Ostriches are cheap to feed and breed at lightning speed. A cow takes a year to produce a solitary weaner calf; in the same time, your ostrich is hatching twenty-five babies and raising them to slaughter age.

'Sir, you're looking at the livestock of the future.' He placed both hands on his hips and gave his pitch a millennarian curve: 'You heard it here first: this bird is gonna be the cow of the twenty-first century.'

I returned to the coliseum, where the riders for the next race were grappling with their mounts. This event involved bareback ostrich riding with a vengeance: no saddle, no bit, no bridle, no nothing. Biped on biped, the ostrich jockeys seemed grafted to their birds, whose legs lengthened the riders' own thin pins. This was how humans rode birds in Greek myth and across the horizon of my childhood dreams.

The starter bell rang and the ostriches streaked off. As the competitors pounded round to my side of the course, a girl centaur sped into the lead, her knees and thighs buried deep in her rooster's wings, her hands vanishing beneath a sea of black velvet plumes. She seemed less mounted on her bird than half inside it, linked by invisible joins.

The sound system, crackling with age, hailed her as the winner: fifteen-year-old Halley Hedrick of Nickerson, Kansas on a headstrong rooster called Hardboiled. Halley, the only girl in the contest, flicked her strawberry-blond ponytail and jogged to the podium. She stood there decked in white cowboy boots, carmine jeans and a shimmery top with a slanting design, one half disco silver, the other a wedge of stars and stripes. She swivelled round, waving to each corner of the coliseum, then dipped her knees and made a backward exit on the run, palms upturned, lifting them up, up above her head, pumping the crowd as she went: a National Velvet for the Nineties.

I eased my way back through the festival crush: the avenues of gazebo salesmen and tattoo tents, Garth Brooks watches and ostrich egg découpage; past the Orbotron ride, the Big Dipper and a medley of Greek, Bavarian and Kansas cuisine. Flagging parents trailed flagging kids, who in turn dragged their winnings – pink panthers, polar bears and fluffy killer whales – through the Arizona dust. The vendors, however, were up in arms about the cuddly ostrich prizes, specially available for this event. Or so I was told by an irate booth owner in dungarees, his arguments perforated by pistols popping pirate ships at our back. The toy birds suffered, he says, from a basic design flaw: too little oomph in the neck. He tried to coax a toy ostrich into standing on the counter. Despite its orange smile, the bird wilted into spinelessness. It just couldn't keep its neck up, as if governed by an urge, as irrepressible as gravity, as persistent as myth, to bury its head in the sand.

Chapter Twenty-two

Wandering back across the fairground, I passed a K.I.B. Ostrich Ranch sign inviting me to 'Make a Million Off Five Acres'. The K.I.B. stand boasted an elaborate display of bolo ties – those informal, Western string ties with sliding gems or metal clasps at the top. Perusing them, I caught the tail end of a conversation between an ostrich hand and a customer – a fiftyish woman squeezed into a salmon shell suit. The woman was clutching her burnished helmet of high-combed hair and sighing agitatedly: 'She just had to leave some pretty obvious footprints, she just had to.'

The guy manning the booth seemed sceptical. 'You'd be surprised, lady. In this hard desert, they don't leave much of a print. She'd be darn hard to follow.'

They could only be talking about Sadie.

The sheriff's posse had gone out on the trail of a tearaway ostrich. Three weeks back, Sadie had broken a fence over at Cave Creek; the sheriff had gotten out his helicopters and was scouring the desert hills. All I knew were the basics: the paper I'd been reading over breakfast had profiled Sadie's getaway.

The K.I.B man pushed back his hat and filled me in. As he talked, he toyed with his bolo tie, which bore a silver figurine of an ostrich travelling rapidly across a slab of smooth, grey agate.

'Now don't get me wrong, ostriches can be dangerous. But this guy, he *really* played up the danger. The bird had to be made a public threat for them to bring in the posse. I'd probably do the same if I had a thirty-grand bird on the run. It's not just the thirty K; it's those eggs. She just started laying. A good hen can spit out eighty a season. Right now she's probably spraying $1,200 eggs right across the South Central Desert.'

The subject of Sadie kept cropping up in Chandler. Some ranchers got shifty and po-faced at any mention of her saga. They were afraid the whole ostrich enterprise would get laughed out of court. But others adored Sadie: saw her as a marketing bonanza, a big boost for the big bird, the first step towards national name-brand recognition. The whole scenario was an adman's dream: one mutinous ostrich, a helicopter search, state troopers, a showdown with the sheriff's posse, that awesome desert backdrop. Everything but sex.

I was beginning to appreciate the walk-on part the ostrich had landed in the cultural theatre of the New West. Maricopa County seemed, at first glance, an unpromising setting for any *mise en scène* of the tough picturesque. The county's 9,200 square miles – spanning Phoenix, Chandler, Scottsdale, Glendale and Cave Creek – register as a seamless blur of crab-grass lawns, golf links and shopping opportunities. After Vegas, Greater Phoenix is America's fastest growing metropolitan area. Many of the newcomers in the 1990s have bounced off the California coast, fleeing whatever it is that made them mad – Mexican immigrants or mud slides, riots, fires, crowds or quakes. Mostly they are white and shifting their dreams to sparser, more conservative states: Arizona, Nevada, Utah, Colorado. They're in search of the future and the past, and heading East is the best way they know of trying to get back West.

The inventor of the posse hunting Sadie in the desert is playing this new mood to the hilt. Maricopa County Sheriff, Joe Arpaio, knows all about angry, nostalgic hope. A hefty Italian-American weaned on cowboy 'n' injun movies, he is a maestro of the retro publicity stunt. Sheriff Joe sports a 1950s cow-lick of fading black hair and a tie-pin moulded into a revolver. He specializes in big, brutal, media-minded gestures to show that he is serious about taking back the West from big government and other known criminals. That's what he is best at: *visibly* fighting crime.

Joe Arpaio is starring in and directing his own Western, an adaptation of some boyhood movie scrolling through his head. But every production needs a supporting cast. So Sheriff Joe has conjured one from the past: he is bringing back the posse. He is going to show that the old ways work – and at no cost to the taxpayer. He has gathered 3,000 volunteers – armed, unpaid, barely trained crime-fighters. They call themselves QAPs – Qualified Armed Possemen. The sheriff's department gives them one free bullet a week – fifty-two a year – but they have to bring their own guns, holsters and cowboy hats and buy their own tan uniforms. Top posse-men get a trusty steed and a gold Deputy Sheriff star. In return, they are at liberty to ride the range in the Phoenix malls, harass hookers and protect the citizenry from rampaging ostriches.

Phoenix is cursed with the fiercest summers of any city in America. The dial can squat above 100 for a month, then surge to 140 – a far better climate, in fact, for ostriches than humans. So when Sheriff Joe wants to look telegenically mean – which is most of the time – the weather backs him up.

His vigilante fighting machine has shown no sign of denting serious crime: the county homicide figures keep soaring like the heat. But the tough-love crowd embrace his style. So Sheriff Joe's posses keep storming the shopping strips to declare another frontier 'war on graffiti'.

I was watching the sheriff on the TV in my hotel lobby, while waiting for Susan Franck – president of the Arizona Ostrich-Emu Association – to arrive. He was spouting about his infamous Tent City, a low-budget outdoor jail composed of army tents. Tent City is virtually a media installation, a backdrop for Sheriff Joe's barking lectures on the good ol', tough ol' days of rough justice that he was bringing back again. When inmates bellow complaints about the heat and rotten food, they are acting like his extras – showing the world that the sheriff is man enough to give those varmints hell. Most of the inmates held in Tent City have committed no more than misdemeanours: unpaid parking violations, drug possession, alcohol offences or shoplifting. None have sentences of longer than a year. Still, the heat and dust and overcrowded tents make them look pretty criminal for the cameras. Between Tent City and his posses, Sheriff Joe is getting all the photo-ops he needs to become the Western hero mirrored in his dreams.

The crowd clamour from a hundred yards away told me the *Ben-Hur* ostrich chariots were still hurtling round the bend. I began to wonder which of the sheriff's specialist posses he had sent in after Sadie. Pictures flipped across my mind of the 'executive posse' – lawyers, doctors and corporate leaders only – sweeping the desert hills for one mutinous ostrich, armed and dangerous, cameras in hot pursuit.

Then Susan arrived – president of the Arizona Ostrich-Emu Association and founder of the consultation firm Focused on Ratites. We moved onto the patio. It was cooler there, viny and cross-hatched with pergolas. Small, black birds clambered about, creaking through the eaves. Susan was petite, flaxen haired, in her late thirties. She was hedging her bets: she'd invested in both ostriches and emus which she kept at a ratite boarding house not far from her Scottsdale home.

'Sadie,' Susan announced between sips of diet coke, 'has been so good to us. A total boon. Every event, every media interview I give always goes back to Sadie. My guess is that she's tripped over a rock or run into a cactus or was eaten by coyotes.'

Susan had emerged as the state's leading political advocate for the ratite cause. 'Right now all my energy is going into lobbying the Arizona legislature. It's my job to persuade the lawmakers that ostriches are not three-hundred-pound turkeys and they're not feathered cows.' She paused and leaned forward to press home her case. 'This bird's gotta have laws of its own.'

In her ostrich advocacy, Susan needed all the ammunition she could find, from Sadie to Sesame Street. (Although privately she doubted whether Big Bird is really an ostrich at all.) But her trump card, she believed, was the past: 'People act as if the ostrich is some wacko new idea. It isn't. It belongs here. It's a piece of Arizona heritage. That's gotta be part of our product profile. This bird is almost native.'

Her approach was radical: almost everyone I'd spoken to treated the ostrich as history-free. Susan revealed that the ostrich possessed an Arizona past that she'd traced back to the nineteenth century. Chandler, it emerged, had once been the epicentre of the Western ostrich dream – America's answer to Oudtshoorn – much as Willcox was today.

Susan's passion for mining the past was paying off: she'd recently struck gold. She tidied her napkin and explained.

'A few years before Arizona joined the union in 1912 the value of land around here went from pennies to $1,000 an acre. All because it was good for ostrich grazing. Senator Carl Hayden was so impressed that in 1914 he steered a bill through the House of Representatives that ensured federal funds for ostrich R & D. Carl Hayden later chaired the Senate Appropriations Committee. He's a piece of Arizona history, a classic name around here.'

Susan's voice tailed off. She peered absently into her glass and clicked a pale pink nail back and forth across the concertina in the middle of her straw. When she looked up again, hope illuminated her face: 'Now with Carl Hayden on our team . . .'

But she wasn't happy with the product as it stood. She was a dog-show judge in her spare time and a stickler for fine breeding. 'I'd love to buy my ostriches with pedigrees attached. We've gotta do more work on the genetics. It's surprising how little time it would take to make an all-American ostrich.'

That was the key to reclaiming the ostrich for the West: genetics, genealogy and history. Plus smart marketing. Arizona, she said, has something the competition in Texas would die for – a state capital called Phoenix. 'It's great when I go to Phoenix to testify. I give the legislators our slogan straight away: "Let's bring this bird back from the dead." '

Susan reached for her purse on the marble floor and scrabbled through it: 'Here, take a look at this.' She slipped me a magazine article, pointing to the accompanying photograph. It was black-and-white and very old. Streaky-looking, made streakier by the rough paper of the print. I could see the main image fine, but the background, lost to age, was an impenetrable mesh of grains.

I found myself peering at a man in an immaculate ice-cream suit astride a coal-black ostrich rooster. The man was sitting in profile, staring straight ahead. Everything in the photo looked perfectly erect: the bird's long legs, the starched white line of the rider's back, the ostrich and the human necks both held stiff and high. Who was he, I wondered, this Janus-faced birdman? And who was he out to impress?

'Meet John Williams. The only photo we have.'

Susan had conjured this strange heraldic man as evidence for her cause. A nineteenth-century cattleman who ranched just south of the Grand Canyon, Williams was America's first ostrich booster, the first frontiersman to pursue that dream. In 1875, he sailed to South Africa where he hazarded a journey on horseback across the Karoo's immensity. His route led him to Oudtshoorn, where ranchers had just started breeding the giant birds. Williams left the town with one image ingrained upon his mind: the spectacle of a South African farmer herding his sheep on ostrichback. This, he wrote in a letter home, was an idea whose time had come.

Before leaving Cape Town, Williams purchased a troupe of ostriches. He arranged for them to be dispatched, at great cost, to the Grand Canyon. It was an exacting trip: by ship from Cape Town across to Buenos Aires, all the way up the Americas to New York, then by rail to Chicago, Omaha and down to Arizona. Fourteen thousand miles in all. Only a handful of the birds survived the ordeal.

Back on his Grand Canyon ranch, Williams faced a twofold challenge. He had to train his ostriches to accept a rider, and persuade his cattle to cooperate with a cowboy on ostrich-back. Williams persisted; he gave it his best shot. But the scheme proved calamitous. The sight of mounted ostriches spooked his steers so bad that he had to revert, reluctantly, to the more traditional horse. Picturing the scene, I find it hard not to summon a certain sympathy for his cattle. The indignity of being corralled by such a creature – Marlboro Man on stilts, sporting a fluffy tutu – would surely have plunged any self-respecting Western cow into apoplexy.

Williams soon found himself floundering in debt. He slaughtered some of his birds, let the others loose. He did, however, retain his finest ostrich, a strong, glamorously plumed rooster. This bird he reserved for riding into town, which he did with panache, head held high above failure and bankruptcy. There is something about the ostrich's high-stepping gait that gives it a regal, arrogant air. Even so, Williams failed to impress the locals with his sense of style and became the object of derision.

One day, a passing cowboy taunted him, then challenged him to a race. Williams shook his head; he wanted none of it. But the cowboy kept mocking him and raising the stakes. Goaded by the crowd, his debt and pride, Williams finally relented. The odds were stacked skyhigh against the ostrich. But from starter's pistol to the finish line, birdback Williams left the horseman in the dust. With his winnings Williams raked back the money he had blown on his hopeless herding venture.

I peered again at the photo Susan had given me. The man's vanilla suit, in the dying desert light, was turning a lurid strawberry pink, as if the silent movie that he was starring in had suddenly been colourized. There he sat astride his triumphal bird, straightbacked on his steed, the granddaddy of Arizona's ostrich jockeys. John Williams: intrepid forebear of all the speculators and visionaries riding their luck today across the deserts of the New West.

Chapter Twenty-three

Inspired by Susan's revelation, I lingered in Chandler awhile and started rummaging through old newspapers, magazines and the local museum. I became entranced with the history. I discovered that a South African immigrant, Dr Charles Sketchly, first envisaged ranching ostriches for fashion out West. (Unlike the dreamers who succeeded him, Williams was just an ostrich rider: he showed no interest in the plumes.) Sketchly's Karoo operation had already made him a tidy pile. But one trip to California in 1882 convinced him that, from the ostrich point of view, he had visited the future. Cheap land, great desert climate, the American market huge and growing. The South African promptly emigrated to Anaheim taking with him a bunch of his finest birds.

Sketchly and a consortium of backers launched the California Ostrich Company. The enterprise proved a quick success. The concept caught on and eggs poured out. So, long before Disney's arrival, ostriches promised to put Anaheim on the map. Imitators of California Ostrich sprang up in San Diego, Phoenix and San Jose. Los Angeles became a budding ostrich town. By the mid-1880s, the dinosaur bird had become a mainstay of the LA economy, the fourth biggest money-spinner overall.

The LA press greeted this African novelty with tones of high euphoria. 'The demand for ostriches in the present state of feminine taste is insatiable,' one writer blazoned. An 1885

145

editorial in *The Los Angeles Times* hailed the advent of a risk-free enterprise: 'The ostrich plume, like the sealskin saque, has achieved a permanent place among the elegant fashion of the day. It is no longer subject to the caprices which cause violent and sudden fluctuations in so many articles of fashionable female attire.'

As permanent as seal-skin saques? A simile lost to time.

However, LA's ostrich optimism proved well-founded for a while. In the dry reaches of Arizona and Southern California, ranchers clamoured to cash in on the lively profits from the feather craze. One of those profiteers, Dr Alexander J. Chandler, looms above the rest. When he founded the town of Chandler, he was careful to build into his plans an elaborate ostrich scheme.

In 1887, the twenty-eight-year-old Chandler emigrated from Canada to central Arizona to become the territory's first veterinary surgeon. Chandler traded a country which is virtually afloat – twenty-five per cent ice and water – for a territory of life-throttling aridity. The brute contrast between Ontario and the Sonoran Desert gnawed at him. He became obsessed with conjuring water by any means possible. Obsessed, more precisely, with that fundamental bit of pioneer alchemy whereby water added to land equals real estate.

For the next sixty years Chandler would remain in Arizona, dreaming and scheming, pitting his wits against the desert. He soon abandoned his flourishing veterinary career to focus all his energies on the conundrum of water. His dream was to take the Salt River – which ran near the future Phoenix – to places it had never been. But operating on a major arterial system proved more exacting than animal surgery.

In 1892, Chandler launched Consolidated Canal Company, harnessing the latest technologies of frontier hope: steam dredges, electric pumps and hydro-electric generators. He devised a simple dodge for using water to bankroll land. This land, in turn, funded the expansion of his irrigation empire. The Desert Land Act became the linchpin of his plan. The act offered settlers federal territory at $1.25 an acre, but only if they could bring water to it. Like so many Western speculators before and after him, Chandler bent the system to his advantage. Poor homesteaders couldn't afford to enter the scheme even at $1.25. So Chandler filed the fee for their land then piped in water from his canals. In return, he demanded a slice of the realty that the homesteaders thereby acquired. Chandler then borrowed against this land at a rate of $25 an acre. These loans he invested in Consolidated Canal.

And so his irrigation empire grew, opening the prospect for yet further real estate. Within a few years, he'd pieced together an 18,000-acre ranch. Long before he'd dreamed of converting ostriches into greenbacks, Chandler was in the frontline of frontier necromancy, turning land into water and water into further land.

Chandler's sense of timing proved providential. Bringing water to the West was becoming a glamorous cause. When President Roosevelt unveiled his eponymous dam in 1911, the desert acquired a new aura of redemptive promise. A year later, Arizona entered the Union as the forty-eighth state. Chandler was waiting in advance. Within three months, he'd sold his 18,000-acre ranch to speculators as a fully planned city-to-be. The local paper (which he owned) trumpeted that 'Chandler is destined to be the Pasadena of the Salt River Valley, a city of a thousand beautiful homes, of palatial hotels, the finest pleasure resorts in the southwest, the cleanest home life in the land.'

When the first speculators arrived by rail on a May morning in 1912 they saw nothing more tangible than three wooden shacks and a lonesome billboard. The billboard promised that the ultimate desert resort, the Hotel San Marcos, would soon be appearing there. Hundreds of speculators jostled and wrangled to claim their plots, their dreams more alive to them than the little they could see.

Out West, most towns sprang up chaotically around prospectors' lots. But Chandler sold his city as a futuristic novelty – modern and meticulously planned. The ostrich became a cornerstone of his ultra-modern pitch. This ante-diluvian bird may have looked like some saurian throwback, but in 1912 it was glamorous, totally à la mode. Ostrich plumes evoked the elegance of Paris, London and New York, the romance of haute couture. A proven money-spinner in the Karoo and California it stood as the perfect symbol for Chandler's city-to-be: a plain old ugly bird, redeemed from the desert, bountiful with promise. The ostrich was a visitor from the world to come.

The arrival of this creature, Chandler believed, would boost valley real estate. So he began touting his imminent city as ostrich paradise. He decided to make the running himself by buying 550 ostriches as an investment and a lure. But he wasn't only dreaming ostriches – he had other birds in mind: the wealthy human migrants he dubbed 'winter swallows' who flitted south in winter to contrive lives of seamless sun. Chandler's icebound Canadian youth gave him a gut feeling for the swallow outlook – that yearning for heat, light, longer days. Now that he'd added water to his property he was convinced he could sell not just desert land but desert sun as well.

Chandler wanted to sell in style. So he hired Arthur Burnett Benton, the celebrated California architect, to create a seductive setting for his swallows. Benton's name was synonymous with the Mission Revival movement, launched in California after the 1893 World's Fair. Like the ostrich idea, this style, which Chandler revered, was both retro and forward looking, blending Spanish mission design with modern construction methods.

On 22 November, 1913, Thomas Marshall, vice president of the United States, unveiled the San Marcos Hotel. Ostrich ranching's most powerful backer, Congressman Carl Hayden, was among the 500 guests who danced all night on the hotel rooftop beneath a brilliant desert sky. Guests thrilled to the hotel's spirit of repose: the winding walkways, coral colonnades, pergolas, secret gardens. Vines festooned the Tuscan columns and heavy timber trellises, creating shady passageways.

Chandler exhumed the name for his hotel from deep in local history. In 1539, a Spanish friar, Marcos DeNiza, had led an expedition up from Mexico – the first Europeans to set foot on what is now US soil. A fantasy of gold had lured them north. San Marcos sought to uncover the Seven Cities of Cibola, his quest leading him all the way to Kansas. But he was chasing an ignis fatuus. There were no seven cities, there was no gold. So Chandler named his hotel after a like-minded spirit – a pioneer who foresaw abundant riches where more prosaic minds saw just heat, rock, emptiness and aridity. But San Marcos has gone down in history as a less auspicious name: the first in Arizona's long line of hallucinating settlers.

Chandler parked his 550 ostriches in a paddock adjoining his hotel: a promo, as he saw it, for his town's coming metamorphosis. From my third-floor room in the San Marcos, I could peer down at that spot through rows of tamarind trees and lanky, bald-stemmed palms, tipped with feathery fronds. But Chandler's ostrich paddocks had long since vanished beneath the greensward. By day I listened to the pock, pock, pock of golfers and their humming carts, like kiddie cars, buzzing up and down the links. By night, I could hear – just below the susurrating air conditioners – the sprinklers' incessant hiss. It was loud enough to trouble my sleep: along with the inaudible sound of heavy-drinking grass sucking at the aquifers, draining them more dangerously every minute of every year.

This, too, was a Chandler innovation: golf as manifest destiny. Until 1914, Arizonans played golf on gravel. That year Chandler seeded the San Marcos links with bermuda grass, later adding the state's first sprinkler system. And so he began the relentless green fantasy that has converted Maricopa County into a 175-course empire of golf. Midsummer, one course alone may slurp up a million gallons a day, while the surrounding desert plants and creatures survive on seven inches a year.

As I stood on my San Marcos balcony, the image came back to me of Oudtshoorn's palace lawns, emerald archipelagos in a sea of dust, some of them still glittering with peacocks. There as here, green was the official colour of hope, luxury and amnesia. The links and lawns keep rolling on, smothering the subtle-coloured desert floor – amber, honey, umber, sepia, senna, auburn, roan and mustard hues all vanishing beneath a mat of solid green. It's as if all traces of the desert were obstacles to establishing a permanent St Patrick's Day. The aquifers sink to desperate levels. But the putters and mowers continue to dream green in suburban protest against the indignity of scarcity.

Immigrants are skilful illusionists, recreating their pasts in the most unpromising terrain. Scottish memorabilia litter the map of Greater Phoenix: names like Glendale and Scottsdale, as if the Highlands could be shipped to the South Central Desert and replanted there on a rainfall budget of seven inches a year. Golf has become Arizona's most lucrative Scottish import. Watering-can Celtic skies are the meteorological antithesis of the Sonoran Desert's sheer-blue clarity. Yet underfoot, Maricopa County could be St Andrews, verdant and spongy, plush with denial, an infinity of green.

The ostrich was a stranger to Arizona. But it felt less alien than crabgrass. The bird chomps stones, can live off dirt and scraggly plants. In 1913, Chandler had every reason to believe that ostriches would make him wealthy faster than his investment in that most implausible of desert pastimes, golf.

Chapter Twenty-four

J ust how precious were the plumes in America back then? Al Wiatr, I hoped, would know. So I paid him a visit at the Chandler Museum, where he was curating a show on his city's ostrich legacy. Al brimmed with casual erudition. American ostrich ranchers, he explained, had turned a profit for about twenty years: from around 1894 until World War One. Al waved me towards a cabinet at the apex of the hall: 'Take a look at this lovely French curled feather. It's about seventeen inches long.' It hung there, ice-white, perfectly still behind its glass, a frozen cascade of *fin de siècle* sumptuary.

'Well, we looked it up in a 1908 Sears catalogue and a seventeen-inch feather was going for three seventy-five and a twenty-four-incher for ten dollars. Now in 1908 you could buy a top of the line shotgun, a bed, a sofa, or a cook stove for ten dollars. And we're talking a single feather.'

I peered at a yellow clipping beside the plume, dated 24 September, 1914, from the *Chandler Arizonan*. The African-American Ostrich Company, one of the biggest operatives back East, had just ordered another 120 lb. of Chandler's finest feathers.

I found myself travelling down a seductive corridor of ostrich memorabilia. The walls dripped with billowy hats, pink boas and sensual, cotton-candy fans in a carnival of colours. The mood felt otherworldly, the air scented with Parisian refinement, immaculate *belle époque*. I realized that emotionally I'd stood in that exact place before.

The first time I entered Oudtshoorn's ostrich museum as a boy, I felt as if I'd fallen through the floor and awoken somewhere else. I wasn't used to sensuality displayed so openly. Plumes tumbled from hats, cloaks, fans and tutus – the lush foliage of immorality. The word Granny would have used was wantonness. But that inviting underworld allowed me some deep release from the severity that hemmed us in.

For a whole afternoon, I sank, entranced, into a low-lit featherbed of dreams. Then the ostrich museum closed for the day and I was ejected onto Oudtshoorn's staring streets. To my amazement, the world outside hadn't changed at all. Everyone was still dressed in dust. Passersby wore dark Calvinist clothes as punishing as the morality and the heat. I saw the same old fisted faces, the same drought-and-sin-and-pleasure-fearing eyes. But something inside me had moved – irrevocably.

The raw, new town of Chandler was severe in its own way. That much was scrawled all over Alexander Chandler's face. His portrait presided, rather incongruously, over the Parisian ambience of the Chandler Museum, his profile as impassive as a Mount Rushmore bust. He cut a picture of zealotry: his tight face seamed with schemes, his high, almost clerical collar forcing up his chin. The overhanging eyebrows gave him a shaded gaze which stretched past and through me in a dissolving stare.

But Chandler wasn't just some luminous outback visionary – he had a darker side. He stood accused of harbouring a miscreant who could have earned his keep in any gallery of saloon rogues: Roughneck, the most villainous ostrich in the West. Chandler had other famous birds, like Brigham Young, a rooster who took and kept several brides. But Brigham Young was basically law-abiding outside the bigamy clause. It was Roughneck, a killer four times over, who stewed up all the trouble.

Chandler bought him cut-rate after he'd kicked a pen-attendant to death on the Pan-American Ostrich Farm nearby. Roughneck was one of 200 ostriches that Chandler purchased that day in November 1914. To avoid clashes with humans and hounds – or so he said – Chandler and his wranglers herded this huge flock of birds in an arc from Pan-American, skirting the Salt River Mountains, all the way to downtown Chandler, some fifty miles away.

He could have taken the quick, obvious route and transported them by train. But Chandler had a theatrical eye: he knew the value of publicity. What better ploy for showcasing some hot new livestock than to take them on a three-week cavalcade through the district with coverage (from the newspaper he owned) every step of the way?

Chandler did his best to naturalize his ostriches by insinuating them into American English. His newspaper explained that big-bird handlers, like those on the looping drive, were officially called 'ostrich-boys'. (Those were the days before cow-boys had lost their hyphens.) A photographic series illustrating Chandler's ostrich trek hung on the museum wall. In one blurry photo, a bunch of cowboys were rounding up what appeared to be a flock of outsize feather dusters.

Ostriches are not easy creatures to drive – they have a mindlessness all their own. In keeping with his character, Roughneck fomented a mutiny. The stampeding birds stormed across the path of a pair of newlyweds returning by carriage from their ceremony. Roughneck and his gang panicked the horses, which reared up in fear, spilling the buggy and killing both bride and groom. Roughneck's homicidal habits didn't stop there. He soon claimed victim number four, obliterating one of the world's few genuine ostrich-boys with a kick that caved in his chest.

Locals bayed for the bird's blood. But he lived so fast and loose he was bound to self-destruct. On 19 March, 1915 the *Chandler Arizonan* announced in its boldest typeface: 'Roughneck, Mankiller, Hangs Self'.

'Roughneck,' the obituary opined, 'ran into a fence. He wrapped his long battle-scarred neck around a strand of wire in such a way as to twist the neck into a knot, cutting off his wind. He slowly choked to death.'

Just below Chandler's museum portrait, there hung a grainy mugshot of this lawless homicide. I peered into his wild-eyed stare: he sure looked mad and mean.

Roughneck was trouble for Chandler, but good trouble – the kind he liked. Like today's ostrich boosters, Chandler battled to integrate these misplaced, goofy birds into the Western imaginary. To seduce more settlers to his dreambird mecca, he needed to peddle ostrich ranching as a manly enterprise, tough enough for the West. What kind of stirrups, hat and holster does a man need to go wrangling birds?

Roughneck worked hard to give ostriches a bad-assed name. He helped prove that being an ostrich-boy was one of the huskiest things a man could yearn to be. Bird ranching was, after all, tough, macho work. Certainly, tough enough to stake a claim today on the macho-lite New West.

So Chandler worked Roughneck's violence into his broader plan. But there are accidents of fate no image-management can finesse. Chandler got into golf ahead of the game, but with ostriches, his timing proved abominable. In 1913, plume prices rocketed; the next year they crashed. Like his South African counterparts, Chandler hung on as long as he could. But World War One, Henry Ford and Coco Chanel all bore down on America's ostrich ranchers too.

On 4 March, 1915, Harry Chandler – Alexander's cousin, the *LA Times* editor and one of the most influential men out West – sent a glum note to a business partner about their ailing venture. 'The subject of ostriches has been sticking in my gullet. I'm afraid the enterprise is not destined to be a success.'

That year, many of the Karoo's spendthrift millionaires were reduced to touting for work. In the Jerusalem of Africa, women wearing imported silk gowns joined soup lines and begged on the streets. Their American counterparts soon followed. Ranchers opened their gates and shooed their worthless birds into the wilderness. Well into the 1930s, travellers reported encountering feral ostrich families wandering Orange County and the Sonoran Desert, cast-offs from the crash.

Max Rose spent almost thirty million dollars in today's money buying up feathers after the market had collapsed. He warehoused them for a future that never came. In Arizona, Alexander Chandler also believed the slump was temporary. But in 1918 he was forced to sell off the last of his remaining birds. Top breeders that had once fetched $800 a pair he managed to flog to a local zoo for $7 a head.

Chandler remained determined to move on. The Hotel San Marcos was flourishing, and he always had backup schemes. In 1927, he invited his close pal, Frank Lloyd Wright, to design a companion to the San Marcos, even grander than the first. Two years later, Wright submitted his final plan for the San Marcos in the desert, a 200-room resort that would jut out from Salt Mountain, offering sensational vistas of the desert floor below. Chandler proved as evangelical about his latest scheme as he'd once been about ostriches. The San Marcos in the desert, he exclaimed, would tower over Eden itself: 'The plentiful scattering of native saguaro cacti, the giant ocotillo and the cholla will be reinforced by transplanting more of those species – to make this spot a desert garden such as God in His own lavishness might have planted there.'

In October 1929, just as groundbreaking for God's garden was to begin, the stock market plummeted. Chandler's backers called in their loans. The San Marcos never acquired its ghostly twin. Scrambling to stay solvent, the crash-cursed Chandler was forced to sell the original San Marcos. But he kept a small cottage on the grounds, close by his old ostrich paddocks. That's where, at the age of ninety, he passed away in 1950 – one year before Max Rose.

Some dreams die reluctantly. Like Rose, Chandler felt in his bones that one day the fashion would turn, bringing feathers back again. So he didn't abandon his dream entirely – he merely moved it into the basement. An aged bellhop at the

San Marcos explained as much to me one morning, dropping to one knee and drumming his knuckles on the hotel lobby floor. He cocked an ear, as if listening for an echo from below.

'Down there,' he said, 'down there. Boxes and boxes of them piled high, holding up the ceiling. A basement full of feathers. Weighed nothing, worth sweet nothing. But old Mr Chandler, even after he'd sold the place, he kept ahold of them. Said their time would come again and he'd get all his money back.'

The plumes sat there and sat there long after the boom had crashed. Through the Teens, the Twenties, the Thirties, the Forties, waiting to rebound. When Chandler died, somebody recognized them for what they were – a basement of bad memories – and finally chucked them out. The ostrich past, like the couture that sustained it, seemed irredeemably passé.

The plumes gone, only stories and shreds of stories remained. Mostly, they too, went underground into those cavernous basements and boneyards where we dispatch all our big futures that have turned into dead hopes. Ostriches were added to the dream debris of the West, a part of the world with more than its fair share of quickly buried, anxiously forgotten past. Small wonder that today's ostrich revivalists were rushing towards the future, without ever looking back.

Part Four

Chapter Twenty-five

After my stay in Chandler, I headed back to Willcox along Interstate 10. I wanted to spend more time with the town's new wave of ostrich hopefuls. But I was also curious, while in the Willcox vicinity, to visit Tombstone, home of the OK Corral. When prospectors discovered a rich silver lode there in 1878, the place soon grew into the biggest city between San Francisco and St Louis. But Tombstone's boom lasted exactly eight years. By 1886, the place had exhausted its possibilities. Nowadays, Tombstone only managed to stave off a ghost-town fate by hanging on as a tourist haunt instead.

The road I chose to get there was a mistake. It had looked straight forward on the map. A smooth parabola looping down from Willcox: drive east out of town, go south through Pearce, stop at Gleeson for lunch, coffee and gas, then head on to Tombstone. At least that was the plan. I chose this route to avoid the interstate and explore the backcountry where the Chihuahuan Desert rolls north from Mexico.

After about ten miles, I passed a sign – 'Unimproved Road Surface Ahead'. The ensuing dirt road was so badly washboarded that even at twenty mph it threatened to wreck my back. Each culvert carried a warning not to attempt a crossing in wet weather. I'd heard about drivers getting washed away in spring by torrential monsoon waters roaring down from the border peaks. The route I'd taken was either, it seemed, impassably dry or impassably wet. I'd been taken in by another desert chimera: a notional road built for a season that didn't yet exist.

By the time my odometer suggested that Gleeson should be approaching, the corrugations had jackhammered my spinal column to smithereens. The landscape had blurred: not the usual lateral blur from speed, but a juddery image of vertical vibrations as if the cosmic movie-projector had run amok.

Gleeson never appeared. It proved to be a spectre: the highlight of the town was a sign announcing 'Gleeson'. I passed a peeling trailer and a few memories of shacks, none offering a full complement of walls. There was certainly nothing here as ambitious as a human being or a coffee stop. Not even a ghosted gas station. I was learning that map-reading is not a universal art and that in southeastern Arizona, cartographers treat living towns and dead ones evenhandedly. Towns that are and towns that were each earn a small white dot. You can easily run out of gas pinning your hopes on some outpost of the vanished past.

I eventually adjusted myself to this cartographic idio-syncrasy, even warmed to it. To grant equal solidity to places that still flourish and places that have gone reminds us that what we have can vanish in a flash and what we've lost spring back in unexpected forms.

Tombstone was receding as a prospect. Yet I felt a craving for a destination, somewhere to mark down that I'd been. Then a couple of miles beyond the Gleeson sign, a second sign appeared, hanging at an angle and written in a wobbly or exuberant hand: '1½ Scenic Miles to Arizona's Largest Selection of Rattlesnake Crafts'. Then a further sign: 'Primitive Road. Use at Your Own Risk.'

It sounded ominous. I thought primitive was where I'd been. But I took the turning and the risk. The road, such as it was, dipped down through humpy arid rangeland. It petered out at a couple of trailers. Beyond them stood a peculiar semi-circular fence about twelve-feet high and sixty-feet long. Several hundred metal objects hung suspended from the fence's heavy cables, clanking in the breeze. It was hard, from a distance, to make out quite what this was: it resembled some figment of a druidic junkman's dream.

I eased my back out of the car and walked on over. Somebody had hoisted things – farm things, kitchen things, hunting things – in various states of dereliction all along the fence. Pitchforks, coyote traps, butter urns, tractor seats, steamer trunks, potato mashers, branding irons, mission bells, mangles, chaps, typewriters, ploughs, shoe-horns, egg-beaters, wagon wheels, scales, gas cookers, saw-toothed stirrups, pots, washing machines, miners' lamps, coal shuttles, shovels, hoes, hacksaws, stamp machines, gold miners' pans, binoculars, hammers, clocks, mincing machines, colanders, a tin toilet seat, a chicken snagger . . . and a myriad other things whose names and purposes I couldn't even guess.

I lingered there awhile, absorbing this object lesson in the weight, the detail, the jangling music of the past. So many things shadowed by the vanished hands that had worked them. The mood was one of labour and abandonment. A sieve, an urn, a lamp, a jagged jaw of spurs: all that remained of some individual industry, desperation, hope or foolishness.

Whoever slung these objects up had clustered them within striking distance of each other, so the fence doubled as a giant wind-chime and a heavy-metal history of the white settling of the West. But I'd never heard a wind-chime speak so many different voices, have so much talk in it. As I stood there, at the centre of the arc, a breeze whipped through, rousing the stirrups, traps, tractor seats and typewriters back to life. Soon the whole place was full of whispers, gasps, clanging and keening.

The desert yawned all around; no traces of anyone. But the fence was company, rich in old-time conversation. And wit as well: a pair of handcuffs groped noisily at a pram, while a harrow, goaded by the wind, beat the stuffing out of what appeared to be the world's first pop-up toaster.

The smaller of the trailers – an eight by twenty-four – had a sign up inviting visitors to enter. I found nobody inside.

Snakes and snake parts filled every corner of the trailer – nothing but scales, skins, skeletons and fangs. They'd all been turned into accessories: snakeskin holsters, belts and money clips, comb pouches, knife sheaths, earrings, barrettes and Alice bands. Rattlesnake steering-wheel covers for people who like to drive feeling a reptile slip through their hands. A set of diamondback-rattler vertebrae made an exquisite necklace, weighted at the centre by the creature's pendulous skull. Arizona is unusually rich in poisonous life forms and a good sampling of them – scorpions, tarantulas, coral snakes, diamondback and Mojave rattlers – resurfaced here as campy craft. In a corner fishtank, a bloated rattler slunk up through the eye of a coyote skull, caught permanently in the self-ironic melodrama of a desert Gothic pose.

I was pondering buying a seven-snake-skin Alice band for my twelve-year-old English niece, when a grey-haired, barefoot man entered the trailer to add an arrowhead to a display. He introduced himself as John Weber. 'When you've got what you want, just stick your money in the box outside.'

I'd noticed the box nailed to the trailer door: the business ran on the honour system. It was strange to emerge from that indoor air of menace to a sign inviting you to pay on trust.

At John's invitation, I sauntered back to the larger trailer where he lived. We sat on the patio for the afternoon, talking snakes and ghost towns, accompanied by the banging of the metal choir. John and his wife, Sandy, had moved down to Arizona from Rockford, Illinois, fifteen years before as newlyweds. At the time he'd been forty-four, Sandy forty-three. Sandy had worked as a secretary for a cable-TV company, John for a firm that built nothing but the gadget that stops an airplane's lights from going brighter when its engine roars.

The Webers lived in terror of becoming perpetual papershufflers. They fantasized escape. John tugged at his luminous white beard and chuckled: 'We dreamed of earning a modest living by doing something lazy.' The snake-hunter life-style gave them the idleness they craved.

When they first arrived in Cochise County the Webers lived

in the ghost town I'd just passed through. Gleeson, John explained, had been an old turquoise mining settlement, active for a few years in the late nineteenth century. Probably didn't even last a decade. It never ceased to amaze me, the speed with which communities rose and fell around here. Even faster than in the Karoo and South Africa's mineral rich hinterland, where so many high hopes flashed and then were gone. Here people hit paydirt or – more often – hit rock bottom. Either way, they moved. Mostly, they disappeared real fast, forgetting what they'd left behind. But their legacy stayed to haunt newcomers like the county's ostrich folk, who lived in earshot of the wind that whistles through the shells of abandoned prospects past.

The Apaches call ghost towns *Sno-To-Ha*, meaning 'Just Lying There'. The more of those empty-eyed towns I saw, the more apt the phrase began to sound. They're places that die without disappearing; they have a tenacious afterlife. In the desert air, the skeletons of memory last and last: without rampant foliage, without humidity, the past just lies there, finished, stripped bare, but reluctant to decay.

I asked John what life in Gleeson had been like. For nine years, he and Sandy had lived in the mini-trailer they now used for selling snake-goods from. He chuckled: 'Can you believe it? Five years, two people, in an eight by twenty-four? No air-conditioning. No heat either. In winter, we used a fan to blow warmth from the cooker towards the bed.'

There had been no other people around – just plenty of signs they'd had the foresight to leave. But John and Sandy didn't lack for company. A large and lively reptile population remained in residence. Diamondback rattlers, mostly. John had done some snake-catching as a boy in Illinois and again at college in Florida. So he decided to use it as a fallback career. At the time, Sandy responded enthusiastically. 'We're total partners. She's in Illinois right now, visiting the grand-kids. Normally we do everything together. It's not every wife who enjoys a life of killing and skinning snakes.'

But after nine ghost-town years in Gleeson, they were happy to move to their current ranch. For one thing, snakes were even more prolific here. Also, John stressed, the new ranch felt more desolate which was what they liked. With a lift from their small pensions, the Webers found they could stay afloat killing around 120 snakes a year. Their greatest financial asset was the rattler's natural arrogance. John tugged at his beard: 'Most reptiles – whip snakes, blacktails, garter snakes, coral snakes, bull snakes – they see you and they scoot. But the rattlesnake won't. He won't eat coil for anyone. He'll just keep on going proud and slow like a caterpillar.'

John disappeared inside to fetch some beer. When he returned, he explained that August is peak season – the hottest month, when the rattlers are out each night. 'It's a little cool right now. We only hunt at night, it's not worth it in the day. In August alone, we catch half the snakes we need to keep us alive during the year.'

At first John and Sandy used a golf putter, dancing around, trying to pin the rattlers down. That, they decided, was tempting fate. So they bought a professional snake catcher's stick. John hauled it out for me to see: a four-feet-long aluminum rod with a pair of pliers at one end, a pistol grip at the other. One partner clamps the snake, the other holds its head down with a stick and chops it off instantly with a knife. 'We don't mess with bags, boxes, cages. Rattlers are Houdinis. They'll push their nose through anything. That's how trouble starts.' Even when its head is severed, the snake can still deliver one last lethal bite, a ghost-bite from beyond the grave.

John was turning sixty, Sandy was one year away. Neither of them had been bitten yet. Working with rattlers for a living and having no health insurance, you had, John insisted, to take that little bit of extra care. Diamondbacks kill more Americans than all other snakes combined. 'Even if you don't die, the agony is such that you wish you were dead.' John fell quiet for a minute, perhaps thinking about that rattler bite he'd never had.

'Down here, as the years go by, you get lazier and lazier. We could never go back to work now. That's for people who want to be upwardly mobile, and we've always wanted to stay down-wardly mobile.'

I pictured the Webers playing life like a game of snakes and ladders. While all the other players were hoping the dice would send them soaring up a ladder, John and Sandy were sliding down their rattlers and relishing the freedom of being back at GO again.

John cracked the beers. He offered, as his best approxi-mation of potato chips, a bag of rattler jerky. It had, as it were, a bite to it. Genuinely tasty, in a smoky kind of way. Before I knew it, I'd chased down half a snake with my beer.

What was the spicing?

'Garlic. Loads and loads of garlic. Most folk who make this stuff, don't put enough garlic in the marinade.'

I stared out across the desert's sprawling quiet. A thin mauve line of grass added a determined glamour to the land's creased and aged face. As the sky darkened, I noticed a distant sulphur haze – the lights, John explained, of the border town, Agua Prieta, over in Mexico. Somewhere, 10,000 feet above us, a US satellite searched permanently for 'aliens'. Douglas, Agua Prieta's American twin, had become a favourite crossing point for illegal immigrants. It was strange to feel so isolated and yet so monitored, some FBI agent charting every human movement down here as it blipped across his screen.

The sun set in a swirl of sugared sherbet. Behind us, the heavy metal fence pinked and clinked incongruously. I closed my eyes and heard moored yachts talking to a marina breeze.

I asked John about the fence. 'It was Sandy's idea.' In their Gleeson days, they'd used a metal detector to hunt down old things buried in the sand. Horse-shoes, plough-blades, rail-road spikes, things that helped them piece together, in imagination, the ghost town's human past. They'd strung the stuff up and become obsessed with getting more. Made it known to neighbouring ranchers that they'd trade rattler goods for relics. And so the fence had grown and grown.

I didn't relish tackling the Gleeson Road in the dark. John

hauled out his map and showed me a less tortuous route. I thanked him and headed for my car, clutching a ziplock bag of freeze-dried rattler, and a photo – pulled from an old German biker magazine – of John and Sandy dangling a six-foot diamondback.

As I turned to leave, I paused beside the arcing fence of memory. I closed my eyes and listened to the cacophony as a rising desert wind clattered through the metal. Working the wind, the suspended past reclaimed its ancient business.

Chapter Twenty-six

On the seventh day after my return to Willcox, an edginess sets in. How quickly a town of unfamiliar faces has become a town in which I seem to recognize them all. And they know me. Familiar sun-tightened eyes have started to subject me to a different scrutiny. I feel the onset of an old airlessness.

In the Oudtshoorn of America the wagon-wide streets stretch as huge and vacant as the streets of the Karoo. The sensation returns to me with unsettling speed. So much space, so little room to breathe. I feel no stranger here than I did as a child in small-town South Africa. But that is strange enough. The one-mistake towns of my youth still possess the power to reach me here, to make me nervy at the memory of being different and living over-observed.

Small things begin to get to me. One morning, at the supermarket checkout counter, I start leafing through the selection of magazines for men: *Shooting, Bowhunting, Bow Bucks, Deer and Big Game Hunting, Deer and Deer Hunting, Modern Gun, Guns, Military and Technical Journal, S.W.A.T., Soldier of Fortune, Combat Handguns, Knives, American Handgunner,* the *Journal of American Bladeware.*

I pay for my groceries and decide to spend the day driving out of town. I'm seduced by all that space beyond – it seems like an extra lung.

For the first few miles, I trail behind a pickup kicking dust and bearing a bumper sticker that explains: 'A man without a gun is a subject, but a man with a gun is a citizen.' Then the citizen turns down a farm track and is gone.

I continue down the Kansas Settlement Road that points south to Mexico. The road leads me past Willcox playa, fifty square miles of dead lake with an alkali crust that has been building since the Pleistocene age. The playa gives off a watery glare like burning magnesium, a *fata morgana* painful to the eye and to the imagination. Local lore brims with cautionary tales about pioneers and prospectors tricked into the heart of the playa by mirages of liquid and the hopeful hootings of ghost trains.

Between the road and the waterless lake I can see no sign of life, except for skeletal bushes that seem charred less by fire than by the inner combustion of staying alive. After a few more miles, I swing east along a corrugated gravel track that takes me past an abandoned house, defeated-looking and full of ragged gougings where the wind has sawn through. After that, no further signs of human occupation. Then, just at the point where the track runs out, I notice a distant figure hammering at a post, his efforts swallowed up by the wide, slack-jawed sky. That's all I can hear when I stop: the solid whumping of a mallet, wood on wood.

The man watches my approach, made slower by the space and solitude. As he knocks back his black stetson, I can see that he is young, with a faint mustache and a sun-reddened skin; his jeans are agape at the knee. He is putting up a dog pen and staking out some ostrich runs, Chris Morgan tells me. Ostriches, he says, have more promise than cattle these days; they do OK on less acreage and poorer land; feed-to-flesh they give you a better conversion ratio. There is a quiet formality to his answers even though, or perhaps because, we stand alone on the plain.

This is ostrich ranching from scratch: 'I don't have a well, power, telephone; last time I was here I was camping out in a tent until I set up the shed and put in the posts.' Chris has moved down from Castle Rock, Colorado. One day he'd driven into Denver for an ostrich seminar and heard all about

168

Willcox: that you could get your birds to start laying earlier down here and spit out bigger clutches.

Chris once worked for the forest services in Wyoming and carries with him, as a kind of talisman, the elk horns that lie at his feet. He shifts from one leg to the other as he talks. Then he gazes towards the black pleats of Cochise Stronghold and falls quiet, as if blown off course by some inner weather. A turkey vulture lazes above us, floating and tilting on the thermals, quartering the range.

Desert land for $1.25 an acre is a vanished pioneer dream that belongs to Chandler's era. Still, Chris has gotten his spread of ostrich heaven for half what people are paying along the Fort Grant Road. Out here, a ghosted place is beginning again: it seems a retake of an older drama, a homesteading scene of sorts. One man, one dog, 280 acres; a wife and three ostriches to follow.

Chapter Twenty-seven

Towards dusk that day, after a long, looping drive, I rejoin the Kansas Settlement Road and meander back towards Willcox. I'm hoping to glimpse some of the 10,000 Sandhill Cranes that I've been told roost on the playa. The cranes are migrants and spring is already stirring. So they may, I realize, have already abandoned Arizona for Canada's thawing Arctic north.

I spend an hour scouring the playa's fifty square miles of shimmery strangeness with my binoculars. Even in this late, low-angled light, the playa dips and dances before my eyes. The cranes are gone. I know instinctively they've vanished for the year, probably within the past few days. As I trudge the scrubby shoreline, the dry lake seems not just empty but ghosted by this ancient, ritual abandonment.

I picture the Willcox cranes dancing across the tundra's ballroom floor as their courting season begins. Each couple performs a remarkable long-limbed pas de deux. The partners face each other, bobbing and weaving. Then together they leap into the air, feet thrust forward, wings flung wide, tubular necks thrown to the sky as they rattle out their cry: kar-r-r-r-o-o-o, rolling their 'r's like Scots. The dancers land and bow, then begin their dance again.

I feel these absent dancers powerfully. Their prancing shadows flicker across the playa. All that remains is the promise of return. I try to think of their loyalties as not so much divided as rhythmically redoubled: they'll always belong here, there and inbetween. These are birds of place and birds of passage that turn towards home in the very act of leaving it. Twice yearly, they respond to the steering stars, the moon, the curved earth's gravity and the urgent inner tuggings of crane hormones and genes.

So much remains unknown about migration's necromancy. Will the parents of this year's Arctic brood teach them to yearn for Willcox playa next fall, setting a lifelong pattern of return? But if parental training is fundamental, how do we explain the migratory urge in young cuckoos that are raised in the nest of another species, often a nonmigratory bird? On their first inter-continental migration, cuckoo offspring will mysteriously 'return' unguided to their parents' territory, a place they've never seen.

The enigma of migration has inspired some lively scientific fictions. On observing geese flying high in a bright night sky, one eighteenth-century scholar decided he'd solved the mystery of seasonal disappearances. Birds, he deduced, migrate vertically, spending each winter on the moon.

However poorly we understand the bird logic of departures and returns, we've come a long way since Pliny and Aristotle. Both men contended that swallows didn't migrate, but spent the winter snoozing underground. Aristotle's alternative theory proved equally flamboyant. He noticed that some species, like redstarts, arrived in Greece in summer soon after winter visitors, like robins, had departed. The redstarts and the robins, he concluded, were in fact identical, just seasonally metamorphosed.

Aristotle's theories of hibernation and transmutation weren't randomly deranged. Within the limits of his day, they made a certain sense. Human migration back then remained a modest thing: *Homo sapiens* was a far less mobile species than we've since become. Travel was ponderous, the known world a diminutive place. Nothing in human experience suggested that distance could exist on the scale birds flew biannually. Incompetent to imagine moving rapidly across continents themselves, the ancients denied birds the fullness of their powers. It was easier to believe that vanishing swallows spent the winter swaddled underground or could change from one shape into another, than it was to credit them with flying from earth's end to earth's end and back again each year.

Persuaded that the cranes have gone, I begin to feel the playa's overpowering hauntedness, its sudden solitude. As the sun sinks, it colludes with the arid lake to produce a glaring sheen exhausting to the eyes. I return to the car and head back for town across the scrub desert plain.

A few miles on, I pass a field of ostriches, necks crooked like question marks. I stop and watch them idly. The surrounding landscape is so reminiscent of the Karoo that these misplaced birds look for a moment as if they might belong. But it isn't just flightlessness that has made their presence in Arizona implausible. Birds typically migrate north to south, temperate to tropical and back again. No species migrates sideways across the Atlantic. Why risk those oceanic hazards only to arrive in a place that looks and feels just like the place you left behind? Unlike people, birds when they migrate normally insist on better weather.

I wonder how Aristotle would have explained the cranes' departure and the appearance of these ostriches. Would he have invoked the abracadabra science of metamorphosis? And concluded that these are the missing cranes in seasonal disguise, turned by the magic turning of the year into ostriches?

Then one of them begins to dance.

He is a soloist, twirling and twirling with a prancing gait then falling to his knees, pumping his wings from side to side, stirring up a haze of dust. As children, we called this ostrich ballet or, sometimes, ostrich waltzing.

Suddenly time slides. This dance isn't happening in front of me but 10,000 miles and thirty years away.

On one of our Karoo pilgrimages, Dad sees a thorn tree up ahead, pulls off the road and stops to rest beneath it. He doesn't need to explain. True to form, the Opel Kapitan is boiling over again. The radiator has become one of our regular stations of the cross. Dad wanders off in search of succulents for his rockery. My brother and I stand around in the spotty shade, waiting for the car to cool. Even under a tree, it's a stungun heat.

Then a quarter of a mile off, a male ostrich hurtles across the desert floor, wings outstretched, twirling all the time and trailing storms of dust. At ten years old, I've never seen anything so spectacular. The world falls away: all I can see is this dancer highstepping it at speed across the plain, as if the earth were too hot to handle. The bird runs, then whirls and pirouettes some more, in a velvet blur.

Suddenly, the ostrich stops and sinks to his knees, collapsing onto the bright red earth. A drab female looks on absently. He squats there, chest pushed forward, legs thrust ahead of him along the ground. He flings his long neck over his shoulders in an arching loop, until his head touches his spine. Then he begins to thrash about in an exquisite theatre of agony, striking his head against first the left then the right side of his rib cage, left and right again, until I cannot count the blows. As he hammers his skull against his ribs he rocks and rolls, pumping his outspread wings like a dying swan struggling to reclaim the air. By the time the ostrich finishes his courting dance, the desert earth has painted his white wing-tips blood-red.

The female seems unimpressed. She pokes at some pebbles with her beak and saunters off, in search, perhaps, of a real man.

Dad has missed the dance. When he returns with his succulents, I'm still deep inside its thrall. Dad traces one finger across the sky, saying something. I can't hear his words, but his lips are legible. What I read is 'Listen, boys. Dead silence.'

For me, that silence is deep and merciful, that silence is alive.

And now, remembering the dance, I'm starting to remember why this landscape once meant so much to me. For much of childhood, I stumbled through the world in a state of semi-deafness. I grew to be a little old man of a boy, a junior Gaffy, craning to hear, but often falling through the gap between the faint world of human sound and the clarity of language. My life was filled with far-off murmurings, strict voices and loving ones, just this side of silence.

I wasn't wholly deaf, just very hard of hearing. My mother escorted me from one ear-and-nose-and-throat man to the next. Tuning forks. Syringes. Tetracyclene in mega-doses. The blanket of anaesthesia falling across my face as surgery began. I inhabited a world of hammers, anvils, stirrups and canals, of quarrying, blasting, pumping and draining. My problem was fluid build-up.

I lived a high tide, low tide kind of life. I would wake from an operation hearing brilliantly, the world solid underfoot, feet back on dry land. Then, slowly with the passing weeks, the tide would creep up again, washing the world away and leaving me with that underwater feeling of drowning from within.

So I learned to live with the ebb and flow of sound and silence, sound and silence. When there was noise around, I'd miss things; and missing things was dangerous. Punishment, I learned, was tidal. Mostly it came when my canals were flooded, when I hadn't seen the doctor in a while. At the deaf end of the month.

'Your problem, young man, is that you never listen.' But I knew otherwise. I was listening, listening and treading water, listening for more than I could ever hope to hear.

At the highwater mark, I watched people, guessed and pretended, listening to the soundtrack on their faces: a loosening in the lips, a jaw tightening, eyes shifting mood, any flicker of this or that. But the Karoo was different from people. It stayed silent, said little, spoke volumes. You could hear nothing and miss nothing and not be punished for it. It was a quiet world, large-hearted, that fell softly on bad ears.

All those early years, I felt swamped by my inner wetlands. I dreamed and dreamed of drying out, of living water free.

Watching this twirling Arizona ostrich and behind it that shadow dancer, I feel the need for a deeper word than memory. Suddenly, I'm back on dry land, touching the childhood place that salvaged me. It's a quarter of a century since I last entered a desert. Here as there, it is perfectly quiet, perfectly arid. I've returned to the first landscape that let me trust its silence when I couldn't believe my ears.

Chapter Twenty-eight

After the ostrich dance, I drive straight back to my Willcox motel room. I close the door, pour a Scotch and begin to write. About Gaffy and Granny's migration from Biggar, the missing mavis, Karoo plants that mimic rocks and ostriches that eat time. This becomes my rhythm. By day I roam old ghost towns and new ostrich ranches. By night I return to my motel, which suddenly seems a perfectly congenial place from which to summon back the past. I can feel the memories move, memories which for all my adult years have been lying still as stones.

The ostrich ranchers, in their way, help me reconnect, by reminding me of the kind of man I'm not. In Willcox, I often get mistaken for a prospective rancher myself. 'Thinking of moving down here, fella? Be sure to get yourself a nice one-hundred-and-eighty-acre parcel along the Fort Grant Road . . . I tell you, best place to get your slick-wire fencing is this guy I know in Tucson.'

I want to say to all these fence-fixing, barn-building men I meet out on the range, 'You've got me muddled up: you're thinking of my father.' He could ranch ostriches if anybody could. Mr Fixit. The man who could make and mend anything. I'm deeply drawn to the desert. But I boast none of my father's practical ingenuities without which one would soon go under in this forbidding world. Out here, I'd be a disgrace: worst frontiersman in the history of the West. I'm a class-A incompetent in the company of things. At my merest approach objects turn moody, unco-operative. Perhaps because they can sense, ahead of time, that's what I expect of them. That I'm wary of what they'd do to me – the kind of man I would become – if we worked together as a team.

I find myself thinking back to the rattler-catchers' metal fence: the traps, the tractor seats, the branding irons, the harrows . . . all those implements used to subdue the land. I am awed by the practical skills they memorialize, and at the same time, I recoil from them. I have chosen a life where I work with words – as far away as I can get from metal and wooden tools.

One evening, the emotions underlying that choice, that sentiment, return to me. I'm sitting in my motel room transcribing my interview with the ostrich 'homesteader', Chris Morgan. After speaking to Chris, I must have forgotten to switch the tape-recorder off. I can hear my scrunching tread as I retrace my steps across the range. And in the background, I can hear Chris resume his hammering. Whump, whump, whump, driving another fence-post down. That hammering sets off in me some deep emotional echoing. An image returns: of my father, mallet in one hand, face locked in defiance and pain, hammering at the recalcitrant surface of our car, trying to fix a dent in the hood.

I'm thirteen and it's Sunday. The males in our family – my father, Andy and I – are following our holy day routine. Dad will drop us off at church where we'll be singing in the choir – seven o'clock evensong. Then he'll drive on to review the Sunday concert at the Feather Market Hall which stands in our town centre, just a hundred yards from St Mary's. At the bottom of the hill, my father will part company from his sons.

I insist on sharing the front seat with Dad on the drive. My little brother, Andy, sits solo, playing with his yellow yo-yo in the back. It's already 7.03 as we pass the Albert Jackson School clock tower. We're still a few blocks from church and I'm badgering Dad to drive faster as we descend White's Road. This, too, is part of our routine. For Dad, to be a bit belated is to be perfectly on time. He's busy, hates waiting. But our choirmaster (Mr Music) has a military vision of punctuality. He was a sergeant-major in World War Two and believes that lateness is lateness. He's hellbent on making men of us – he's vicious with the cane. If you're not perfectly on time, you'll be thrashed for it the next day. His eyes flash that message as you slink into the choir-stalls after the seven o'clock chime.

Of course, it's sissy, unthinkable to mention punishment at home, the global epicentre of 'grin and bear it'. So my mission in life is to harass Dad into changing the way he sees time. And periodically to turn all the clocks in our house, surreptitiously, seven minutes forward. Nothing works. Dad and I, it seems, will never be in synch.

White's Road ends in a steep hill that looks out over the Indian Ocean. So steep that from the top, I often think, maybe the car will run away with us, plunge straight down through the scraggly cannas in the mayoral garden and drag us all to the bottom of the sea.

The night is black, the moon curtained by clouds. We're almost at the old, blind lighthouse now, whose flashing eye shut long ago, stopped witnessing anything. As we crest the hill, Dad revs a little, a half-hearted gesture to my demand for speed. But we're still not going fast. I'm thinking: 'Mr Music will kill me, he'll kill me, I know he will.'

We've just cleared the ridge when I see a dark shape shuffle into the road, angling in front of us. I let out a shout. Everything slows down and I have all the time in the world to watch Dad swinging his eyes left and right, left and right, not seeing what I see.

There's a thud, then a tumbling heap, high above us, of struggling clothes. A long, almost leisurely wait then another thud, as the heap smacks the tarmac ahead of us and begins to roll.

I leap out and start chasing the body. It's getting away from me, it's rolling and rolling, gathering speed, heading for the church. There's a leather briefcase skidding fast as well; it bumps to a halt against a parking meter halfway down the hill.

If only I can just reach it and return it to the man, maybe things will be OK.

I get there panting, pick up the briefcase and see a name on it I recognize shimmering in cracked gold. I race uphill again, uphill towards my brother.

'Andy, it's Father Keats, it's Father Keats.'

I wrap my arms around Andy who buckles into a heap of sobs. 'Don't cry, little brother, please don't cry.'

I feel helpless. I can't stop him. What good are you in this world if you can't stop your own brother from feeling pain?

Father Keats is the priest at church. He should be preaching tonight, lisping out his sermon just before us choristers stand up, red anthem books cracked open at 'Jesu, Joy of Man's Desiring'. Father Keats is a warm man with a fleshy face and a laugh that swells like his middle. After communion this morning, Andy and I caught the No. 7 bus home with him. He told us jokes, took out a penknife and split a green apple into wedges for us all to share.

First the crowd appears, then an ambulance to carry away our dead priest. My father disappears with the police. Eventually, Uncle Lindsay arrives and drives Andy, me and our badly dented Opel Kapitan home.

Our family life fell into two parts: before and after the crash. We were already a shrinking unit. Gaffy, my great-grandfather, had recently gone to the grave; my sister Sheelagh had vanished soon after to England. Ruth, the eldest of us five children, had emigrated as well, to Melbourne, down under. After the crash, Dad, or some major part of him, also disappeared.

Dad became silent and distracted. He'd sit on the veranda staring at the newspaper, holding it for ages at the wrong distance from his eyes. When family and friends joined him and tried to goad him into small talk, he simply held his silence.

179

Early one morning, a week after the event, I was woken by a succession of banging noises, like an off-key dinner gong. I got up and traced the sound to our backyard. Dad had his head buried beneath the hood of our car. He was hammering and hammering at the huge hole where Father Keats had been.

He stopped his hammering when he heard me coming and removed his head.

'I'm trying to fix this dent in the bonnet.' He spoke abstractly, as if neither of us had a clue how it had got there; as if, perhaps, a meteor had fallen on our Kapitan in the night, leaving behind this cavity.

There had been a mishap; things would be repaired. Something had been dented, so something needed to be straightened out. It was all impersonal, shaped by the passive voice.

Dad continued banging and straightening until the shadow of the dead priest's bulk started slowly to recede.

'Here, would you hold this for me?' He handed me a bowl of putty. He held the spatula. Everything would be smoothed over now, the memory, the fear would go away. He didn't want me to get directly involved. But he wanted me there, I could tell, as a witness to his work.

He was being a man for me; I was watching how to become one. This was my emotional apprenticeship. Learning to do what men are meant to do with grief and other big emotions: putty over them until a crust hardens above the hole.

I stood there in the posture of an altar boy at some ritual sacrament, cradling the silver chalice, stretching it towards him in my hands. I can still smell the incense flooding down from the vine above us, the passion fruit that clambered uncontrollably all over our carport. It was late spring, and the vine was bursting with wide open, starry-eyed flowers.

I stood there holding the bowl, trying to help him fill the cavity. The silence I couldn't fill. We had no words of consolation for each other. Man to boy, boy to man, we had no words.

Then Mom appeared and stood where she often stood, in the kitchen doorway on the threshold of the yard. She wasn't treading on the men's territory. But her hands were hooked onto her hips, elbows jutting out in a way that made her big arms – strong from domestic chores – seem bigger. In our crowded household, this was her way of clearing some space before she spoke.

'For goodness sake, Bob, take it to the garage. Let the garage-man do a proper job on it. You can't tackle that yourself.'

She spoke with love, with pity, with pain.

I saw him turn and stare at her with a look of blazing anger; and just beneath that, a look of the most terrible fear. He said nothing. Silence: his heavy artillery. Mom was driven back over the horizon and into the kitchen, where Granny was bottling fruit again.

We continued our fixing. The job was taking longer than I'd imagined, the putty vanishing into the cavity like butter into toast.

Then Dad stopped and turned to me. 'My boy, don't ever pay to fix something if you can fix it yourself.'

We passed the rest of the time in silence, until we'd finished with the hole.

Job done, Dad went inside and changed for the office. He spat on his shoes and brushed them. He always did this, it saved, he said, on polish. But this morning he kept on brushing, back and forth, back and forth, spitting and brushing, long after the shine was so high that he could see himself down there.

Then he climbed into the Kapitan and drove off to face the world.

For a time, when I could, I went everywhere with him. Mom would say: 'Dad's going to Settlers' Park. Why don't you go along for company?'

We always travelled there and back in dead-silent turbulence. I was the only one who'd spotted Father Keats in time.

So I kept my eyes gripped tightly on the road ahead, on the lookout for more priests.

Dad's driving changed completely. He developed an erratic, surging style behind the wheel that he never overcame. He would brake and rev in the wrong places, couldn't settle on a speed. He drove hunched up now, peering over the grey pool of putty on the hood, as if wondering what might rise up from it next.

Something had vanished inside of him. All I could see was a man who wasn't coping, but who felt that if he hoped to be – to stay – a man he could never admit as much. As a boy approaching manhood, I grasped something of his predicament.

One day, weeks after the crash, Mom found me alone in the bedroom that I shared with Andy. Her face looked troubled, desperate. She stared at me, gave me a hug, then said: 'You're the man of the family now.' And left, closing the door.

I changed instantly. Stopped acting up, became a model family citizen. Took up religion, took on responsibilities. Held back from pleasure, held my feelings down. I felt powerless to protect the family the way a real man should. But I did my best. From what I saw around me, my main task as a man was the obligation not to show. I let nothing get to me; for ten years I never wept.

I shared my brother's bed for the next six months, cradling him when he cried. He was a child, three years younger than me, I was now a man. Officially, I was comforting him. But he helped me more than he could tell, doing all that grief-work for us. He seemed to have a huge gift for sadness and for joy. He was my lightning conductor, absorbing all the emotions I felt but didn't dare show.

At night, as I held my brother deep in sleep, Father Keats would come to me, usually bottled in a jar. His black vestments flapped like wings in the fluid. I couldn't tell if he was alive and swimming for his life or just one of the floating dead. Either way, he never spoke a word. He always came with an apple gripped tightly between his teeth.

***

When Dad's trial finally came round, it made the front page of *The Eastern Province Herald*, the newspaper where he worked. He was, in the end, acquitted of culpable homicide. Extenuating circumstances – dark night, black-cassocked priest jaywalking beneath the crest of a hill. But the judge roundly condemned my father nonetheless: he became the occasion for a sermon on the blight of reckless driving. The judge was a man Dad knew from the Dahlia Society.

I couldn't see back then, how deep his shame must have gone. How his dented public image and, with it, his dented sense of self could never be puttied over. Priest-killer. Exhibit A of antisocial recklessness.

In this small, tight, white community, where it was hard to pass unknown, Dad had worked all his life to achieve a municipal renown. Among charity organizers, school principals, gardeners, photographers, dahlia judges, music-lovers, theatregoers, conservationists and the like. That's where he'd put his pride, in his vision of civic-mindedness, his belief that a man ought to belong with the full responsibility of roots.

From the evening the priest died until Dad's death a quarter of a century later, we never spoke about the fact that we'd had a crash together. It felt strange to kill the family priest without ever getting round to talking about his sudden disappearance from the pulpit. I always thought the killing was something we'd done together, our joint responsibility. But from the instant the crash happened it was past, and the past for Dad was useless, just a place for burying things.

I came away from it all with an understanding and a fear of the way men often hide. Dad had always been a handyman. Our tight budget had demanded it. But after the crash, he stepped up the work. Whenever the family threatened to get emotional, there was something to fix outside, some broken thing would call.

He had nowhere else to put his fear, his courage and his

shame. We lived surrounded by box-jawed men who knew cars, washing machines, lawnmowers, tree-pruning, roofwork and plumbing inside out, but had no words for saying how they felt. We lived among men who banked their emotions so long that when the time came round to draw on them, they'd misplaced the key.

Already I knew, as the man of the family, that's what I was supposed to do, to be. A lockjawed fixer of things, the surest sign that I could hold my own as a man among other men. But, whatever I became, I didn't want it to be that. Even as I held my emotions down, I feared that once I submitted to those codes of speechless practicality, I'd disappear for ever into a fixer's world of emotional disrepair.

As children we see so much, so little. What I saw after the crash was a dark shape, bigger than me, but somehow ghostly. My father: the silhouette of a man on the horizon, vanishing into broken things. Feet busy, busy, busy; head in the sand.

Part Five

Chapter Twenty-nine

In Willcox, people kept probing me: did I have any inside information about Nelson Mandela's policy on the ostrich? South Africa's first democratic elections were just two months away. If the elections went ahead, no-one doubted the ANC would win. But would they lift South Africa's ban on exporting live ostriches, which dated back almost a hundred years to the feather boom? As one Willcox rancher worried aloud to me: 'If Mandela opens up the Karoo, ostriches will be coming out of everywhere.' Then America's protectionist prices – $60,000, $70,000 a pair – would come tumbling down. Across the southwest, ostrich ranchers were sleeping badly, afraid that Nelson Mandela would embrace free trade and drive them to the wall.

A month after my return from Arizona, I met a delegation of ANC economists at the Algonquin Hotel in midtown Manhattan. The economists – some old friends of mine, others new acquaintances – were on a reconnaissance trip to Washington to lobby for the New South Africa. We sat in the Edwardian dimness of the Algonquin's oak-panelled lobby, talking about peace and violence, mostly. From one news bulletin to the next, South Africa's prospects veered between chaos and an epic hopefulness. I was leaving shortly for a return trip to South Africa – a pilgrimage of sorts. To vote for the first time, to do some reporting on the changes and, in a more personal vein, to explore the past.

Faizel Ismail gave his cocktail a vigorous swirl and turned to me: 'So what kind of things will you be writing about?'

I told him. 'The Zulu conflict in KwaZulu Natal, the white right, the challenge of land redistribution.' Faizel gave a furrowed nod. 'Actually,' I added, 'I'm also thinking of writing something else, something completely unconnected. A book about ostriches.'

Faizel brightened visibly. 'The ANC has that one covered too. We've got some people working on a plan. By the year two thousand, we want to bring blacks and coloureds into this ostrich business. They've got the skills, you know, they just haven't had the opportunities or the land.' Faizel rummaged through his briefcase. 'Here, when you get to Cape Town, call this number. If you're interested in ostriches, he's the guy who knows everything the ANC is up to.' I took the number eagerly.

A few weeks later, I found myself driving across the Karoo towards Oudtshoorn for the first time in a quarter of a century. I clung to the backroads to slow time down. I wanted to make the journey last. I watched the Karoo deliver the same vista again and again. What I saw I recognized, but it had been so long I couldn't quite make the memory mine. The whole trip felt suspended, as if occurring in a tense grammarians hadn't yet described.

Politics had gutted the present. Like most of the nation, I was living in units of an hour – from one news bulletin to the next – my sense of what was possible veering between ecstasy and hopelessness. We swung with every Zulu massacre, every outbreak of peace, every bomb, every heroic handshake between enemies. On the worst days, I feared that the future would be over before it had arrived.

Farmhouses were few and far between along those Karoo backroads. Each one announced itself as a distant promise of molten light, where the iron roof caught the sun. Then I would drive some more before I could discern the blue-gum tree and poplars clustered around each yard. Only later would the house itself emerge.

Poplars, like aspen, have two-tone leaves, darker above than below. They shimmer in the slightest breeze. As a child, I used to think of them as dancing. But now they looked different, appeared to quake neurotically. The tree's Latin name came back to me from Dad's 'Growing Things'. *Populus tremula.* The name seemed right for these agitated times.

On the radio, they were talking about people hoarding things. There had been a run on supermarkets for emergency supplies. Rice, flour, tinned foods. Candles, especially. Whatever the future held, the fear was spreading that it would be candlelit. The nation was running out of candles as it fumbled for democracy.

Slowly, the Karoo began to turn on me. Perspective drained away; the clarity started to seem desolate, the big, burned silences too silencing. Space in such quantities no longer felt expansive, just humiliating for human things. I recalled how this was as a child. Those days when my vision blurred and fizzed in the sun, and the heat got trapped inside me until my skin felt like a duvet I couldn't kick off. I did now what I did then. I reached for the discipline in detailed things: the rhythmic rumbling of gravel on tyres; a dust-plume rearing in the mirror; the slow clock-curve of the sun. I concentrated on three crows picking at a jackal corpse smeared across the road. As I approached, they flew off, their cries as sharp as stones.

I found myself driving through sub-hamlets that clung to the map long after the people had fled. Places where hopes had soured, places with bitter names: Oven, Verlatekloof (Afrikaans for 'Desolate Ravine'), and Volstruisleegte ('Ostrich Emptiness'). I drove for an hour beyond Volstruisleegte without seeing anyone. Then a funnel of dust delivered a donkey cart. Two grey donkeys pulled a family of seven and a mountainous jumble of hessian sacks. Blue paint clung to the cart side in patches; the clothes that clung to the family were scarcely more solid than that. They looked like evacuees.

The scrub desert started to appear not so much empty as

abandoned: like the set for a post-Apocalyptic remake of *Road Warrior*, starring South Africa. The soundtrack from the radio didn't help. Although there was talk of the elections (despite Chief Buthelezi's boycott) going defiantly ahead, there was also a lot of talk of Armageddon in the air.

As I approached Oudtshoorn, crude stick tents began to punctuate the plains. Each tent was A-shaped, about ten-feet high at the apex, open at the front and back: a cross between a lean-to and a wigwam. En masse they resembled a makeshift refugee encampment.

Farmers erect these structures as breeding shelters for ostriches. Beneath each wigwam, an ostrich rooster makes his nest – though 'nest' is a grand flattery for his perfunctory scratch in the dirt. By day, the tawny hen sits tight, merging with the sand. By night, the male takes over, his chiaroscuro patterning turning him into just another shadow thrown by the desert moon.

I passed by tent village after village, bivouacked across the plains – the sign I had entered ostrich country proper. It was early afternoon as I swung into Oudtshoorn from the east. A thunderhead was building above the Swartberg Mountains – the northern rampart of the bounded plain known as the Little Karoo. Oudtshoorn lies at the centre of this plain, between the Swartberg and, to the south, the Outeniqua range.

Whatever else changes in the Karoo, the sky normally stays steady. The same big, bleached blue from one month to the next. Clouds are rare, an earnest talking point. Will they, won't they? Usually they don't.

But on the afternoon of my return, I entered Oudtshoorn under strange skies. Cloud castles perched above the 9,000-feet Swartberg peaks and started tumbling towards town. People huddled in groups on street corners, pointing heavenwards. A religious sky bore down on us; less a sky than a firmament. Raven black, yet blinding, as sheets of desert brilliance sheared through the gloom. Thunder, lightning, then the hail began.

I joined a crowd scurrying for the town library. We watched hail strip trees, rip flower beds, flatten the municipal cannas to a violent refrain of stones on iron roofs. After such a long absence, it was an unsettling return. Within half an hour, the once familiar landmarks around me – the oxwagon wide streets, Victorian houses, palaces, lacy ironwork – were deep in mothballs, as if some overseeing preservationist were embalming them.

Then the hail abruptly stopped. And the sun came out, burning as hot as ever. The air felt washed, the light cleansed. Torrents, stained red by the earth, hissed and swirled knee-deep through the streets. The times were too tense, too tumultuous, for weather, good or bad, to remain merely weather. The heavens had shown they were full of auguries. In this sermon-saturated town, the storm – the heaviest hail in half a century – was a bonanza for the preachers. And for other people too. Three days later I overheard a mechanic talking about God's anger at the way 'us whites' were giving the country to the communists lying down.

It wasn't just humans whom the weather left disoriented. The hail concussed some ostriches; others simply drowned. Like turkeys, they tend to gape at the sky when it rains, forgetting to close their beaks. It's not uncommon, in a downpour, for ostriches to drink themselves to death.

The hailstorm had shattered my car windscreen, and (according to the local newspaper) the windscreens of 400 other Oudtshoorn cars. In the 1980s, smashed windscreens became a trademark image of South Africa's civil war, as schoolchildren turned stone-throwing into an insurrectionary art. For a week after the hail, Oudtshoorn resembled a town recovering from an uprising. The recovery was slow. The town's auto repairmen were all overworked. I had to wait my turn. So for my first few days, I drove around this half-strange, half-familiar town peering at it through a screen of jagged glass.

Chapter Thirty

I decided to remain in Oudtshoorn while researching some articles on the challenge of post-apartheid land reform. One evening, on returning to my hotel, I poured myself a drink and stepped onto the third-floor balcony. The day's dust hung heavy in the air, though night was falling at shutter speed. I'd forgotten how fast it fell. None of those twilit shades I'd grown accustomed to, living in the north, where afternoon politely eased into evening. The childhood sensation came back to me of feeling overexposed all day, followed by this sudden, plunging dark.

Then I saw a blazing cross etched into the black sky. It was a long way off, hanging above a hilltop on the far side of town. It had to be immense to burn so brilliantly from so far. To my returning, now half-American eyes, it had a sinister air. Here, I knew, men didn't peer through slit white sheets, didn't cluster beneath flaming crosses. Those weren't the rituals of local bigotry – that was the other country. But there was something ferocious about the glowing cross that still left me on edge.

I walked to my car and drove through the night streets, uphill towards the light. I was drawn by something deeper than curiosity, some desire perhaps to face the lingering unease I felt about returning. As I drove, I kept one eye on the cross. It led me up a road that rimmed a military base, one of the maze of police and army camps that coil through the town. Halfway up, the road steepened and turned to dirt. Driving became difficult: the runoff from the hailstorm had wrecked the track. I passed a cul-de-sac sign, then crested the summit, where the road came to a halt at the foot of the lit cross.

It towered above me, a mass of brilliant bulbs, perhaps one hundred-feet high. The cross was mounted on a huge cement plinth; a sixteen-feet-high barbed-wire fence barred any further approach. I stood there for a while, peering down at the town, listening to gravely voices rising from the army camp. Then the voices stopped and there was nothing. Just the night air pulsing with cicadas and the cross's electric sizzling.

As I turned towards the car, I suddenly found myself facing a second cross, gouged into the sky above the opposing hill. I drove back through the town centre, watching this other cross flit in and out of view. Eventually, I reached the hillcrest, where the road came to a halt before a metal gate and another barbed-wire barrier. A sign hung from the gate: 'No Entry. Oudtshoorn Correctional Services.' From behind the fence, just beyond the prison yard, soared the second burning cross.

So this town was guarded by two huge crosses, one rising out of an apartheid army camp, the other out of a prison. I stood there for a while in the insistent white light. I felt a haunting pass through me, an old one-mistake town fear of glaring intolerance and conformity.

Then I let my gaze drift deeper, beyond the cross-scalded surface of the sky. The night was almost moonless. But the stars led me further out, into the depths of space, where a third, more ragged cross sprawled across the sky. If you've lived beneath it as a child, the Southen Cross never disappears. It glowed, as it always had in memory, with an ecstatic brilliance beyond religious or political intent.

Then a guard shouted at me and I left.

Chapter Thirty-one

The route from my hotel into town each day led me past the caged white man. He lived in a corner house along Baron van Reede Street. Or rather, he lived in the veranda jail that bent around the house. Between him and the world beyond, stretched row upon row of metal bars, impaling the veranda roof at the top and, at the bottom, a knee-high wall. The man was making the future safe by turning himself in, a pre-emptive prisoner of the times.

Whenever I passed, he was there, pacing leanly up and down and round the bend, until the far wall turned him back. I'd once seen a bony polar bear pace like that in a tropical zoo. It didn't slow down as the wall approached but jack-knifed violently at the last instant, to be sent back the way it came.

The man's face was sucked in. His jaw moved constantly, giving the impression of someone gnawing at a raw place inside his cheek. A wicker chair slumped in one corner of the stoep. But I never saw the thin man pause to sit in it. He lived on his feet. He was ready. If the future wanted him, it would have to come and get him, drag him from this lockup he called home.

What everyone shared, regardless of race or politics, was this gnawing wait. Until the elections happened, we would all be prisoners of uncertainty. The town, the country lived on edge. On the white side of Oudtshoorn, these anxieties got tangled up with the state of the ostrich market. Over and over people said to me: what the Americans are doing is unreal. Eighty-thousand dollars for two ostriches? People spoke with trepidation of a second ostrich crash. Bad history has made white Oudtshoorners as sensitive to ostrich inflation as Germans to an inflationary mark.

Chapter Thirty-two

One morning, an interview I had set up with some local activists was cancelled at the last minute. I had time on my hands and decided to spend it visiting Cango Ostrich Farm, one of several show farms that catered for tourists. While waiting for the tour to start, I browsed through the curio shop, an Aladdin's cave of Oudtshoorn memorabilia. Ostrich-egg brandy-kegs, replete with elegant wooden taps. Ostrich feet, amputated eighteen inches from the ground, stuffed with cement and topped with copper ashtrays. (Noticing my peering curiosity, the vendor assured me that he owned several himself: 'They're heavy enough to work nicely as doorstops on a windy day.') Electric flex was threaded through one ostrich's grey, scaly toe and up inside its sawn off leg. A pink lampshade crowned the effect, teetering on top.

Some curios were multipurpose, multitiered affairs. For a hundred rand (about thirty dollars) I could have owned a shiny, yellow-wood map of Africa, with a two-toed ostrich foot sprawled across it. The foot supported a brandy egg-keg, which in turn supported a lime-green lampshade. An ostrich foot – from toe-tip to toe-tip – measures about twenty-eight inches. On all the maps, the back toe-nail impaled Ethiopia, while the larger, lethal front toe stretched down the long body of Southern Africa to pierce the map at Oudtshoorn.

Then I noticed something strange. Without exception, every ostrich curio was left-footed. Someone, somewhere was amputating and preserving the left feet of dead ostriches. But whatever happened to all those missing right feet which were nowhere to be seen?

Our guide for the day was Veronica van Wyk, a lean, bright-faced Afrikaner in her early twenties. I was the only non-Taiwanese member in our group. The others had tumbled out of a bus and through the curio shop, just in time for the nine o'clock tour. One elderly Taiwanese man made the mistake of buying an ostrich leg lamp before we all set out. He kept startling his compatriots by accidentally stabbing them with the bird's claws which poked from beneath his arm.

Veronica was a knowledgeable enthusiast. Pulling down a big rooster's neck with her shepherd's crook, she showed us the bird's sophisticated breathing apparatus. She explained how the ostrich has four nostrils. In a sandstorm it seals the two large ones with membranes and breathes through two tiny backup holes that filter out the sand.

Then Veronica passed around a broken egg, the shell as thick as a dinner plate. Twenty Taiwanese visitors waited patiently to learn from their translator that the unborn ostrich lacks a handy little egg-tooth. Most bird embryos have one for chipping their escape. But ostriches prefer to head-butt their way to freedom: they hammer at the egg wall with a soccer hooligan's indifference to the impact of brick on cerebrum. So the baby ostrich's means of entering the world gives the first clue that the brain is a marginal organ for this bird. Sixty-five per cent of ostrich cranial space is reserved for the eyeballs. Clearly, a creature designed for vision not for insight.

After several Taiwanese tourists had enjoyed the chance to ride an ostrich, Veronica gave us a lecture on the bird's economic versatility. I listened to a similar spiel to the one I'd heard a few months before at the American Ostrich Association convention in San Diego. How the skin, feathers, meat, eggs, toenails, corneas, eyelashes were all proven money-spinners. But Veronica's list contained a few uses the

Americans had overlooked. 'Even ostrich heads come in handy,' she announced proudly. 'We sell them as crocodile food to the crocodile farm down the road. And for those of you who haven't visited our shop yet' – she gestured encouragingly – 'you'll notice that ostrich feet can be turned into lovely curios.'

I saw my chance to crack the riddle of the missing feet. 'Is there a reason why the ashtrays and lamp stands are all left-footed?'

Veronica blushed slightly. 'Well, that's true. The right foot . . . well the right foot is a problem.' She explained that it had all started with the crash. Oudtshoorners felt haunted by that calamity. Veronica's voice sank; it sounded less official, more personal. 'The past can be frightening,' she said. 'Rich people were thrown onto the streets.' In her edgy backward glance, I sensed some hint of future fear at the country's coming transformation.

But in her answer she stuck to ostriches. Now that the farmers were making money again, they were afraid history would repeat itself. People worried about being too greedy, about trying to make a profit from every bit of ostrich. So whenever they killed one, they threw the right foot away. Some farmers believed that tossing the right foot of an ostrich over the left shoulder would chase away bad luck.

I was asking too many questions, overtaxing the Taiwanese translator. So I waited until the tour was over before asking Veronica about the crosses on the hill. Her eyes narrowed. Her face darkened. She pulled me to one side and started talking rapidly in Afrikaans. Oudtshoorn had become a den of Satanists and nonbelievers. They'd descended on the town from across the land. Cats had started disappearing. Everyone with blond hair was afraid.

Then, she said, in 1991 Oudtshoorn had staged a Passion Festival – a sort of Karoo Oberammergau. It had been held in the bowels of the nearby Cango Caves, a natural amphitheatre with excellent acoustics. Hundreds of Christians had marched eighteen miles from Oudtshoorn to the caves. All the way, they'd sung hymns, carried palms and crosses, and prayed.

The Satanists – every last one of them – had fled before the light of the Lord. After the festival was over, the town fathers met and voted to keep the two largest crosses, one on each hill, burning for ever more. That way they could be sure the Satanists would never dare return.

'They're like a halo,' Veronica said. 'Now Oudtshoorn is a very safe, very nice place to live.' She smiled and swept the blond fringe from her eyes.

Chapter Thirty-three

I had gone to bed late and slept badly. All night a high-pitched dog dipped in and out of song. When I woke the next morning I noticed, from my hotel window, a woman across the road. She wore owl glasses and was sipping coffee on her stoep, watching me intently. I stared back. She allowed herself one bonus stare then slid off her chair and vanished indoors in a lemon crimplene swirl. Within seconds, her front bedroom curtains had gone into a lacy spasm of surveillance.

When I went down to fetch something from my car half an hour later, the crimplene spy hadn't left her post. I couldn't see her, but I could read the small-town morse code as it started up: twitchety, twitch, twitch, twitch, twitchety, twitch, twitch, twitch.

Sometimes, this town of tight faces and watchful windows still unsettled me. I found it easy to confuse the adult and the child. Every now and then I needed to hit the road and decompress, remind myself that things were different now, that I could choose to leave. And so I'd drive out of town and exhale in the Karoo's immensity.

Along those roads, a chanting goshawk would appear every few miles with incantatory regularity, sitting on a fence-post or a thorn tree not much taller than itself. Elegant, official-looking in a uniform of pinstriped grey. And watchful, in that blank way that men on duty have. From across the years an odd detail came back to me: this goshawk is the only polyandrous bird of prey in Africa. Each lady-goshawk gets to have (or endure) two men for life.

I sometimes stopped my dust-encrusted car, got out and wandered through the veld. The ground felt flinty underfoot. The vegetation was miserly – mostly the grey end of green. A bonsai treeline clawed at my ankles. The stunted trunks, when I knelt to examine them, appeared tortured with aridity. Everything lay flat: even the bushes, grazed down to perfect crewcuts by the goats.

One dusk, my veld wanderings led me to a tiny dam that reminded me just how alive the Karoo can be. A desert hare, the colour of the earth, sprang from nowhere and hared off. I watched it go, a dead metaphor suddenly bounding into life. A chacma baboon patrolled the dam's edge with a stiff-legged gait. He barked at my approach, sized me up and down, and barked again. Then walked off slowly enough to keep his pride intact, a parody of arthritic masculinity.

I waited by the dam. Twenty minutes passed, then thirty Namaqua sandgrouse landed nervously. In the deeper deserts to the north, these pigeon-sized game birds settle in vast flocks – 7–8,000 at a time – on even the feeblest pan of water. They're fast-flying, edgy things. When startled, they rise in unison to a massive applause of wings.

This bird's unique adaptation to the desert made an early impression on me. During the breeding season, the female sandgrouse leave their nests twice daily, at dawn and dusk, and fly to the nearest water, sometimes thirty miles away. The mothers wade into the dam where they remain until their speckled chests are sodden. Then they fly the thirty miles back. The fledglings bury their heads in the returning mother's chest, drinking their fill. What I saw, in my mind's eye, was half-mammal and half-bird: offspring suckling at a feathered breast.

My aimless ventures into the Karoo and my encounters with once familiar birds, helped me maintain a modicum of equanimity. I was travelling widely during this time to other parts of South Africa – to report on the violence in KwaZulu

Natal or a bombing up north. Each time I would return to Oudtshoorn disturbed; it only takes a few dismemberments to shake the mind. Deep down, I was afraid that some calamity would plunge the country into a downward spiral of carnage, the bottom of which lay beyond imagining. My vanishings into creature-time gave me some respite from the bloody images that kept my fears awake. Memory can be a useful way of forgetting excruciating things.

Chapter Thirty-four

One morning, I awoke to exhilarating news. The elections were definitely on – Buthelezi had finally agreed to participate. Bloody feuding between Zulus loyal to Chief Gatsha Buthelezi and ANC Zulus had threatened to derail the elections and Buthelezi had sworn he would boycott them. But now all major parties were on board. Whatever happened, the country would queue to vote instead of exploding into the next Lebanon, the next Bosnia.

The waiting game felt less gut-wrenching now, the future clarified. I was still looking, though, for some local sign that Oudtshoorn was ready to open up. I had made some preliminary enquiries about the ANC plan to get coloureds and blacks into ostrich farming, the scheme Faizel Ismail had mentioned to me at the Algonquin Hotel. But I'd met with no success. So I decided to try Bishop Eddie Adams next.

A close friend of mine – a college roommate who'd gone on to become Archbishop Desmond Tutu's chaplain – had suggested I contact Adams. Bishop Eddie, as everybody called him, was Oudtshoorn's first coloured bishop. For seven years, from 1983 to 1990, he'd been the only coloured or black person resident in central Oudtshoorn, an area strictly zoned for whites.

The dome of Oudtshoorn's Catholic church was low-slung and as cobalt as the sky above. Surrounded by square Karoo houses and Calvinist spires, it looked utterly incongruous: like a blue spaceship that had descended on St Saviour's Street.

Certainly, when Bishop Adams moved into the Catholic manse in 1983, white Oudtshoorn couldn't have treated him with more hostility if he'd been visiting from another planet.

The manse bell didn't work. So I waited awhile outside the siege-like iron grid, eventually rattling the bars and crying out. The bishop's assistant arrived, bearing an enormous key.

I found Bishop Eddie sitting behind a circular conference table engrossed in paperwork. His square, black-rimmed spectacles and peering nose gave him a scholarly air. I asked him about the gate. He nodded. 'Even though the elections are just around the corner, we still lock ourselves in. You can't be too careful. We lived with threats for so long: police raids, constant surveillance, stolen files whenever I left town. People promising to kill us, bomb us. We lived under a cloud of dirty tricks. They loved to make you aware that you were being watched. They made you live on edge. In this little town of Oudtshoorn, everyone was so vulnerable, so exposed. At one stage under the state of emergency, the government was crushing everybody. The church was people's only real cover.'

Bishop Eddie came across as a mild-mannered but stone-willed man. He was fifty-nine years old and had been a priest for thirty years. I asked how he'd ended up in Oudtshoorn. He shook his head, tucked two fingers inside his dog-collar and tugged. 'You know, God has a great sense of humour. Put it this way: coming here after a big city like Cape Town – it was a challenge.'

What had the town been like eleven years ago? Bishop Eddie handed me a scrapbook the nuns had put together documenting his Oudtshoorn years. On the first page, a newspaper clipping from the Johannesburg *Sunday Times*, dated 28 May, 1983 and headlined: 'Black Bishop Storm Rocks Ostrich Town'.

A white neighbour, Hestelle Swart, asked to comment on the bishop's arrival, said 'The Lord above made the coloured people, too. But I just don't want to have to live next to them.' A keen golfer, Bishop Eddie was told he could use the links two days a week, 'The days open to blacks and coloureds.'

The scrapbook gave some sense of the white town's priorities in 1983. The police raid a public pool to round up students who are charged with the crime of swimming on a Sunday. The white foreman of an ostrich farm dies and twenty coloured labourers who worked for him travel to his funeral. But the Dutch Reformed Church turns them away, denying them permission to mourn inside its doors. Even in grief, segregation doesn't bend.

This wasn't the 1930s or '40s, this was the mid-Eighties. Before moving to Oudtshoorn, Bishop Eddie had spent his whole life in Cape Town. At one point, he'd lived in a cottage attached to Cape Town Cathedral – a whites-only area, but no-one had bothered him about that. But when he came to Oudtshoorn, all hell broke loose.

The Oudtshoorn Town Council had led the assault, people like the town clerk, Michael Schmidt, and a man who later became mayor, called Seppie Greeff. They'd declared the bishop an illegal resident. He couldn't stay without a permit. Bishop Eddie had countered bluntly: 'I will never apply for a permit, whether it be to live in a black, white, coloured, or pink residential area. A bishop is a bishop for his people and that's that.'

He stayed. But at first, as he explained to me, he lived a monastic, almost ghostly life. Every café and restaurant in the town centre was for whites only. He ate in the church house with the brothers of the Pallotine Order. He spent most of his time inside the manse or on the road, ministering to the fifteen-thousand Catholic families strewn across his desert diocese of 80,000 square miles. 'Sometimes,' Bishop Eddie said, tracing the lean ridge of his nose, 'I have to travel two hundred miles to see two families in an outstation, just to remind them that other people know and care that they exist.'

As South Africa came close to civil war in the 1980s, Bishop Eddie's work became more political. He helped establish a regional peace committee, tried to get enemies to talk to each other. 'Without it, this town would have been in flames.'

Under cover of the church, he was instrumental in collecting and publishing affidavits from residents of Oudtshoorn's black and coloured townships who'd been tortured or detained.

Since Nelson Mandela's reincarnation from prison, things had begun to ease. Bishop Eddie sighed back into his chair: 'When that happened, I felt a load falling from my shoulders. We began to feel a bit freer in Oudtshoorn to say what we had to say.

'What I was fighting for has come about. There's an election next week. The church will face different challenges now. It's important that people don't see us as the church of a particular political party. Back then, morally, we had to do what we did. But now we're thinking of the future. We've got to be here for everyone.'

Bishop Eddie was in a rush, heading off to a convention. But as I left, he turned to me: 'Here, take this number. If it's the past you're after, he's the man you should be speaking to. His name is David Piedt. He'll know about that ANC plan to get coloureds and blacks farming ostriches.'

It had once been possible – many decades earlier, before the full force of apartheid had been felt – for coloureds, blacks and whites to live in Oudtshoorn all mixed up together. Bishop Eddie's stubborn presence on St Saviour's Street was a reminder of those times, a collective memory in solitary form. But his presence also possessed some future force, promising that he was just the first of many, the harbinger of changes that would surely now begin.

Chapter Thirty-five

I called David Piedt and arranged to see him when I returned from the elections. As 27 April approached, I knew I didn't want to vote in Oudsthoorn. I needed a different kind of augury. So set off for Cape Town, which sprawls across the Atlantic peninsula known as the Cape of Good Hope. More specifically, I wanted to vote in Vredehoek ('Freedom Corner'), a Cape Town community whose name commemorates the emanicipation of slaves in 1838, when the British ruled the Cape. Vredehoek seemed the right place to be for this long dreamed of second unshackling.

This way I could vote among friends, many, like myself, returnees voting for the first time anywhere. People who, through compulsion or choice, had emigrated abroad and returned now, decades later, as semi-foreigners. We'd all struggled in our way with memory, some forgetting this place too fast, others not nearly fast enough. What we shared was the simple desire to be here, to join the line in this great pilgrimage of hope. We'd come to vote for the future and to reckon with the past.

On the morning of the 27, the whole country was on the move. TV showed people queuing for miles; some would shuffle forward for most of the day – seventeen or eighteen hours – before placing their cross. At Vredehoek, the line was shorter: we waited six hours.

The day proved blustery and wet. Table Mountain, towering above us, belched black clouds. There was something ceremonial about the gathering: any society's first ballot box is a kind of shrine. The crowd's mood was quietly exuberant. People talked and talked. We started telling stories about ourselves, stories we wouldn't otherwise have told, sharing them with the strangers who, for six hours, lived as our neighbours in the queue. There was a touch of Chaucer about the scene: people from all walks of life who would normally never meet telling each other stories to help speed time. And to show goodwill – that barriers could and should come down.

Each raconteur tried to upstage the last. The best story-teller among the pilgrims in our vicinity was Jasmine September, a stout coloured seamstress in her mid-thirties. She heaved herself in and out of her stories, her whole body getting involved. Her tales were elaborate; she tailored them perfectly to the patient progress of the queue. She'd start with something straightforward involving a priest and a pregnancy, then add frills and fancy stitchwork until she'd embroidered something intricate.

As we listened, 3,000 feet above us, a hang-glider with a sense of occasion threw himself off the mountain. It was crazy weather to glide in, but we all applauded as he tilted his pink wings and headed for the shore.

Jasmine pulled out her hang-gliding story which included, in passing, her views on the old government, gangsters, globalization and gardening. And a little aside on ostriches.

Her uncle worked on an ostrich farm near Calitzdorp. 'Tough work. Terrible pay. And those birds.' Jasmine clapped her head in her hands. 'Man, they've got such a goddam nasty nature.'

December last year, the farmer took her Uncle Petrus to one side. And told him he could have an injured ostrich as a Christmas bonus if he slaughtered it himself. 'Now my uncle is a kind-hearted man. But he knew if he killed the ostrich outside, everybody on the farm would be wanting some meat and there'd be nothing left for his family.' So he decided to kill it secretly. He tied up the bird's legs, just tight enough so

208

it couldn't kick, but loose enough so he could march it into his little cottage.

Then Petrus got out a huge knife to slaughter the ostrich on his cement kitchen floor. But as he brought the knife down on the neck, the ostrich panicked, kicking out wildly and breaking its thongs.

'The ostrich head lay there on the floor. But the rest of the bird was running around crazily, like a decapitated chicken. That ostrich smashed the house to smithereens. Broke a chair, cracked a table, kicked in the damn TV. Uncle Petrus had to jump inside his wardrobe for safety's sake.' As the ostrich rushed about, its long, headless neck swung round and round like a garden hose, spraying all the walls with blood.

'Eventually, that damn ostrich collapsed on Petrus's bed. Made a helluva fucking mess. It fell down right there, dead on the bed. *Net soos a dronk witman*' – just like a drunk whiteman.

We all threw back our heads and laughed. Jasmine nudged me in the ribs. 'Ja, just like a drunk whiteman.' She smiled and gave me an extra nudge while edging her way forward in the queue.

Three days after voting, I drove through the operatic mountain passes beyond Cape Town, back east towards the Karoo. Soon the land flattened, the foliage thinned, the light clarified and the Great Dry stretched wide beneath a huge sweep of sky.

Part of me was already wondering whether the coming transformations would be bold enough. The country's challenges were forbidding. But there would be time enough to think of those. For now, I wanted to live in the deep present, just driving and listening as ecstatic voices on the radio poured out their hopes. So I drove and listened and kept my eyes trained on the horizon, resting in the prospect of ever-widening space ahead.

Chapter Thirty-six

On returning to Oudtshoorn, I visited David Piedt in the so-called coloured community of Bridgton. Coloureds outnumber blacks and whites in Oudtshoorn by a ratio of three to one – so Bridgton is where most people live. Each time I visited the community, I was struck by how near it was and how far. Just three minutes drive from the town centre, yet it appeared on none of the maps available at the tourist office. Every street, every historical site on the white side of town was meticulously marked. But Bridgton existed only as an arrow and a name on each map's perimeter. Alongside the arrow, the road leading into the community was sawn through, like one of those unfinished overpasses left suspended in mid-air when the money runs out. This week, Bridgton's people had finally voted for the first time. But they still weren't on the map.

I made do with the instructions David had given me on the phone. A horseshoe bend opposite the golf course fed me into a maze of mostly dirt roads where cramped, zinc-roofed shacks mingled with solid concrete houses, each with a small, parched patch of lawn. As I passed David's school, a yellow poster, hanging by one corner to a fence, flapped in the breeze. There was going to be a concert Saturday, Afro-D-Ziac would be playing.

David lived some fifty yards beyond the school gates. A nine-foot front wall gave his house a maximum security feel. I knocked and waited. I wondered if he'd keep the wall up now that apartheid was coming down. A lanky, beige-suited man came to the door and welcomed me into his living room. Inside, the light was a thick yellow-brown. It had that bruised quality I associate with churches. Midday almost, yet the curtains were all closed. I remembered this from childhood: the way Karoo people shuttered themselves against the all-invasive sun. Surplus light is a problem here: Southern California receives 2,600 sunshine hours annually, Oudtshoorn 3,900.

David folded his long frame into the couch. His bullet-bald style of handsomeness mixed a bit of Yul Brunner with a bit of Omar Sharif. His ample ears tilted slightly forward, giving him the appearance of permanent attentiveness. We sat and talked for hours in the gauzy heat, the curtains seeming to concentrate our conversation, as did the sense of balancing on history's cusp, of living almost out of time.

David Piedt was born, he told me, in Oudtshoorn in 1940. For fifty-four years, he had lived nowhere else. In 1964 he had qualified as a school teacher, and ever since had served his community as a leader and activist. First, as a teacher, then as principal of Colridge Primary, an Afrikaans language school for coloureds, across the road. David had a teacher's way of speaking, emphatic and demonstrative.

'I know this ostrich town. I was born here, I grew up here. This was really, really one of the most conservative towns in South Africa. The white people were super-*verkrampt*.' Ultra-cramped, ultra-reactionary. 'But even Oudtshoorn has begun to move.

'This peaceful transformation in South Africa . . . there aren't words for it. We were all afraid this thing could only end in extra blood. The international community sent thousands of election observers. I'm sure they thought: OK, we're going to watch these people destroy each other.

'That man,' David said. Then he fell silent, pointing, with chin and eyes, towards a painting of Nelson Mandela

211

suspended above his mantelpiece. 'That man. Twenty-seven years inside. And when he came out, he was ready for history.'

The Karoo is one of the few regions in South Africa where coloureds outnumber both blacks and whites. It also proved to be one of the few regions where, in that week's elections, the old apartheid rulers, the Nationalists, had gained an electoral majority. I asked David why so many coloureds had voted for their old oppressors.

He nodded, then explained. On isolated Karoo farms, people – all voting for the first time – had no access to information. Often, their white bosses intimidated them. Voting was something new and strange, he said; people were afraid. Whites had always had the power of knowledge. Most farm workers were illiterate. They assumed the farmer knew exactly what they were up to. So if he said vote Nationalist, they would be afraid to vote ANC. Afraid they would lose their work, their homes.

Stories, David said, were coming in of what had happened. Stories of farmers trucking their workers to the voting station, then pointing to the red smoke-detector light above the booth. 'That red light,' they'd said, 'will tell me whether you voted Nat or ANC.'

David shook his head. 'We're talking about people who, for generations, have been under the white farmer's thumb. They grew up thinking the white man knew everything. Why, now, would that have changed?

'Of course,' he added, 'that's not the whole story. The coloured community is deeply religious, devoted to the church. Many people bought into the smear-campaign against Mandela as a godless communist. There were also fears about the fate of Afrikaans, the people's language around here, under the ANC.'

Mainly, though, it was fear: fear and intimidation.

'I'll give you an example. Friday morning, day after the elections, I hear this knocking on my door. I open it. There's a man standing there, a dirt-poor farm worker. He has walked ten miles to come and see me. On Thursday he'd gone to vote. When he got back to the farm, his boss asked him, "Who did you vote for?" The man said he was so happy to have voted, he just said, spontaneously, "Mr Mandela." The farmer looked at him and said, "OK. Let Mr Mandela find you work." And he chased the man and his family off the farm for good. So now, the man tells me, standing in my doorway, he has nowhere to go.'

David told this story in the subdued way of a man holding down great pain.

'At least now we could report the farmer to the electoral commission. But there's no way those people can go back. The farmer would make their lives a misery. We're trying to find new homes, new work for them with one of the more liberal ostrich farmers in the area.'

David pressed his palms together, his long fingers pointing upwards.

'But the first victory is to vote, even if people are misinformed. Education can come later. The process must be respected, otherwise our struggle for justice was for nothing. Yes, just voting: that's the first victory.'

David began talking about his family and his ancestors, beginning with the Khoikhoi, whom the colonials called Hottentots. As he talked, he used his long, expansive arms to gesture across history. The Khoikhoi were itinerants: they trekked away from the Cape in the eighteenth century to escape predatory Dutch settlers. Some Khoi, he said, migrated along the arid west coast into Namaqualand, others ventured east, crossing the barrier mountains until they reached the Little Karoo. They arrived in the Oudtshoorn area in the mid-nineteenth century. The scrub desert was excellent for sheep. The Khoi were herders so they stayed. They also hunted the plentiful wild ostriches.

'So the brown people were here first.' Before Oudtshoorn existed as a town; half a century at least before the Jerusalem of Africa.

'My great-grandfather on my mother's side emigrated to South Africa from Holland in 1824. He was a Coetzee. He took a Khoi woman as his wife. There's a strong resemblance between him and my grandfather. The height, the profile. In photographs they look like brothers. About my grandmother, we don't know too much.'

David's grandparents were born near Oudtshoorn in the 1860s and '70s. His grandparents and his parents all grew up within twenty miles of the town, working on ostrich and tobacco farms. They had to labour in the farmer's house or on his land. They lived off food they grew beside their shacks and wore handouts from the white man's family. Out there on the farms, money was something they never saw, utterly foreign to them.

'These were the stories my parents told me. If you showed any initiative the farmer would block you. There were donkey carts on the farm. But they couldn't use them to sell firewood in town. The farmer would get suspicious and say: "What do you lot want with money?" There was no hope of uplift, no hope at all.

'They were always riding in those donkey carts, bringing ostrich feathers, vegetables, lucerne bales to town. But always for the farmer. They got nothing out of it themselves. They were bound to him for life. Except, he could get rid of you. When my grandfather got old, he was chased off the farm, so the farmer could give his room to a younger, fitter man.

'At the turn of the century, brown people flocked here. Not to Oudtshoorn, but to the farms outside, because of the feather boom. Then things got very bad. First the ostrich slump, then the depression. By the Thirties, most people had fled the farms. They came to town and squatted.'

His parents joined the exodus. His mother started ironing and washing white people's clothes in Oudtshoorn. That's what she did most of her life. His father found piecework as a handyman. Bit by bit, in an informal way, he taught himself to build. By 1948, David's father had achieved his dream of working as a builder. But that year something happened in the wider world that would shake their family to the roots. For the first time, the hard-line National Party triumphed in the white elections. It rose to power on the vision of apartheid.

David peered past me, through the crimplene twilight. He squinted, then widened his eyes, then narrowed them again as if struggling to find the right focus for such a calamity.

'In 1950 they began to impose rigid segregation. They gave themselves ten years "to make South Africa clean". Before, everyone had lived mixed up in Oudtshoorn as one community. Coloureds, blacks, whites all together. On the West Bank and in North End where my family lived. But after 1960, everybody was chased out of there and the place was turned over to the whites. There had been removals before, but nothing systematic. 1960 – that's when they came for us.

'We owned a house in Adderley Street, near the centre of town. We'd moved in there in 1947, when I was seven years old. A simple house, two bedrooms, raw brick. We couldn't afford proper, baked brick. It wasn't a grand place, but it was our own. Then one day, the officials came and told us: "Out. You have to go." They gave us eighty pounds for the house. You couldn't negotiate.'

Those men were sent by the Department of Community Development which, under apartheid, was set up to destroy communities.

'Same year, same thing happens to my grandma on Draai Street in North End. Two white men knock on the door. They give her a poor price for a nice big house on a large property. Then they give her three months to leave. That was the mentality of those times.

'Suddenly, we had no home, no land. We'd lost both houses to forced removals. Now we had to live as renters in Bridgton where they put all the coloureds. My grandparents were already in their seventies. Both died – died from heartache – the year their house was seized. Two aunts also died after they'd been pushed out of their homes. In two years, we lost five family members. All passed away from the strain. People just couldn't see a way to go on living.'

Adderley Street to Bridgton: just a few miles up the hill. But sometimes the shortest journeys carry the heaviest burden of pain.

As I listened to David's family story, I thought back to the story he'd first told me when I walked through the door. The story about the man who had knocked on his door the day after the elections, whose family had been thrown off the farm for voting for Mr Mandela. Now I heard that story differently. It had another layer.

David took up where he'd left off. 'So we had to start again in Bridgton. Eventually we got together the money for a plot. Every Saturday, month after month after month, the whole family came together to help to build a house. For someone from my father's background, it really meant something to build your own family house with your own family's hands. That gave us a hell of a lot of pride. Despite all the restrictions, you've done something for yourself.'

David turned to me. 'Do you still understand Afrikaans? OK, then, let's talk in Afrikaans. Otherwise' – he jerked his head towards the cemetery up the hill – 'this language will soon be heading for the grave.' It would be a big mistake, he added, if there were now a backlash against Afrikaans. Most people remembered it as the language of prisons, bullets and brutality. But for the great majority of coloured South Africans, it was their mother tongue.

Afrikaans had started as a slave language, centuries before. It had grown up as a patois in the kitchens and on the farms, among the poor and uneducated. Afrikaans was to Dutch what Haitian creole was to French, and Yiddish to Hebrew.

'It was our language first. Later white people insisted it was their own. They took it from us and used it for their police state.

'Sure, Afrikaans was the language of oppression. But here in the Karoo and in the Cape, it was also the language of the oppressed. It mustn't disappear. Remember, we fought our fight in Afrikaans.

'Those forced removals, those injustices – the kind our family suffered – inspired a tremendous history of resistance.' Those hardships became his inspiration. 'And the fact that, growing up on those ostrich farms, neither of my parents could read or write. That gave me an incredible motivation to learn. It was a huge responsibility too. We were seven children. There wasn't enough money for us all. I was the one chosen to be educated all the way.'

He qualified as a teacher in 1965. Two years later, he went to jail for the first time for organizing. He was back inside in 1974. And in 1985, and in 1986 and in 1987 again. Detained and released; detained and released; detained and released; detained and released; detained. Then released for the last time.

They did similar things to so many people in that town. They refused him a passport. They sacked him as unfit to be a principal, unfit to lead a school. But he took that battle to court and was reinstated.

'Through everything we kept protesting. We couldn't take it lying down.'

David paused and shifted on the sofa. His body tightened, bending into a hunch.

'One Saturday afternoon, second of July, 1986. I remember the date exactly. I've just got home from Cape Town. I've just driven all the way. Two hundred miles. No sooner have I arrived, than I hear this knocking.'

David cocked his head, as if listening for some trace, some echo of that day.

'I open the door. It's my little niece. My sister has sent her. The little girl says: "Uncle David, you must get out of town. There's a swoop taking place in Oudtshoorn. The security police are picking up all the ministers of religion and all the activists. They've already put forty people in detention."

'I'm going to a teachers' convention in Kimberley starting Monday. So I decide to leave early, to escape this town.

'It's five or six o'clock. Wintertime, getting dark. I'm still tired from the long drive, so I put a blanket in front of the window and think, first I'll just have a tiny nap before I hit the road again.

'I fall asleep and, I'm so exhausted, I sleep through the alarm, all the way to midnight. Then I hear this heavy knocking, this doof, doof, doof, doof and people screaming my name. Lights are flashing against the window. Just this doof, doof, doof in your head and there's nobody to tell you whether you're asleep or awake.

'Voices are shouting: "If you don't open up, we're going to kick this bloody door off its hinges."

'I keep the light off. And sit there. I hear someone say: "*Nee, man, hy's nie hier nie*": "No, man, he's not here." Someone else says, "No he's here. We've got him."

'I had a car that was an unusual colour. Petrol-coloured. There was only one other car like that – a white man owned it, Kobie van Dyck. So one of the security policemen says, "He's not here. I know that car, it's Kobie's car."

'Then I hear loud singing coming from outside. *Nkosi Sikele*, the liberation anthem. I peer through a corner of the window. There's a street lamp outside my house. Under it I see a police truck full of people inside the cage. Thirty, forty people singing their lungs out. The police get distracted. One of them says: "We can come back later. Let's go pick up Reggie Olifant." So they roar off to look for my friend Reggie.

'Then I'm out of there. I hit the Kimberley road just as I am, in my pyjamas. Someone rides after me, overtakes me to tell me that, six o'clock, they're going to be putting up a roadblock at Beaufort West. Ten to six I make it through there.

'Reggie and I had to leave for a while and go into hiding in the Cape. Things became impossible in Oudtshoorn. Life was like that, then. It was a time of tremendous struggle. Those were the *Saamstaan* years.'

Saamstaan means 'stand together' in Afrikaans. It was the name that David, Reggie Olifant and other Oudtshoorn activists gave to the tiny newspaper they founded in 1982. Bishop Eddie joined the board.

David shrugged. 'None of us had any journalistic experience. Editing, writing, layout . . . nothing. We wanted to reach ordinary people who couldn't afford a newspaper, people who'd never even read one before.'

They wrote stories about the plight, the courage of ordinary people in the coloured and black communities of the Karoo and Southern Cape. For twelve years, *Saamstaan* gave the voiceless a voice. Politically, it put Oudtshoorn on the map. Despite what people in Johannesburg and Soweto thought, this wasn't the middle of nowhere. Out here in the scrub desert, people were taking a stand.

The ANC in exile found Dutch sponsors for *Saamstaan* who covered costs so the paper could be distributed for free. But first David and his friends had to get it printed. Oudtshoorn's only printers were white. They wouldn't touch the paper. So they had to try in George, a town forty miles away. Same refusal there. Then Mossel Bay. Again, the same response. Eventually, they had to travel to Cape Town before they found a printer prepared to do the job.

'When that first *Saamstaan* came off the press, the security police were waiting. They seized all twenty-thousand copies of issue number one. In our first ten years, the building that housed the newspaper – a few blocks from here – was burned down three times. Of course the police never found any suspects, never brought anyone to trial.'

No newspaper in South Africa had to operate in quite such an exposed and hostile environment. But *Saamstaan* soon started winning awards for independent journalism.

David straightened the lapels on his jacket. 'Our newspaper kept spreading. We reached people, we really reached them. Dirt-poor people, out there, too, on the ostrich farms. We made a difference, I know we did.'

'And then came the second of February, 1990. There he was walking out of that jail.' David gestured again with an outstretched arm towards the man in the painting on the wall. By this stage, Mandela had become a third presence in the room.

David acknowledged him constantly as he talked with little glances, nods, subtle consultations.

'This week, he's president. Friends from here are going to Pretoria for the inauguration. I wish I could have been there. It's amazing to us, who fought so hard for this day. I'm glad I lived through all that dirty history, I really am. Just to reach this moment.

'Things are changing, things that matter. Oudtshoorn's first integrated school started up recently. Now you can see coloured and white children walking the streets together. Even white kids, for the first time, sleeping over with their friends in Bridgton and vice versa. The parents, as a result, sometimes become friendly and start visiting each other. And look' – he parted the curtains and peered out the window – 'the sky hasn't fallen yet.

'I work with children. Monday morning I stood in front of them all at school assembly and said: "This is the first gathering of the New South Africa. In the past, there were restrictions. You could always say, I want to but they won't let me. Now, those restrictions are out the door. Starting today, it's up to you to say, I want to and I can. I can become a lawyer, a magistrate, a bank manager, or the president, like Nelson Mandela."'

David recalled an angry exchange he had with one of the old *verkramptes*, the outgoing white mayor, Seppie Greeff. I remembered the name: Seppie Greeff had led the campaign against Bishop Eddie when he'd moved into a white neighbourhood.

The time had come, ex-mayor Greeff had recently told David Piedt, for everybody to forgive and to forget. David threw up his hands. 'Forgive, yes, I need to forgive in order to grow. But forget? Never. I will never, ever forget. I can't: that's history.'

He slowed down as he spoke, leaning on his last two words. What I heard wasn't just a history teacher speaking. I heard the voice of someone whose nameless ancestors, grandparents, parents, students and neighbours had all lived lives that lay outside official history, had never made it into books. For thirty years, David had faced a daily dilemma at school. How do you give young people a sense of self-worth when the state prescribed textbooks required for passing their exams contain no record of their history?

The Czech writer Milan Kundera once invented a character called the President of Forgetting. South Africa had suffered through plenty of his sort. Just that week, it had elected a leader with an almost superhuman capacity for forgiveness who was also the country's first President of Remembrance.

Memory – or at least the power to go public with it in textbooks, museums, films, tourist guides – was a novelty. The way David said 'that's history' left an impression on me. It conveyed a sense that the past wasn't something receding into irrelevance, but something that lay ahead, for which fresh, urgent forms of storytelling still needed to be found.

Yes, the elections had given people hope. But huge obstacles remained.

'Like this ostrich business. Around here, people see ostriches and they see money. So many of our people have the experience, generations of experience with these birds. They're impatient to get farming. They're queuing up. Especially now that the Americans are going bananas over ostriches.'

But they didn't have the capital, didn't have the land. For four decades the *Broederbond* – the super-conservative, Afrikaner 'brotherhood' – has dominated the ostrich business. The *Broederbonders* were clandestine, creating a closed, hostile atmosphere, never admitting any blacks, coloureds, Jews, English-speakers, or women to their ranks.

David gave his coke a swirl. 'This will – this has to – change. But the big problem remains the land. To break in is extremely difficult. Even for people who have the skills. People with a great love for farming, who know this world back to front. The government will have to sell off some state

221

land. Make it available to promising farmers from our communities.'

I asked him about the ANC's ostrich-farming plan. No, he hadn't heard of that. Nor had anyone else I spoke to. It was just a dream-scheme with no more solidity, it appeared, than a very deep desire.

A knock on the door interrupted us. It was OK, just a friend. David rose and chatted to him for a few minutes about school business. How often, over the decades, had David's door been knocked upon in every imaginable and unimaginable emergency? How many years, how many knocks would it take, I wondered, before knuckles rapping on wood became a safe, a normal sound?

The friend left. David turned to me.

'It's been one hell of a struggle. But, really, these changes have come much faster than I dreamed.

'Let me tell you about Michael Schmidt. He was the town clerk here for thirty-eight years. I've been politically active just about that long. Through all those terrible times he ran this town like a dictator. A very efficient bureaucrat. But he gave us such nightmares. He had no feeling whatsoever for coloureds and blacks.

'Well, recently, he's had some big sufferings of his own. His wife died from cancer, then his son drowned and his daughter is disabled. Soon after all that happened, he was driving back to Oudtshoorn from Cape Town in his Mercedes 230. He got home, parked the car in his garage and started helping his daughter towards the house. Suddenly, the car exploded behind them. They survived, but the Mercedes was wrecked.

'Next day I went to visit him. He was standing outside his house with the white mayor and some town councillors. It looked like they were having a meeting of some kind. So I went up to them and said, "Gentlemen, I don't want to interrupt you. But I just wanted, Michael, to extend my people's sympathies. We've heard about your troubles and I wanted to say you are in our prayers."

'Michael looked at me. He said nothing. Then he grabbed

me by my lapels. He pulled me towards him and started crying. He just cried. And he wept my jacket wet. I realized it was the first time that a white man had embraced me.'

'Since then we've talked a lot. I said to him: "I'll respect your beliefs, but you must respect mine. You cannot continue dehumanizing people the way you did all those years." So we've become friends. He comes over to chat about things going on in town. We watch TV; he falls asleep on the couch. If a man's ready in his heart . . .

'Now he's pushing me to stand for council. I don't know, I'll have to talk to my community. If the people want me to stand, I'll stand. There's still so much to change.

'Here in Bridgton, we'll have to think differently. Leave the torpedo mentality behind. Before, we were always scheming to undermine authority. Resist, resist, resist. Bricks were things kids threw at the police. But now we must learn to build.'

David held up both hands, his fingers and thumbs squared off at top and bottom to shape a brick. A gesture shadowed by his father's work. I thought back to that moment in 1960 when the Piedts had suddenly found themselves dispossessed, declared 'undesirables' – which, in Oudtshoorn, meant non-white. I tried to picture all those Saturdays David had spent as a young man putting up their house, working beside his father, mother, sisters, brothers and cousins, resurrecting what they had lost. Thirty-four years ago, one brick at a time, building and resisting.

Leaving David's place early that afternoon, I took a detour past the *Saamstaan* office, which arsonists had returned to scorch again and again. A tiny, peeling building, smaller than a country store, burn marks still visible on the corrugated-iron ribbing that constituted the roof. Padlocked metal grids barred the windows and doors.

As I got out of my car, I was engulfed by a reeking flatulence. An awful, smothering smell. Half-chemical, half-flesh. The stench clawed its way inside me even as I held my breath. I climbed back into my car and went looking for the source. On the far side of Bridgton, I arrived at a large, industrial-looking building in the midst of an open lot. The chimneys spewed charnel-house fumes that left me nauseated and dazed. I felt unfit to drive.

A sign said: 'No Entry'. And another sign: 'Ostrich Abattoir'.

Once a week at the abattoir they burned the bones. A journalist, who worked for *Saamstaan*, later told me this. He pointed out something else as well. That they'd built the abattoir on the border between the coloured zone and the zone for whites. In other towns, people grew up living on the poor side or the rich side of the railway tracks. Here they lived downwind or upwind of the ostrich slaughterhouse.

'Downwind for coloureds and blacks. Upwind for the whites. You know,' he said, 'those apartheid town planners, they used to think about those things.'

Chapter Thirty-seven

Ifirst met Larry Markus at a kosher Oudtshoorn *braaivleis* (barbecue). When I joined him and the other youngish ostrich farmers around the grill, conversation was stilted at first. Why was I interested in this ostrich stuff? A book? Somebody wondered aloud if I wasn't 'spying for the Americans'. The man laughed uneasily, but the laughter didn't quite escape his throat.

Towards evening's end, Larry turned to me: 'You must meet my dad. He's somebody who can tell you all about the past. My grandfather came from Lithuania. He was one of the Jewish ostrich pioneers.'

Next day, towards sundown, I drove out to meet Larry's father, Monty Markus. A barrel-chested man with floppy silver hair met me at the door, gripping his left thumb in apparent pain. 'Excuse me while I find my pills. I've had a hellluva pain for a month. I went to buy some birds, beautiful birds. Beautiful, but so wild. One of them kicked me and broke my thumb.'

Post-painkiller, Monty suggested we talk at Jack and Rosie's place. Jack Klass's father, like Monty's, had emigrated to Oudtshoorn from Lithuania before World War One.

Jack was waiting. Stiff-hipped, he led us into his living room, where all the windows hung wide open, without denting the heat. His dark-haired wife, Rosie, joined us. When we were all seated, Monty tipped forward in his chair, as if ready to spring. Then he leaned towards Jack, as he would all evening, in a gesture of consultative memory.

'Jackie, our parents came here with nothing, isn't that so? They'd all heard about Africa, ostriches and gold. But they never dreamed that the gold and the ostriches were so darn far apart.'

Jack coughed: 'A lot of those old Jews, like my dad, thought they'd come for two years and return to the *shtetl* a millionaire.' Two years in the Jerusalem of Africa would be enough. But they came and they stayed.

Sol Markus, Monty's father, had escaped the *shtetl* for Africa while still in his teens. He'd already been forced to serve four years in the Russian army. Smugglers slipped him across the German border and from there onto boats bound for Southampton and South Africa.

Sol reached Cape Town in January 1910. That same year, my great-grandfather, Gaffy, and my grandmother also sailed into Cape Town harbour from Southampton, full of their own immigrant hopes and apprehensions. The Christmas lights amazed Sol, as did the upside-down seasons and the overwhelming heat. A horse-drawn cart jammed with immigrants bone-rattled him to Oudtshoorn where, as a greenhorn *smous*, he began to pay his dues in foot leather. Sol started at the bottom of the ostrich business and walked his way to the top.

Monty Markus rose from his chair. 'You must remember, my friend, they walked.' Monty heaved some fantasy sacks of feathers, eggs, pumpkins and tobacco onto his shoulders and slung them over his back. As he talked, he trudged around the room, in empathy, in commemoration, bent double beneath his father's load.

'My dad and Jack's dad, Bennie, used to walk the same route each week. All the way to Ladismith and back again. Two hundred miles round trip in that heat. But a chap called Wilkes, he had the worst journey: to Prince Albert and back to Oudtshoorn over the Swartberg Pass. Have you ever been that way?'

I had often, as a child. The Swartberg: the Black Mountains. They reminded me of the sky islands around Willcox, huge, unexpected peaks ringed on all sides by the desert. Ecologically, a world unto themselves. Their peaks lush and cool, brimming with temperate plants and creatures that seemed incongruous so close to the desert floor. The ascent up an Arizona sky island resembles a one-hour trip from Mexico to Canada. The Swartberg Pass of childhood was a bit like that: I'd feel dizzy from the hairpin bends and sudden altitude. And at the top, I'd find a cold, foreign dreamland that wasn't the Karoo, but could have fallen from the sky or from a book. Every week, the *smous* Wilkes had to scale the Swartberg's sky islands twice on foot, dragging his feathers through the clouds.

'My dad used to sleep most of Saturday,' Monty continued. But the minute *shabbat* was over, he'd start working on his feathers, styling them so he could get a good price for them on Sunday. My dad and Jack's dad and all the other green-horns had to sell their feathers to the wealthy ones – blokes like Sadofsky and that crowd. Then Sunday night, he'd set off with his bags again, napping on the road.

'After a while, my father had saved enough for a bicycle. Then a one-horse cart, then a two-horse cart. Eventually, he'd sold enough feathers to buy a motor car.'

Sol's first few years were hard, yet hopeful. Then came the ostrich crash. Monty's voice changed, becoming somehow both more passionate and more hushed, each time our conversation moved within range of those disastrous years. Although Monty was only born in 1924, a decade after the events that he described, he spoke as if he'd survived them personally. I noticed this among Oudtshoorn's ostrich fraternity: how the crash retained an ever-present force.

Jack held up his right hand, palm towards me, thumb sticking out at a right angle. He touched the tip of his tallest finger: 'Ostriches are like this. We're up here now. At the top again.' Then he stared at the drop from that fingertip to the valley of the thumb, tracing the gap with a finger from his other hand and shaking his head. 'You just never know with ostriches,' he said. Then he fell silent. While Monty talked, Jack kept fingering the graph he'd improvised from his hand, peak to trough, peak to trough again.

Monty whistled. 'I'm telling you, of those speculator guys, I don't think one survived. Even Max Rose went bust. Actually, he went bust twice.'

'Max Rose – they sold the ring off his finger,' Jack interjected. 'When he went bust the first time, he had to auction everything he owned. And at the auction, somebody noticed he had a gold ring on. So they made him take it off his finger – they auctioned it right there on the spot.'

Around 1950, when Jack was young and starting out, he'd bought some of Rose's birds shortly before the ostrich king had died. For £3 each he'd acquired such impeccable ostriches that in America today they would probably fetch $30,000 a throw.

Jack's jaw tightened as he reminisced. He toyed with the stubble on his chin. 'Max Rose, he never spoke much. Same with my father. Those old Jews they didn't talk a lot. They only spoke about ostriches and *shul.*'

'Just before World War One,' Monty recalled, 'my dad, Jack's dad and Judel Lazarus went into partnership. They owned some ostrich farms together and a feather dealership. The three of them could have been the richest Jews in Oudtshoorn. One day, they hired a gentile to drive them around from farm to farm and bought a massive amount of feathers for a hell of a good price. Then they became greedy, they wouldn't let them go.

'Another speculator wanted to buy the lot. But they argued all week about the price. Friday morning they woke up and the bottom had fallen out.' The market was finished. And they were stuck with 204 crates of worthless ostrich plumes.

'Not boxes,' Jack wagged a finger. 'Crates. Each crate weighed a hundred pounds. That's a hell of a lot of feathers.'

'So what happened to all those crates?' I asked. Twenty-thousand pounds in weight of unsellable ostrich plumes?

'Well,' Monty continued, 'the three partners divided them up. Sixty-eight crates each.' Sol Markus took his sixty-eight crates to a barn at Wynensrivier. Then he locked the door. 'Those feathers just lay there and lay there. Jack's dad, my dad and a few other Jews always swore the ostrich would come back. Meantime, when school holidays came, he'd make us all get up early before it got too hot and help him unpack the crates. Just so he could admire his feathers again. And to give them a little air. We had to take them, walk a bit and chuck a bundle, a bundle, a bundle.' By morning's end, feathers covered the whole road.

After World War Two, plume prices began inching up again. So whenever Sol Markus unpacked his crates, he'd set aside some feathers which he'd sell to A. J. Pudney and Co. in Port Elizabeth. He wouldn't dream of letting go his finest plumes. Those he was saving, for he remembered what they'd once been worth. Sol Markus was a nostalgic and a hopeful man. Patient too, like the world around him. In the depths of the Karoo, seeds can lie dormant for seventy years waiting to be sprung by rain.

Monty's eyes took on a distant look. 'One more thing about those feathers,' he said, as if in afterthought. 'Whenever we repacked them, Dad took a crayon and wrote on the crate in Yiddish. So no-one else would understand. He was a very private man.'

'Then, one day, after we'd worked the feathers together, he handed me the crayon. And he said: "Now you write."

'I couldn't read or write Yiddish, even though I could understand when people spoke it. So I looked at him, not knowing what to do.

'And he said, "Write. Write it in English." And he told me what to write on every crate.'

Monty wandered over to the living-room door. His back towards us, he planted himself squarely beneath the jamb.

'My dad went to the barn door and stood like this. And he said to me: "You know, I'll never unpack those feathers again."'

A couple of months later Sol Markus was dead. He'd known that he was fading. And that Yiddish was fading too: the lingua franca of a feather age that never would return.

As Monty told his father's story, I thought back to Alexander Chandler of Arizona. How he'd clung to his feather fantasies long after he'd dumped his ostriches. How in the 1940s, the San Marcos Hotel basement and Sol's barn at Wynensrivier were both bursting with the promise of stored plumes. How the two men, in deserts 10,000 miles apart, had waited in vain for thirty years for the past to come back again.

The Arizona feather dream finally ended in the 1950s, when somebody chucked out the last of Chandler's feather bales. But in Oudtshoorn the reverie held, if precariously. When Sol Markus died in 1957, he still had fifteen crates hoarded in his barn. Those feathers became Monty's inheritance.

Monty threw up his hands. 'What could we do? My brother, my sister and I each took a third. They sold theirs to Pudney. But me, being the farmer, I kept mine for a long time afterwards.' So Monty ended up doing what his father had done before him. He returned to those crates obsessively: unpacking, regrading, repacking those forty-year-old ostrich plumes. By now, he had children of his own to help him spread and sort the bundles. He sold the worst ones, stored the rest. A hedge against the future and the past.

Jack leaned back and snorted. 'Agh, you don't get quality like that these days. Beautiful, beautiful feathers.' He closed his eyes and for a moment we lost him to a plume swoon.

Monty stooped to sip his tea. Then for the first time all evening, the heavy heat gave way to the shadow of a breeze. Nothing much, just a reminder that air can move.

Rosie fluttered her dress: 'Ah, a bit of cool.'

The room stayed quiet for a while. We all sipped silently. Then our conversation turned to the subject of Afrikaners and Jews.

When Sol Markus had arrived in the Karoo speaking only Yiddish, an Afrikaans farmer called Serfontein had helped him to his feet, selling him feathers every week. Monty's dad had spoken well of Serfontein. The two men had developed a strong mutual regard.

In the beginning, Monty explained, the Jewish immigrants impressed the Afrikaners. 'The Jews kept themselves apart from other people. The Afrikaners respected that. They were that way themselves.' The Afrikaners embraced the Jews as people of The Book. Unlike the dissolute British, these newcomers were pious – they gave the sabbath its due. By the same token, Oudtshoorn's religious earnestness suited the *shtetl* refugees perfectly.

It was thanks to Afrikaner magnanimity that the Jerusalem of Africa acquired its first synagogue in 1889. The Jews were still too poor at that point to pay for it themselves. So an Afrikaans ostrich farmer called Vorster donated the land; other Afrikaners provided building materials free of charge.

Jews and Afrikaners both saw themselves as God's elect, peoples of the Covenant. The Afrikaners were Old Testament stoics to the core, mistrustful of the softness of the New. That God had brought them to this punishing landscape confirmed his testing love. The Karoo: a mythic Promised Land for Jews and Afrikaners, a place where His Chosen bent their knees in supplication for mercy and rain.

Each time I heard the rudiments of this story, I was reminded of how its telling depended on a will to silence. For Jews and Afrikaners, remembering involved a stubborn forgetfulness. No-one mentioned that this Promised Land was also stolen land – stolen from the people who were living there before the whites arrived.

So Jews and Afrikaners bonded: over deserts, myths, religion, ostriches and colonial amnesia.

Through a quirk of colonial migration history, the Lithuanians had arrived in the one corner of Africa where most inhabitants – the coloureds and Afrikaners – spoke a language which shared Yiddish's Germanic roots. Many

Afrikaans words, the Litvaks found, half-echoed Yiddish ones. '*Leffel*', for 'spoon', was '*lepel*' in Afrikaans. '*Kleyn*', for 'small', was '*klein*'. '*Tante*', for 'aunt', was identical in both languages. '*Fenester*' – 'window' – was '*venster*' in Afrikaans pronounced with a soft, feathered 'v'. Jews and Afrikaners discovered just enough linguistic kinship for them to grope towards some improvised middle language. (Certainly, for both communities, English felt – in the mouth and to the ear – a far stranger tongue.) One Afrikaner Oudtshoorn mayor, Johnny de Jager, spoke such flawless Yiddish he was repeatedly mistaken for a Jew. And the Jewish ostrich farmers, fluent in Afrikaans, became known as *boerejode* – Jewish boers.

But slowly the goodwill between these two colonial communities started to erode. At first, Monty explained, it was just jealousy. 'The Afrikaners saw the Jews building big shops and houses. And then the Nazi Party came.'

The Nazis called themselves the *Ossewabrandwag* – the Oxwagon Sentinel. Many Afrikaners became German sympathizers. By 1939, the Oxwagon Sentinel boasted 400,000 members nationwide. They lashed out against foreign imperialism and 'Jewish money power'. But at the root of it all was the battle over gold and diamonds, over African labour and African land. Afrikaner and British colonialists warring over the right to the spoils that came from subjugating Africans.

Monty shook his head: 'You see, the Afrikaner hated the Englishman. Hated him. Couldn't forgive him for the Anglo-Boer War. Those concentration camps. Where were they? Ceylon? All those Afrikaner women and children who died.

'Those camps were a terrible thing. So at first the Afrikaners weren't so much pro-Germany, they were anti-British. So the Afrikaners wanted Germany to come here and give their enemy a *klap* (a hit) and knock the British right out of South Africa.

'Now the Afrikaner sees his friend, the Jew, siding with the British. And he feels betrayed. But I mean, you had to see things from our side.' Blacks and coloureds continued, nationwide, to bear the brunt of the bigotry, the mining greed and the white landgrab. But some Afrikaner politicians also began campaigning for all Jews and Indians to be deported as 'unassimilable immigrants'. South Africa had served as a minor haven for Jews escaping the pogroms. But during World War Two, the white South African parliament introduced laws making it almost impossible for Jews fleeing the holocaust to enter.

The Oxwagon sentinel praised Hitler vocally. One leader, a Dutch Reformed Church preacher (and brother of future South African Prime Minister, John Vorster), proclaimed that '*Mein Kampf* shows the way to greatness. Hitler gave the Germans a calling, a fanaticism. Only by such holy fanaticism can the Afrikaner nation achieve its calling.' For a time, that mood of 'holy fanaticism' had Oudtshoorn in its grip.

Jack nodded. 'Man, there was a lot of anti-Semitism around here. In one month in 1944, they burned down twelve Jewish shops in town.'

Monty shifted closer to the edge of his chair, a story twitching through his body.

His father hadn't just owned ostrich farms, he'd had a store in town. 'The store was open to the street and on one side there were two little *shopkes* owned by someone else. I used to go there to pick figs. Then the Nazi Party rented one of those shops. Suddenly, we as children were frightened to walk past there. They'd shout at us: "*Ons sal jou doodmaak. Ons sal jou keel afsny.*" We'll kill you. We'll slit your throat.

'And in the window there were these massive drawings. Hell, I remember that like it was yesterday. There was a Jew sitting on a little milking stool like this.' Monty moved his tea-cup and straddled the coffee table.

'He had a nose like this. And red, bloodshot eyes, as if he was going to murder, and teeth like this. And big ears, hairy ears and hairy, hairy arms. Milking the cow. And on the bottom was written – I still remember it – in English and Afrikaans: "They take the milk and we get the dung."'

Monty took a deep breath, his eyes pacing the room. Then he peered into his tea-cup, as if searching for something there. He picked up his teaspoon and tapped it absently.

'You know where the First National Bank is now? That was a double-story building. On top was a wooden balcony. That building belonged to the Dutch Reformed Church. They had offices upstairs. And they, the bastards, went and let the offices to the Nazi Party. From the top they had a pole sticking out like this and on the end a Nazi flag made from silk. But I'm telling you, that flag must have been the size of this carpet. And as kids – excuse the language – we used to shit ourselves to walk past there in case they jumped out and slit our throats.

'And then old Sam Agnenay – Jack, remember old Sam? Well, one morning, as he came out the bank, Sam walked up to the Nazi headquarters. He took a box of matches from his pocket. He lit a match and put it to the flag, just like that. Then he ran for his life.' Monty swivelled in his chair towards Jack. And smiled: 'Whoosh. Their flag went up in flames.

'Then the threats started to come. They threatened to kill Sam at night when he was alone. They threatened to skin him alive.'

The room fell quiet. Monty slowly poured himself another cup of tea. But it sat there and he didn't drink.

All evening, Rosie had held her silence. Just a few half-nods when Monty launched into a story she recognized. But now her face tautened. 'Did you hear,' she said, 'that Peter Levy is leaving Oudtshoorn? Got a job in Cape Town. How are we going to maintain the synagogue? Those that come these days never last.'

Monty shook his head. 'You must look to the future, it's no good closing your eyes. The writing is on the wall.'

The feather crash had spelled the beginning of the end for local Jews. During World War One – the first exodus. By the 1930s, the town's two *shuls* had shrunk to one. These days it was a battle to keep a single *shul* alive. Oudtshoorn's Jews didn't have their own rabbi any more. Once a month, a rabbi visited from Cape Town, 200 miles away.

Only a handful of Jews remained. Monty ticked them off on his fingers: the two Markus families, the Klasses, the Fisches, old Mrs Kroll, Mrs Lipschitz and her sons . . . Down from 500 families during the plume boom.

Young Jews weren't interested in ostriches any more. Or interested in living in a town like this. They preferred more exciting, more cosmopolitan places: Cape Town, Johannesburg. Some had emigrated to America, Australia, England and Canada, doing what their *shtetl* grandparents had done before them, following hope abroad.

'My son Larry is in the ostrich business now.' Monty's voice was edged with pride but also with anxiety. 'He and his wife, they've got three little daughters. Why would they stay? In another five years time, how many Jews will there be here?' The few who had lingered were doing well. But the Jerusalem of Africa had long since disappeared.

It was already ten o'clock, too close to dawn for people who still kept ostrich farming hours. I stood to say goodbye. Monty walked towards me, then stopped in the middle of the room. From his eyes I could see his mind was somewhere else.

He raised his right hand above his head towards the chandelier, then clicked his thumb against his middle finger to signal the lighting of a match.

He turned to Jack and smiled.

'Whoooosh. Remember that flag, Jackie, remember? Whooooosh.'

Their faces suddenly looked young and luminous in the burning memory of that flag.

Chapter Thirty-eight

A few days after talking to Monty, Jack and Rosie, I went looking for the ostrich museum. The place had changed since I'd known it as a child; it now resided in an abandoned boys' school along Baron van Reede Straat. I entered via a sandstone arch through doors that required a heavy shove. I continued down a narrow corridor: brutally polished floors, dark wood, the after-stench of ammonia cleaning fluids. As I passed the old classrooms on either side, the whack of a ghostly master's cane was almost audible.

I reached the museum's main gallery, what must once have been the school assembly hall. Now, assembled here instead were a few stuffed ostriches and bric-a-brac from human happenings in which ostriches had played a major role. Sketches of bird-pulled Roman chariots, a replica fan from Tutankhamun's tomb, a San rock painting of an ostrich hunt, shiny stones retrieved from an ostrich stomach and a few puffy, once-fashionable hats. A dented Merry Widow hat shaded a mannequin's cracked face. Her hands and cheeks, I noticed, had lost most of their pink to a powdering of dust.

The museum had grown and shrunk. Once it had seemed to me the beginning of all fantasy. I had stood surrounded by scenes like these, listening to the click of heels and dresses rustling, co-conspirators against the rectitude outside. Now what the place principally preserved was the feeling of decay. It resembled a museum of a museum – what museums once used to be. It was utterly without gadgetry. No buttons to press; no sound effects; no headphones, prerecorded voices, videos or computer screens. No storylines told with high-tech assists. Just this taxidermal must, and glass between me and everything.

I left the main gallery behind and wandered down another corridor, past a tall fan that created the noise of circulation without quite managing to move the air; past the glassy stares of sundry antelope sawn off at the neck, stuffed and strung up high along the wall. Beyond the antelope, I stepped through a doorway and suddenly found myself inside a synagogue.

I was peering, through dust motes and umber light, at a Holy Ark crowned by three gold, onion domes. Beneath the domes, two pink-shaded oil lamps stood, flanking an Ark cloth of purple velvet. On the cloth, tricked out in golden thread, appeared the skyline of Jerusalem. This place was new to me. The ostrich museum synagogue, I later learned, is still used during High Festivals. It had that aura – a lingering sacramental feel.

I looked more closely at the objects that dotted the room's periphery: a spice box carved from olive wood; a Lithuanian samovar; a *smous*'s suitcase and the hand-sewn bags he would have stuffed his feathers in; an 1850 tractate of the Talmud addressing laws concerning eggs, and beside the tractate, an ancient basket overflowing with ostrich eggs. Photographs ringed the walls: images of *shtetl* streets, of men and women embarking and disembarking from boats, wagons and trains. I saw faces whose names I knew: Max Rose, Bennie Klass, Sol Markus ... Small, mostly moustachioed, men, proudly brandishing feathers or sheltering in the shadows of their enormous birds.

As I stood there, in that synagogue, I recalled a story Monty Markus had told me of how Oudtshoorn had acquired two *shuls*. The first wave of Jewish immigrants had all come from a single Lithuanian *shtetl*, Shavel. But a schism erupted when a second wave arrived from Chelm, a community with more conservative traditions of observance. The Chelm newcomers seceded in 1896 and built Oudtshoorn's second

237

synagogue, the so-called *griene shul* – the greenhorns' *shul*. In erecting it, the congregants reproduced from memory every detail in the Ark of the Chelm synagogue they had left behind.

After the ostrich crash, Oudtshoorn's declining Jewry could no longer sustain two synagogues. So they closed the *griene shul*, making sure, however, that they preserved the Ark. The survival of that replica Ark was to take on an unforseeable significance. In July 1941 – shortly before Oudtshoorn's Nazis started burning Jewish shops – the German army swept through Chelm, massacring Jews and torching the town's main synagogue.

So the Ark before me, in that recess of the ostrich museum, was all that remained of the original. I began to wonder. Had the Chelm immigrants' nostalgia for the place they'd worshipped in always been more than that? Had the pogroms taught them to remember in such reverential detail? Taught them that the past is never secure enough against future violations? That this shadow place, this tabernacle of memory, could one day become more lasting than the real thing?

That night, unable to sleep, I got into my car and set off past the cemetery under a bone-white moon. The old gravestones – divided by race and religion – stood glinting on the hill: everybody in Oudtshoorn still in their boxes, the living and the dead. I headed out of town beneath a blazing cross, its light dimmed by the moon's brilliance. Some nine miles on, I passed Greylands, one of the old feather palaces, still splendid-looking. The black and white awnings, verandas, balconies and rooftop peaks appeared doubly Gothic on a shiny night like this. I remembered something Monty Markus had told me. That an Englishman called Harry Gavin had owned Greylands. And that in Monty's father's day, Gavin had put a sign up on his gate. 'No dogs, no Jews.' 'Harry Gavin,' Monty had said, 'he also went bust.'

I started thinking back on the museum. How it had not a single word to say about Oudtshoorn's coloured majority. No artefacts, no stories on the walls. Dead silence. The closest it came to embracing any experience that wasn't white was a solitary rock painting and a plaster-of-Paris San family, sitting on their haunches, huddled around a fire in an imaginary cave. The museum was a shrine to *shtetl* memory; but it also turned forgetting into stone.

I headed north along the Beaufort West road, the road David Piedt had fled down eight years before in his pyjamas. Then I doubled back beneath the huge, striated massif of the Swartberg range and continued on through mimosa thorn-veld, past one ostrich farm after another. Near a farm called Onverwagt ('Unexpected'), the moonlight picked out a flock of several hundred ostriches huddled in a yard.

Fifteen miles further on, woodsmoke and a thin yapping of dogs marked the approach of Waaikraal and Dysselsdorp. In the 1960s and '70s, these two old mission settlements became sites of forced removals when coloureds and blacks were driven out of town. Last I spoke to him, David Piedt had said that people hoped Waaikraal would become the first coloured-owned ostrich farm. There was some mission land close by that could be opened up. A place for a forgotten people to put their long-remembered ostrich skills to work. A small beginning, but a model, perhaps. A start.

Chapter Thirty-nine

Towards the end of my stay in Oudtshoorn, I was flicking through the telephone directory when I came across an entry that piqued my curiosity. 'Pappalardo, Luisa. Plume-maker/pluim-maker.' A name like that stood out in the Karoo: Mediterranean-sounding in a world of Pieterses, van Jaarsvelds and Serfonteins. What, I wondered, would a professional plume-maker do in this day and age?

So I called. The woman who answered spoke in a tumbling voice, a change from the standard, white South African squashed monotone. She was busy, she said. She had work to do. What did I want to know? She had nothing to tell me. It would be better if I looked it up in books.

Nevertheless, next morning, I drove to her house, my spirits lifted by the country's political buoyancy and by a sudden soaking rain. A tall, elegant lady in her mid-fifties opened the door. As we stood on the veranda, she stared at the sky with a look of personal affront. 'Terrible rain, terrible.' She was the first Karoo person I'd ever heard complaining about rain.

'All this humidity. A disaster. It ruins the feathers.'

Luisa disappeared indoors, then returned waving a sad-looking ostrich plume. 'See here. Frost and rain. By the time you pluck the bird, the feathers are all stringy and pointy. Useless, ugly things.

'Oudtshoorn is dry, dry, dry. Excellent for ostriches, excellent for health. Lots of people I know came here because

240

their doctors said, "You have to go to Oudtshoorn or you'll die." Excellent, excellent air.'

But that's not why she'd come. Luisa had emigrated to Oudtshoorn because she was a plume-maker and wanted to live at the source. Ostrich feathers were her passion and her destiny.

Luisa Pappalardo was born in Algeria in 1940. As a young woman, she moved to Paris, where she studied the ancient arts of plume-making; then moved again to Rio, working for ten years as a feather maestro at the carnival. But carnival work bored her. Besides, she yearned for the desert. So, five years ago, Luisa had visited Oudtshoorn for the first time and stayed. She'd arrived in January – the furnace month: forty-eight degrees centigrade (118° F) in the shade. A sandstorm was blowing across the Karoo. But she'd felt a surge of pleasure on re-entering childhood weather and at the prospect of living out her days surrounded by ostriches.

I asked Luisa: what exactly does a plume-maker do?

'Ah,' she said, 'my work. The correct term is *plumassière*. I've dated the first use of the word back to the late sixteenth century.' But even before that, camel caravans had carried feathers across the Sahara to North African ports. From there, they were ferried to Livorno in Italy.

'That was going on since the epoch of the crusades. The Christians were wearing marvellous ostrich plumes in the fight against the Muslims.' And then, after the sixteenth century, the demand became so fierce that the professional *plumassière* was born.

Luisa's conversational style was full of somersaults and pirouettes. She would land, suddenly, in the court of Louis Quatorze, then do a backflip into medieval couture. She would whirl from seventeenth-century musketeers to Victorian milliners, then leap across the centuries again, with sidelong glances at Roman centurions, the Mata Hari, flappers, Italian feather-curling, music hall and the significance of bisexual fashions for the Renaissance. She

241

peered at history with a compendious curiosity through the parted fronds of ostrich plumes.

She began to explain to me the arts of feather-bleaching, dying and knotting; how to set a fan; the seven different ways to curl a plume using heated curling knives.

'Come, come, it's better if you see.' With both hands, she waved me through a door.

We entered her bedroom which doubled as her workroom. A white sewing machine, strewn with unfinished garments, squatted in a corner alongside an old metal trellis table. Boxes filled the room: long thin flower boxes piled everywhere. Luisa started unpacking them, box after box after box, carefully folding back the tissue paper inside to reveal plumed fans, boas, pom-poms, *chapeaux*, feather-fringed jackets and décolletage – fashion phantoms from the past.

She draped her creations across the bed, the chairs, the wardrobe door and the armoire, until the room was frothing with feathers in peach shades, apricot, crimson, white, crow-black and ice-blue. Slung over everything, the décolletage, the fans, the boas gave the place a louche, backstage feel. The look was lush and saucy: this could have been Mae West's dressing room. Apart, that is, from the open book face down on the bed: *Learn to Speak Afrikaans.*

On arriving in Paris in 1962, Luisa had studied under Madame Fevrier, one of the last great *plumassières*. The *plumassière*, Luisa explained, was the plume-mistress, the specialist. In the olden days, she'd have had several *plumonieres* working below her to implement her ideas. The Paris fashion industry used to employ an army of *autruchennes* – 'ostrich workers'. This was the collective term for the *plumassières* and *plumonieres* and also the hat-workers who styled feathers for milliners. The Parisian army of ostrich-workers peaked during the *belle époque*, although some women kept going for decades after that. In the 1930s, Madame Fevrier found lucrative work making garments for Metro Goldwyn Mayer as Hollywood fell briefly in love again with the ostrich look.

Luisa lifted and cradled a fan. Her fingers folded around a glistening tortoise-shell handle. 'Here,' she said, 'look carefully.' The splayed feathers were white, but held some memory of pink: like that moment, late afternoon, when the Karoo light turns pale coral, just before the crimsons, the purples, the indigos arrive.

There are twelve feathers to a fan. The *plumassière* generally sets the handle in ivory, tortoise, or mother-of-pearl. Luisa showed me how she had to slice the base of each quill at a careful angle so the feathers could slide smoothly over each other when the fan was closed. It is easy to slice too deep and weaken or guillotine a feather.

Perched on the edge of her bed, Luisa rolled a peach boa around her neck. She flounced a little, striking a pose with an exquisite fan. To make the fan, she had chosen a rare feather type that possessed a natural double hue: white with a soft bluish trim. Luisa gave her two-tone fan a flutter. 'Very glamorous, shows up beautifully at night.'

I sat there, listening to her voice and her talkative hands. In the company of feathers, her fingers came alive, the way a face will suddenly relax and brighten among friends. As we chatted, she would shape from air and memory a particularly fleshy feather or the droop of a cascading hat. Her hands were seldom still. Even in repose, they remained her private centre of gravity.

Where, I asked, did her passion for ostriches and feather-work begin?

Luisa gestured expansively across the room. 'As a little girl, I grew up with ostrich feathers. They were my playthings.' Her Algerian godmother was a milliner by training and had maintained a lively workshop. Each day, after school, Luisa would vanish into this feather-world, playing and watching as her godmother and her fellow *plumassières* created lavish things.

Since the eighteenth century, Luisa's family had amassed some wealth from olive oil, trading between North Africa and her father's ancestral Italy. The family had owned a farm in

Algeria for over a hundred years. It lay south of the capital, in the pre-Sahara, on Algeria's high flats. During her school holidays, Luisa would visit this family farm. It was called Hassi-Naam, The Well of Ostriches.

'Since ancient times, wild ostriches came to this well to drink.' Luisa staged a little pantomime with her hands, imitating the bobbing walk of an ostrich and then the looping neck, as it stooped to scoop up water.

'In 1854, my great-great grandfather, August Hardy, had the idea to capture and breed some ostriches, along with his camels and his sheep. Nobody else had ever thought of that. Before, even in South Africa, when somebody wanted feathers they got on a horse and took their gun.'

The family farm lay near an area called Daya, where pistachios – a delicacy much favoured by ostriches – grew abundantly. August Hardy captured and bred some of these wild ostriches, the coveted Barbary birds. He produced a special strain that became legendary for its splendid double floss.

Luisa peered at me over her tear-shaped spectacles. For the first time, I noticed little clusters of silver glitter brightening the corners of the frame. She pouted questioningly: 'You know about double floss?'

Only vaguely. Double floss, I recalled, was what the Trans-Saharan Ostrich Expedition had been all about.

'Here.' She unfurled a feather, full-bodied as cotton candy. Her long fingers stroked and plumped the plumes. 'This,' Luisa said, a breathy tenderness entering her voice, 'is double floss.

'Look carefully at the barbs.' I bent close enough to focus on the microscopic hooks ranged along the feather's lateral branches. I was beginning to realize why a plume-maker might develop dodgy eyes. By locking into each other, the barbs and minuscule barbules render feathers air-tight and make flight possible by turning them, collectively, into wings. For the *plumassière*, the density of these little hooks is crucial: it sets the limits to her art. Only the finest ostriches produce a thick enough matrix to give plumes this springy buoyancy, this layered sumptuousness.

'You see, it is all a matter of ostrich pedigree.' Luisa began to recite from memory elaborate family trees for the finest feather birds dating back to the mid-nineteenth century. I didn't catch it all: Syrian this crossed with Barbary that; the role the blue ostrich played and the George White Special Bird. Luisa could expatiate on ostrich bloodlines with the detailed passion one might expect from an Irish horse-breeder discussing the genealogy of the Godolphin Arabian.

So August Hardy, Luisa's great-great grandfather was the first ostrich farmer in history. However, by the 1880s, Oudtshoorn had bested Algiers in the contest to become the world's ostrich capital. Hardy's endeavours faltered, then trickled, traceless, into the sand.

Luisa blamed the French colonials. Men like General Margueritte, a notoriously trigger-happy nineteenth-century colonist whose maraudings helped ensure that the Barbary ostrich disappeared. Luisa thrummed her lower lip: 'The French were excellent, excellent at extinction. The famous Barbary ostrich, the famous Sahara leopard, the famous Atlas lion . . . all gone.' Then she turned her finger into a knife, slid it across her throat, and made a gurgling sound.

'Oudtshoorn,' Luisa exclaimed, 'never had those beautiful Barbary birds, until a few were smuggled in.' But Oudtshoorn had something just as invaluable: fences.

At The Well of Ostriches and across Algeria, fencing was impossible. Immense caravans – sometimes 20,000 camels at a time – trailed back and forth along the ancient trade lines that looped from North Africa all the way to the Senegalese coast, then up to the Mediterranean again. For the better part of a millennium – since the crusades at least – Europe had depended for its feather supplies on Arab caravans travelling those routes. But, ironically, for August Hardy and his successors, those same caravans made ostrich farming im-possible. Camels and sheep could be raised without fences.

Luisa threw up her hands: 'Ostriches, no.' They would disappear at speed.

As a teenager, Luisa fantasized about putting up fences and recreating lost feather lines. She had a cousin who shared her passion for ostriches. In 1956, they undertook a journey together through French West Africa, hoping to track down some of the fine old ostrich strains. She was just sixteen.

'You see,' Luisa said, 'I was always a dreamer.' She unfolded her hands and caressed a turquoise fan absently. The feathers streamed through her fingers like water over branches in a brook.

Luisa and her cousin Bernard set off in search of ostriches they had read about in nineteenth-century French and German travelogues, books written by adventurers who'd passed through the great markets of Kano, Timbuktu and Khartoum. The two cousins scoured the African interior from Senegal to the British Sudan and back.

'We were naive. These beautiful birds, they were all finished. They existed only in old books. We just saw sand and stones and more and more poor peoples. But Bernard and me – he was my lover at the time, my cousin and my lover – we wanted to marry and breed ostriches on a big, big scale.

'After the trip, it was over. So here I am in Oudtshoorn and he is farming clementines in Corsica.' She half-chuckled, half-shrugged, but the shrug seemed stronger than the chuckle.

In 1962, the Algerian revolution triumphed, bringing to an end Africa's bloodiest anti-colonial war. Luisa's family lost their farm and fled Algeria for France, arriving in Paris bearing two suitcases. There, Luisa underwent her long, exacting training under Madame Fevrier, learning to shape boas, set fans and create *l'araignée*, 'the spider', a complex tasselly effect that turns feathers into trails of gossamer filaments. Later, she set up her own practice as a *plumassière*. The feather-work answered a deep yearning. But it also bound her to the past, preparing her for an obsolete career.

When Luisa expounded on Victorian couture and the *belle*

époque the passion in her voice became elegiac. Her work had left her captive to a vanished age, gone before she was born. The real world, the past, lay behind her in all its splendid solidity. Like Plato's prisoner in his cave, she was reduced to watching ghostly flickerings.

Luisa wanted to pass on her art. She dreamed of an apprentice, someone younger, someone for the future. 'The Cape coloureds are marvellous artisans. Marvellous, marvellous artisans. But who would want to become a *plumassière* today? To learn everything, to learn to set a fan correctly, seven or eight years it would take. Before the Second World War in Paris, you had to create a Prince of Wales to pass the plume-maker's exam. To reach that level, pah, maybe ten years . . .'

We wandered out into the washed light of her garden. The rainstorm had long since passed. It was almost midday now, and the sun was sucking up the remaining pools of shade. Cape turtle doves throbbed metronomically: troo, troooo; troo, troooo, troo, troooo. The only sound never defeated by the heat. Depending on your mood, a soothing sound or a headache that refuses to go away.

A band of extravagantly tailed mousebirds landed in a fig tree and began gouging pulp from the fruit. From a nearby field, a flock of hadeda ibises let loose volleys of raucous mockery. 'Ha-ha-hadeda. Ha-ha-hadeda.' They're big, bulky birds with scimitar bills and an iridescent sheen – sequins of pink, teal and burgundy flicked on and off as they flew overhead. Their cries startled and delighted me: one of the oldest, boldest sounds I can recall, a sound that, as a child in the Karoo, I would hear every day. Now their voices had a half-exotic ring, in the way of all things familiar yet new.

Luisa and I talked about the other birds that flourished here: like the Egyptian goose and the piebald sacred ibis, revered by the Pharaohs and immortalized in paintings and engravings in the pyramids. Both species are found across the length of Africa: Luisa recognized them from her childhood

247

in Algeria. These were, for her, the birds of memory and return.

Oudtshoorn felt, to Luisa, like the mirror latitude of youth. She vanished briefly inside the house and returned bearing an atlas. Her lean feather-knotter's forefinger pointed to the top and bottom of Africa. 'Look at Oudtshoorn, look at Algiers. Almost exactly the same distance, north and south of the equator.'

Then she turned to talking about her frustrations. 'People here they are narrow, they are tight. They are so cautious. They don't want to speak to you their secret, even when this secret is the secret of the great-grandfather. For them it is like a violation. I cannot understand that. Because it is a pity for the story, the exact story of the feather.

'For example, this man Pietertjie.' An Afrikaans ostrich farmer. She wouldn't give his last name; she was sworn to secrecy. Over generations, Pietertjie's family had kept alive the finest strain of feather-bird in the world.

'Ostriches have made them very rich. But they live like peasants, very simply. Pietertjie's greatest pleasure is to see his name on the front page of Oudtshoorn's little newspaper, when he wins the annual ostrich cup. Fourteen years in a row, he gets the prize for the best feathers. He wants no more than that.

'He is a small man, very, very shy. Blushes when you talk to him.' Luisa gave Pietertjie a few imaginary pats on the head to indicate his size and temperament. 'Sometimes I feel I am, I am . . . too strong for him.' She threw up her hands and pouted: 'He makes you have tea with his mother for an hour first, before he lets you see his secret flock.'

Did she think it might be possible for me to meet Pietertjie? She laughed. 'How much time do you have? No, no. It would be too difficult. He is such a suspicious man.' It had taken her two years before Pietertjie finally agreed to introduce her to his ostriches.

But the wait, she said, was worth it. Pietertjie commanded very little English and no French at all. Luisa had hardly even a beginner's Afrikaans. But somehow they managed to communicate through their shared language of birds. 'He washes the ostriches; makes sure they're perfectly groomed. Ah, the beauty of it.

'He respects, he reveres those birds. To see them – it was the most beautiful thing. A miracle. They were creatures from a dream.'

Luisa's eyelids flickered and her voice went quiet. Her hands conjured first the ostriches, then the detail in the feathers, until just her fingertips were moving, like a pianist playing pianissimo.

We wandered back indoors and sat chatting among the feather garments strewn around her bedroom. Luisa recalled how she had once started to write a book about ostriches and the people they inspired. The loss of all that ostrich past pained her: 'Even Oudtshoorn people, they know nothing about his wonderful past. I wanted to share the history, to cut through all the lies.' Luisa chopped the air with her right hand. 'Then one of the farmers' wives, she said to me: "Will anyone be interested in your romance with the ostriches? That feather-world is finished." And I thought: she's right. And I took the book outside and burned it. Finished. Extinct.'

Luisa's voice faltered then faded. Shafts of sheer light streamed through the window, picking out dust motes in the air and illuminating the detail in her fans, her boas, her décolletage. I watched her plumes burst into bloom, into the tumbling colours of a *belle-époque* gorgeousness.

For a moment, our silence hung there; the past lit up the room and the passage of time was stilled.

Then Luisa began to pack her things away. As she opened and closed boxes, her hands fluttered like hummingbirds over a brightly coloured garden. Slowly, her flowers folded and disappeared, until there was just one pink boa left. Luisa cracked the last box, wound up the boa and wreathed it in tissue paper, before bringing down the lid.

Chapter Forty

After leaving Oudtshoorn for the last time, I swung wide
through the Karoo. En route to Port Elizabeth, I wanted
to see the Owl House in a hamlet called Nieu Bethesda. My
father, shortly before his death, had visited this strange outpost where the Owl Lady Helen Martins and a succession of
collaborators had created a fantasia of statuary from cement
and broken bottles. Dad admired anything done on the
cheap – his definition of ingenuity. As far as 'Growing Things'
was concerned, a flowerless garden where only concrete
statues bloomed was stretching it. But the Owl House made it,
all the same, into one of his last Wednesday columns.

To reach Nieu Bethesda, I drove a couple of hundred miles
east then north across the Plains of Camdeboo. Nieu
Bethesda lies on a dirt road going nowhere in particular;
except in a wild, meandering way it doesn't link one place
with the next. The hamlet is so isolated that it didn't acquire
electricity until 1992. So when the Owl Lady died in 1976,
she'd lived her entire life by gas and candlelight.

The approach road proved steep and bendy. It would have
been easy to misjudge the turns and join the company of
vehicles – donkey-carts, oxwagons, Volkswagen Kombis,
pickup trucks – that littered the drop on either side. The road
passed through the foothills of the Sneeuberg range before
curling down towards Nieu Bethesda valley, a thin, green
velvet strip which, from high up, resembled a girl's hairband
fallen on a field of stones.

Long before the hamlet came into view, the Dutch Reformed Church announced itself. The white-washed steeple was built not just to be seen from far off, but to be observed. For 40,000 years before that spire went up, the Bushmen or San – the Karoo's first inhabitants – must have felt this valley's allure. But by the time Nieu Bethesda appeared in the late nineteenth century, colonial slaughter had driven the San close to extinction here and right across the Karoo.

At the bottom of the hill, I asked a farmer for directions to the Owl House. He turned his head aside and addressed a nearby field: 'You're not the first to ask, you know. People go there now. Before, they stayed away. They thought she was a witch.'

I drove the way he suggested and stopped the car near the Post Office. I got out and stood there, listening to the un-familiar sound of water. A spring bubbled up, cold and clear, gushing through the streets in open stone-lined furrows. I walked along the furrow verge, past pear trees and apricots, quince hedges, roses smouldering in the heat. Willows over-hung the watercourse, sagging beneath the mass of cone-shaped nests woven by golden weaverbirds. Beneath a willow's spread, an old lady dipped her red bucket into the furrow, then walked, sore-hipped, back to her door.

Bethesda, the Bible tells us, was an oasis, a balmy pool that drew travellers to its healing touch. But this new Bethesda lay far from any traveller's route. Shadowed by valley and church, people lived there all their lives, with little knowledge of beyond or prospect of escape. Nieu Bethesda, as Helen Martins discovered to her cost, was an archetypal one-mistake Karoo town.

Her first mistake was to be creative. She crammed her yard and house with concrete camels, birds and strange-eyed votaries. Her art marked her with the stain of difference. Besides, she kept to herself, shunned church, stank of ginger and was said to be missing one toe from each foot. The woman was clearly possessed. So the locals closed ranks

251

against her and her statuary. Small boys threw stones. Larger boys lobbed rocks, sometimes knocking a carved pilgrim from his camel or maiming a concrete owl.

On first sight, I was surprised by how ordinary the Owl House facade appeared. I had seen its likeness all over the Karoo: long and creamy-walled with a wide veranda out front. The corrugated-iron roof was black and sloping, like a forelock of brylcreamed hair furrowed by a comb.

Helen Martins was born in this house in 1898. She died there seventy-eight years later. For a brief time, in her twenties, she got away. She moved to a larger Karoo town, found work as a teacher, felt her world widen. But back in Nieu Bethesda both her parents began to ail. So Helen returned to that claustral house and hamlet, to care for them. Like legions of daughters before her, she put her own living on hold. She nursed her parents through serial sicknesses and saw them to the grave. This took her twenty years: sixteen before her mother died and another four before her father, her special torment, followed in 1945.

The end of the war coincided with her father's death. She felt a double sense of release. After decades tending and waiting, she grew obsessed with passing time. She was almost fifty now; her life's work, long pent-up, hadn't yet begun. So she started to remake her world, simply at first, painting her father's room, which he'd insisted on keeping black, red. She scattered coloured glass across the walls, some shards of brightness to exorcize the past.

Then she started creating owls. All concrete, though that didn't seem to hinder their fertility. Soon, they'd multiplied until they overran her house. The first owls appeared on the veranda. Walking up the steps, I could feel the weight of their gaze on me. Eight saucer-eyed sentinels sitting there, quiet as the dead, but watchful all the same. They reminded me of Gaffy, the way he'd roost on our porch in his pince-nez spectacles, stock-still for hours, but letting nothing pass unobserved. By instinct and infirmity, he was the perfect veranda owl.

These guardian owls were Miss Helen's retort to village life. All eyes: her way of staring back at a prying place where to live eccentrically was to live over-observed. Miss Helen housed her concrete sentinels in a chicken-wire cage. Once it had been an aviary, until she found she couldn't afford the constant topping up that living birds require.

I passed through the veranda owl-cage and crossed the threshold into the house. Inside, each room was radiant. Left behind in her parents' place, Miss Helen had dealt with the past by lavishing light on it. Huge yellow-glass suns shone from the ceiling. Ground glass, in turquoise, saffron, carmine and sea-green, glistened from her walls, her pantry shelves, her dressers, chairs, tables, windows . . . on every surface bar the floor.

Miss Helen lived bone-poor. She dressed in threadbare smocks, walked barefoot, survived on bread and tea. Her paltry pension she reserved for the things she cared about: mirrors, bottles, lamps, thrift-store glitter and cement. Miss Helen used an old-fashioned coffee-grinder to mill her glass – mostly beer bottles. Then she sorted it, by chip-size and by shade, into peach jars which shared her larder shelves with ancient, home-made preserves. Her bottled glass and bottled confectioneries stood there together, like a hedge against hard times, looking equally edible and indifferent to decay.

Mirrors she adored. But roaming the house, I noticed that she'd hung most of them too high for human vanity. Instead, they amplified the glistening and helped her owls proliferate. Owls perched everywhere. Twenty or thirty of them, some one foot tall, others four feet. They guarded doors, eyed their own reflections and flapped silent wings, straining against their solidity. Wherever I wandered, a pair of beer-bottle eyes sunk in concrete followed me.

Miss Helen couldn't have done all this alone. She scandalized her white neighbours by working, over the decades, in close collaboration with a succession of coloured men. Piet van der Merwe, Jonas Adams, and, most productively of all, Koos Malgas. Miss Helen's dependence on them was complete. For although the vision for the Owl House was hers, her hands weren't equal to it. This, she felt, was the cost of her belatedness: that just as her creative confidence was rising, her arthritic wrists and fingers started stiffening into claws.

Before they met her, none of the men had any sculpting experience. But, given the chance, they flourished. Especially the gifted Koos Malgas, who shaped so many of the finest statues in the house and the yard. Koos and Miss Helen worked together for her last twelve years. She was already sixty-four when they met, he thirty-five. Koos was a sheep-shearer who visited every so often to help repair things around the house. But she soon noticed that he had a creative eye and creative hands. Miss Helen adapted images from ornaments, cards, illustrated Bibles and sketches to show him what she wanted. But it was he who built the wire armatures and gave shape to the cement. Is it possible to separate the initial vision from the final hands?

As her arthritis worsened, Miss Helen relied on Koos to help her dress. Prying eyes noticed this, and where eyes pried gossip soon followed. The air of scandal intensified. But the couple continued working together, dreaming and building nonstop, blind to the discriminations of the town. The art itself proved blinding: Koos Malgas, Piet van der Merwe and Miss Helen all suffered deep damage to their sight from glass fragments, spat out by the coffee grinder, or falling from ceilings as they worked.

I left the house and stepped out back, into the place Miss Helen called the camel yard. The atmosphere was frenzied, so different from anything in the hamlet snoring beyond her walls. Concrete pilgrims, seers, votaries and magis massed across the yard. Scores and scores of them: bowing, praying, staggering forward, yearning wide-armed. Some caught in gymnastic arabesques of devotion, others striding on tiptoe, treading air. But most were migrating across the yard on camel-back, heading east.

Hordes of creatures shared the yard with the nomadic

worshippers. Camels, peacocks, storks, lions, giraffes, more owls. Only the birds and animals, I noticed, had been allowed glass eyes. The human votaries peered through orbs of blank cement. They seemed driven in a bewildered way, as if blind or battling some excruciating light. Their frenetic fingers took over where their eyes gave out. No hands lay still: they all pointed, beckoned, implored, signalled despair, blocked ears or fought off the sun's ferocity with open palms.

Along the perimeter fence, Miss Helen had hung a couplet from the Rubaiyat of Omar Khayyam: 'The stars are setting and the Caravan/Starts for the Dawn of Nothing – Oh make haste.' A mood of frantic belatedness prevailed everywhere.

This statuary would die in any indoor gallery – even outdoors in a less ferocious light. The Karoo's unyielding presence seemed essential to the abrasive world surrounding me. In these parts, people lived with their eyes clenched against the sun. But the light was so severe that it brought concrete to life, giving it a brilliance all its own. Miss Helen and Koos had used all this surplus radiance to extract from grey cement a panoply of shades.

Miss Helen refused to take her moral bearings from the Calvinist Karoo. She used liquor store empties to embellish her mangers, cribs and church steeples. These shrines thrived alongside what she called her 'Corner of Debauchery', where a hostess hoisted her brown beer-glass skirt and thrust a half-jack of gin towards a cement figure slumped into a chair. His arms were locked behind his head, his legs crossed, as he leaned back, eyeing temptation, in a pose of unconvincing nonchalance. Alongside this pair, a mermaid sprawled seductively in a translucent gin-glass pool. Her face was masked and enigmatic, her tail scaled with whisky-bottle shards. In her right hand she flaunted a plastic yellow comb of the sort I'd noticed in the village shop. Half its teeth had fallen out, casualties of her vanity perhaps, or the trials of concrete hair.

Miss Helen invented co-ordinates of her own. Like the clock on the imitation Dutch Reformed Church spire, some twelve-feet high, that rose from the centre of the yard. The clock face never moved. The cement had dried at ten past twelve. Two youths struggled to hold back the hands, while below robed men on camels hurried past.

In strict compass terms, her travellers were all off course. The pilgrims weren't really surging east, only towards her version of it. By the time Miss Helen discovered her error, her caravan had grown too vast, too cumbersome to turn aside. So she adjusted nature's compass by reorienting the Orient to suit her needs. She clamped to the back fence two rough-cut silver stars and a simple, remedial sign that read, in English and Afrikaans: EAST/*OOS*.

Some neighbours believed she was satanic; most agreed she was insane. 'They think I am crazy, the village idiot,' she wrote to a friend. It pained her to see her flocking birds and pilgrims pelted with stones. But she gave up trying to shake her reputation for dementia. Publicly, she found a way to live as she was perceived: 'Behaving like that keeps them away, so I can get on with my work.' Meanwhile, she built her high walls higher, to protect her creatures and her creativity.

Cemented to this spot by birth, parental illness, then indigence, Miss Helen took flight through reverie. She wrote as much to a friend: 'I haven't the money to travel. So I must make the world myself.' Yet she didn't fantasize about mountain forests or ocean shores. She sat down in the midst of her thousand-mile sandbox and dreamed herself a deeper desert life. More camels, more caravans, more nomads, pursuing the Promised Land across her yard and into the desert beyond.

I never saw the Owl House as a child. But through the memory of a wish, it seemed a childhood place, somewhere I'd visited in desire long ago during my oasis-hungry early years. Children are seldom literal escapists; they can't go far away. Instead of running from the world, they burrow deeper into it, using what lies to hand. A tin, a stick, a few pebbles, long white mimosa thorns.

It's a special gift that children have, one hard for adults to regain, this readiness to look around, pick things up and use them to make a small, stuck world feel huge. Miss Helen and her collaborators could do just that: stage, from broken beer bottles and cheap cement, this alternative great trek across her yard.

After wandering among the statuary, I stopped to rest beneath the shade of what must once have been the work-shop. I leaned against a bag of cement – half-used, long since solidified. A pile of metal bits lay to one side, mostly unfin-ished stars, alongside an ancient coffee mill with a rotating arm. I found myself ringed by hills of beer bottles, some whole, some smashed, some with their necks knocked off, as if in readiness for the bad end of Saturday night. South Africa's favourites were all there: Castle Lager, Lion, Amstel, Windhoek Light.

Despite the spiritual intensity of this place, Miss Helen and Koos used the rawness of their raw materials with wit. On either side of me stood two bottle shrines which Miss Helen called her Meccas. Hive-shaped, open at one end and large enough to step inside. Inspired by Islam and each built from tiers of Castle Lager dumpies – those squat, brown bottles that express one version of 'the South African way of life'. Dumpies summoned back childhood images of white men in rugby crowds: explosive, thick-jawed types, bleary with drink, teeth tearing into kudu or ostrich jerkey, pelting abuse, oranges and bottles at the opposition or some offending referee. Yet to step inside one of Miss Helen's dumpy Meccas was to leave that boorish culture far behind. I found myself in a circle of benediction, a calm, cathedral light.

On emerging from a Mecca dome, I found a small family group had joined me in the yard: a paunchy coloured man (mid-thirties I guessed) trailing a child – one boy, one girl – on each arm. The Owl House, once totally obscure, had started to draw the curious, people prepared to drive the extra miles. The father stalked around with a hunched,

257

suspicious air. He looked nonplussed; he was making up his mind. The little boy tripped over his own shoe, bawled, dusted his knees and found himself face to face with a wire-whiskered lion. It stared at him with headlamp eyes. (Koos Malgas had retrieved them from a Volkswagen Beetle that had careened off the pass.) The boy was suddenly unnerved and said, in Afrikaans: 'Daddy, I don't like this place. It's creepy.' The father rumbled something impatient that I couldn't quite overhear.

The girl dropped her father's hand and skipped through the maze of statuary towering above her head. She was perhaps ten, slightly older than her brother. She was wearing socks and sandals, a flowered dress and a straw hat with a coarse weave, so that as she ran, a lattice of light and shadow played across her face. The rough grain of the concrete seemed to draw her in. She stroked a magus, a camel, then a man at prayer. She didn't run her hand along them absently, like a child trailing a stick along a fence, but with care and concentration as if trying to get a feeling for the forms.

'*Pappie*,' the girl chirped abruptly. '*Pappie, ek wens sy was my ma.*' 'Daddy, I wish she was my mother.' The man seemed not to hear. But I was suddenly moved and wanted to ask her why. There was no mother in sight. Perhaps her parents had separated or divorced. Perhaps, too, she liked to provoke her brother; they were at an age where they probably didn't get on. But the way she walked and stared and touched, there was more to it than that.

The girl threaded her way across the dreamyard, past a peacock, two men in fezzes, a shepherd shooing his sheep towards Bethlehem. She sidestepped one set of outstretched arms after another, then stopped. Something had caught her eye. '*Pappie*,' her piccolo voice began; then she noticed that her father had retreated to the willow shade at the far end of the yard. But she saw me looking on. 'Look here, mister, this camel's got wings. It's the only one. This camel knows how to fly.' She reached up and touched it, the hump first, then the wings.

Her father called; she scampered off, flapping her naked arms. But I walked over to the statue she'd noticed, which had escaped my eye. It differed from all the rest; the only portmanteau creature in the yard, half-camel and half-bird. A beak-faced desert Pegasus, stony wings held high as if trying to gain the air. A tiny girl stood on the creature's back, perfectly balanced and upright like a rider in a ring. Her eyes were cemented shut, her hands stretched forward, pushing against the light. She was nothing but plain cement herself, just like her steed, except for two tiny nipples done in ruby glass.

Miss Helen had lived all her life in the vicinity of ostriches. Perhaps she took the San view that the ostrich is a border creature, stranded between the mammals and the birds. A view shared by Aristotle, Pliny, and, in his way, Linnaeus, when he baptized the ostrich *Struthio camelus*. European explorers travelling through Africa and Arabia often reported confusing camels and ostriches in the shimmery desert light. Both have long necks and limbs and because the camel walks by moving two legs forward at a time, it can appear two-legged in silhouette. Struthio camelus: a name born of an illusion.

I suspect that Miss Helen, who had a fondness for Islamic myth and art, would have warmed to the Arab fable about the ostrich's identity dilemmas. Allah, we are told, summoned all the living creatures to be assigned a name and a way of life. The ostrich arrived, but stood to one side, not knowing quite when to enter the procession. As the birds passed, he said, 'Clearly, I am not a bird, for I do not fly.' When the beasts of the earth trooped by, he declared 'Certainly, I am not a beast, for I have only two legs.' When all had passed and Allah's work was done, only the ostrich remained. Allah turned to it and decreed: 'You have cut yourself off from all your fellow creatures. You have chosen to be different and to be alone. So you shall live as you have chosen.' And with that he drove the ostrich off to dwell for ever in desert solitude, with nobody but camels for company.

Miss Helen committed suicide one winter morning in 1976. She was seventy-eight. She'd been working on the Owl House for almost thirty years when she died.

Arthritis had already claimed her hands; her glass-ruined eyes were fading fast. The gulf between her near-blindness and her still urgent vision became intolerable. Shortly before her death she wrote to a friend: 'As you get older, you realize that dying isn't the problem . . . living is the problem. That is why you have to live it well and to the full. My agony would be to "live dying" without being able to work.'

In taking her life, Miss Helen used, as always, what lay to hand. On her pantry shelf she kept a tin of caustic soda for cleaning and scouring. She reached for it, spooned some into a glass of water, stirred and drank it down. It took her three days to die, corroded from within.

After her death, Koos worked at the Post Office for a while. Then he left town. By all accounts, he stopped creating things and stumbled into drink. It is said that on her deathbed Miss Helen directed Koos to a note in a draw. The note explained that she was leaving everything – the little she had – to him. He heard her words, but he couldn't read them: he was illiterate. A disapproving white neighbour took possession of the note and he never received a thing.

Part Six

Chapter Forty-one

Nearly four years had passed since I'd first visited Willcox at Charlie Biggs's invitation. I'd kept returning to the area, drawn to its strange, displaced community of ostriches and the landscape they inhabited. But I hadn't been to Arizona in fifteen months when, in some recess of the Internet, I came across what I took to be a bad augury.

'Sheriff Feeds Inmates Ostrich Casserole'. The piece was an update on the antics of Joe Arpaio, Maricopa County's self-described 'toughest sheriff in the world'. Now he was introducing 'equal opportunity chain gangs' for men and women, forcing inmates to wear pink underwear and feeding them ostrich casserole.

Serving gourmet cuisine to prisoners didn't sound like vintage Sheriff Joe. Four years before, his possemen had chased Sadie, the $30,000-ostrich runaway, across the desert and the headlines. Now Sadie's children were being converted into food for felons. Something was amiss.

The article explained that some Arizona ranchers had donated 1,700 lb. of ostrich meat to Sheriff Joe's tent-city jail. The ranchers were keen 'to reduce their inventory'. That sounded like a euphemism for trouble.

So I called Charlie Biggs's Arizona number. A South African picked up the phone. But the voice wasn't one I recognized. Austin Ramsay explained that he and his wife were renting Charlie's house. Charlie had abandoned Willcox, gone back to the Karoo, where he was writing

263

screenplays on one of his family's ancestral ostrich farms.

Austin paused. The long distance line hissed and spluttered. 'When were you last down here?' he asked. 'Well, you'll notice a few changes. The place looks different now. Things are on the slide.'

A week later, I was driving down Kansas Settlement Road. Willcox playa – the town's immense dry lake – shimmered with illusory water to the west. I'd arranged to meet Chris Morgan, whom I had last seen standing on 320 acres of bare land, hammering with a mallet at a fence-post, putting up his first ostrich pens.

I turned onto a dirt road that led me through tumble-weed territory and fallow fields. When I lost my way, I asked a man repairing a centre-pivot sprinkler if he knew of any ostrich ranchers around there. He'd heard of Chris and sent me back the way I'd come.

Chris was waiting, standing propped up against the doorway of his white, A-framed house. He was taller than I'd remembered: six foot two. Thick eyebrows the colour of hay shaded his blue eyes. His wife Debbie, Chris explained, was at her job in town, typing copy for the *Arizona Range News*.

Debbie and Chris hadn't paid for their house with ostrich money. Chris squared his shoulders and pointed with his chin at half a dozen distant, scraggly birds. 'The ostrich business has gone sour. We're finished with ostriches. Seems like everybody around here is just barely hanging on, or thinking about getting out.'

We went inside and sat down in the high-ceilinged living room, curtains drawn to disperse the midday heat. Chris flicked at his straw-coloured hair where it lapped against his collar. He spoke, even emotionally, in a level voice.

'A few years ago, people just thought it was gonna be a huge thing. But the ostrich has been free-falling ever since. People tell me they wouldn't take ostriches for free. I don't think anybody made any money. The ones who have done the best have maybe broken even. Everyone else was just putting money in.

'One time we had thirty-two birds, now we've just got six. We'll butcher them and head back to Colorado.'

Chris hoped to work with his brother and mother who'd started renovating houses. From his four-year escapade with ostriches, that's mostly what he'd gained, he said: plenty of construction skills.

He stared down at his farm-worn footwear. 'Least I could have gotten out of all this was a nice pair of ostrich boots.' His eyes looked strained and edged with pain – trying, but not quite succeeding, to support the smile below.

Nobody I met in the ensuing days mentioned the Oudtshoorn of America. Willcox had dropped its moniker as quietly as, eighty years before, Oudtshoorn's newspaper had removed the ostrich feather from its masthead and the town had ceased to call itself the Jerusalem of Africa.

The sun was dipping fast by the time I left my motel and turned up the Fort Grant Road. Austin Ramsay's house lay nine miles away. I passed through a mix of stubbly winter fields and desert flat, interrupted by a ranch house now and then. But I saw no sign of the bulbous bodies, the questioning necks of ostriches.

As a I swung into his driveway, Austin was muttering to some black-faced sheep as he shooed them into his barn. He was in his early forties; not a tall man – perhaps five eight. But the half-light threw his strength into silhouette.

Later, over dinner, he'd appear to me like two people joined at the neck. A farm-taut body topped with a head that looked ecclesiastical: a swirling white beard, hair in retreat and eyes that peered through delicate, gold-rimmed spectacles as if the world were barely legible.

But the voice belonged to the body. Blunt and gruff, though warm, once I'd adjusted to the man's directness.

Austin shut the gate on his sheep and turned to me: 'I'm the last of the Apaches. The only South African left standing in Willcox.' Plenty had come here hawking their ostrich skills. Now they'd evaporated into America's hinterland or returned to the Karoo where the ostrich dream still lingered.

The crash, Austin explained, had started with the emus, Australian pretenders to the throne. 'Emus?' Austin clamped his hands against his temples. 'What a scam. Those emu ranchers have all gone to the wall.' Farmers just hit their birds over the head or chased them into the desert. Now some ostrich ranchers were starting to do the same.

Austin flicked an arm towards the farm's perimeter. One neighbour had picked up and fled the month before. Disappeared under a cloud of debts, whereabouts unknown. That past week, a second neighbour – patience and cash exhausted – had let 300 ostriches starve to death.

The big boys across the road had been delisted from the stock market. Austin grimaced. 'The flagship is a shipwreck. They say they won't be collecting eggs this year.' Because eggs mean chicks and chicks cost money to feed.

Austin's mouth bunched up tight. 'It's bad. Bad for the reputation of the bird. Let's get this straight: nobody can blame the ostrich. It should have been a success. Now it's finished here.'

All the hype, he said, had attracted totally the wrong type. People who treated ostriches like stocks and shares; folk who didn't have a farmer's bone in their bodies, who splashed out on zany technology without watching their overheads. Too many realtors, ex-professional tennis players, brain surgeons and retired rodeo clowns.

But Austin was a long way from despair. Every calamity creates a boon for someone, somewhere: in Willcox, Austin was that man. An ostrich-leather expert, death was his stock-in-trade. And across America right now, dead ostriches were plentiful. Bankrupt owners, bearing freshly salted skins, came banging on his door.

Austin led me up three wooden stairs and into the small, prefab house that Charlie Biggs had erected hastily when ostriches were hot. Why hadn't the meat caught on? I asked. Austin grunted a laugh and walked to the refrigerator. He glanced for a moment at his Michigan wife's family, whose photos brightened the fridge door. Then he pulled out some beers.

The bird's boosters had lied, he said, about how much meat an ostrich can deliver.

'Listen, my friend. It's not a fleshy bird. There's too much sinew, too much muscle. Less than twenty pounds of prime cuts. No farmer can survive on that. Eighty per cent of his income has to come from the hide.' If desperate ranchers kept dumping ostriches, they could ruin everything. The leather would be driven downmarket, and lose its exotic cache.

But I'd found Austin in a cheerful mood. He talked animatedly, with lively hands, about his new discovery. He'd seen the future and it belonged to Mexico. Mexico was ripe for ostriches.

'My friend, you have to understand the North American Free Trade Agreement and gaucho culture. NAFTA is killing off the Mexican cattle business. The borders are coming down and all those little mom-pop operators can't compete with America. So now the Mexican is looking around for something new to farm. Guess what . . . ?' Mexicans and ostriches: a marriage made in heaven. Most Americans couldn't see the ostrich for what it was – a basic barnyard animal. They saw it as a concept, an investment deal.

Austin leaned towards me from his chair across the room: 'The Mexican, he doesn't have that problem. He comes from peasant stock; his people have always worked with animals, lived close to the land.' Austin admired the people he met down there. They were hardworking, thrifty. When you shook a man's hands they were rough: proper farmer's hands.

'The gauchos go a long way back. Don't forget that the Texan with his spurs and his Stetson is a Johnny-come-lately. The Mexicans were cowboys first.' Gauchos adore exotic wildlife leather. Traditionally, they've turned sea bass, giant lizards, rattlesnakes, bison and marine turtles into boots. Finger by finger, Austin kept ticking off the gaucho's leather menagerie: 'Crocodiles, too. And camels and elephants and diamond-backed pythons smuggled from Indonesia.'

Endangered creatures, mostly. Now almost impossible to get. The ostrich is different: an exotic creature that can be farmed and harvested. Since the 1950s, the gaucho had revered the ostrich look, claimed it as his heritage. For mass, weddings, funerals . . . where a century ago, he'd have pulled on sea-bass boots, today, to make a statement, he arrives in ostrich skin.

So the Mexican farmer, Austin explained, didn't need some hype-merchant to persuade him that the ostrich was the next big thing. All his life, he'd lived enviously among gauchos who could afford to strut their stuff in full-quill ostrich boots. So the ordinary guy was prepared to save all year and pay maybe $1,800 for a custom-made pair.

Austin narrowed his blue eyes and nodded.

'Yes, ostrich is their number one. That's the gaucho dream: white Panama hat, leather waistcoat, flash pair of full-quill ostrich boots and a horse or a 1968 Pontiac.'

Austin drained his beer from the can. Then he leaned across the coffee table and passed me his colour chart for selling hides to Mexico. I skimmed my eyes down the ninety shades of dyed ostrich skin that a gaucho can acquire. Little squares of brilliance, poetically described: jungle green, nicotine, nutmeg, campari, bordeaux, buttercup, African violet, pâté orange . . .

'Cognac and champagne – those are the most popular. Except for the drug lord. He loves his ostrich in jewel colours.' Yellow, lime green, fizzy blue. Austin fetched a boot – toe curled high, heel sliced forward, as turquoise as the Caribbean. He held it up admiringly.

'Mexican drug lords – they're picky as hell. They all demand full quill. Lots of feather follicles, pimples all the way up. A boot without smooth leather.'

It's the bumpy skin that brings the money in. Austin lifted one eyebrow. 'That's where the Americans went wrong.' They became fixated on creating a fat, meaty bird. But a porky ostrich is an ostrich with a stretched skin – fewer follicles per foot. If those little volcanic bumps are thinly spread, the Mexican won't pay.

Austin vanished into the bedroom, past the collage of African wildlife photographs adorning the passage wall. He reappeared with a scroll of skins tucked beneath his arm. These he unfurled, like parchments, across the floor and stared at them with theological intent. We kneeled down together. Then he ran one hand across the surface, encouraging me to do the same, as if I were learning braille.

'Full quill. Feel that, a beautiful piece of work. Twenty-eight dollars a square foot.'

Then he unravelled one of the shabbier Willcox skins. It looked like the Karoo seen from the air: a flat, sepia expanse broken occasionally by *kopjes* – those solitary far-flung hills that rise up every now and then to interrupt the view.

The ostrich crash had created an avalanche of skins. But many proved unusable. Austin flicked his fingers dismissively across the sparse-pimpled Willcox hide. No self-respecting Mexican drug baron would be seen dead in a skin like that.

Trying to farm ostriches had nearly bankrupted Austin. At one stage, he was so broke he was reduced to selling his labour to neighbours – putting up slick-wire fences for five-fifty an hour. The ostrich trade had pulled him through a thorn tree backwards but he'd ended up all right. Things had turned around when he'd returned to basics – to his secret expertise in skins.

Ostrich tanning, as Austin described it, is an arcane art. 'Americans haven't got the curing right. You can't treat it like cowhide.' And the South Africans guard their ostrich-tanning brew as if it were the Coca Cola recipe.

Austin had done some curing of his own. But mostly he had the leather done 'back home', in the Karoo. Austin had decided to go global. As he talked, I counted. An ostrich skin, it appeared, had to cross five international borders before it could become a boot.

First, Austin selected the best of the cast-off American hides. These he freighted to South Africa to be cured and dyed in gaucho colours. South Africa contributed to the process not just curing skills but lax pollution laws. Then the skins travelled back to America where they were cut into boot shapes – to ensure that the final product was 'American'. These bits, in turn, would get trucked to Mexico – to Leon, a city of 300 shoe factories, a cobbling heritage and plentiful cheap labour. That's where the boots were built. Then they were sent back across the border to be blessed with those 'Made in the USA' labels which the gauchos so prize when the boots are trucked back one last time for sale in Mexico.

These days, Austin said, he was spending half his life on the south side of the border. Three times a week he drove through Nogales, two hours southwest of Willcox, his trunk filled with dead ostriches and lurid colour charts. But his crossings had started to arouse suspicion. His vehicle had begun to show up too often on surveillance photos shot from border satellites.

Austin shook his head. 'The Mexican border guards decided I was running narcotics for the drug lords. Each time I went through, they'd check inside my boots, my hubcaps, sometimes make me take off all my clothes.' The strip-searches began to get him down. So he appealed to his friend and Mexican business partner, Ruben Gonzales, to help him finesse his identity.

Ruben spoke to the uncle of a cousin of a . . . So now Austin was officially a Mexican. As a citizen, he could own land down there and ostriches, as well as forty-nine per cent of the company he and Ruben had begun.

Austin smiled. Together, they were creating some amazing designer shoes. He disappeared again into a back room, and returned bearing the world's first full-quill, champagne-toned ostrich sneaker. 'We're calling them Reedocs. Go for a hundred and twenty bucks in the mall. Patrick Ewing owns a pair. Size fifteen and a half.'

I held the sneaker and ran one finger – bumpity, bump,

bump, bump – over all the little molehills bursting out everywhere.

'No leather in the world can compare,' Austin mused.
'Ostrich is so forgiving.'

Midnight had passed by the time I returned to my car.
Austin came out to see me off, his cognac-coloured labrador
by his side. He waved as I reversed. I left him standing there
in the huge desert dark, his head full of ostrich dreaming, on
the verge of something new. An Englishman by ancestry, a
South African by birth, an American by marriage and now
a Mexican by spiritual inclination and necessity.

Chapter Forty-two

Each time I'd travelled to Willcox I'd missed the over-wintering cranes, though even in their absence I felt their pull. This time, I hoped we'd be in synch. Winter was edging towards spring. Soon, the cranes would be ascending on the thermal updrafts created by the warming earth and start following the thaw north to the Yukon, Alaska and Siberia. There they would spend the summer breeding in bogs and tundra. Come fall, the cranes would begin their reverse migration down the continent's central flyway, escorting a fresh generation of three-month-olds to Willcox playa and other southerly destinations. While wintering at Willcox, each new bird would seek and find a mate, with whom to come and go for life.

It was Austin's wife, Donna, who told me on the telephone that, if I wished to see the cranes, the fields opposite their farm were an excellent location. 'Be there early. The birds fly in each morning at exactly seven-thirty,' she said. By night, the cranes roosted on the playa; as day broke, they took off to feed on the wintry stubble fields.

So on my final day in Willcox, I positioned myself opposite Donna and Austin's farm with time to spare. I waited in the predawn frost for the first light and the first cranes. Soon, a soft wash of grey began to spill across the valley floor, pulling my eye towards the peaks, thirty miles away, that ring Willcox and its mirage-making playa. I took the time to absorb this landscape once again. I loved the width and lift in it, the sense of convergence everywhere. A place between places, a border world of desert corridors, migrant flyways and mountain chains. Here two great deserts met – the Chihuahuan and the Sonoran – joined by a third, the Karoo, in memory.

To the west, the Chiracahuas soared to 9,000 feet along the Arizona-New Mexico divide. To the south, the Huachuca range marked the beginnings of Mexico. These sky islands rise abruptly from the desert floor, creating outposts of ecological diversity by enabling plants and creatures from the Sierra Madres to skip the border. Biologists call these sub-tropical visitors pioneer species. They're natural reminders that our maps are brief, transient inventions; that a 150 years ago – before Willcox or Oudtshoorn existed – this was Mexico.

And before that a procession of human pioneers passed through here. Starting with the Clovis people, who roamed the playa at the end of the last ice age, butchering mammoths, bison and camels long before the first cranes appeared. Wave after wave of hope chasers followed them. Sixteenth-century Spanish friars questing after Cibolla's golden cities, silver panners, homesteaders, gauchos, stock men, Mexican peasants and railroad magnates. Mogollon Indians, the region's most enduring inhabitants, remained until the Apaches arrived in the 1500s and drove them out. The US Army in turn marched on the Apaches, removing Geronimo and his people from their sky islands and sending them into exile in swampy, prostrate Florida. I was standing in a place of sedimented hopes. The inspired, the inventive, the desperate, the deluded, had come and gone, each pursuing some lode-star fantasy.

Above the Chiracahuas, the grey dawn turned sudden saffron. The cranes were leaving their playa roost by now: I could hear their deep-throated chattering miles away. I watched them rise in their thousands, clanking as they went. From a distance, their staggered, uneven black Vs appeared like scratchings in a foreign script crowded onto a huge yellow pad. They flew in formation. Each bird travelled slightly lower than the one that followed, creating uplift for those behind. As they passed, I could almost feel the draft from their urgent, migrant wings.

A hundred cranes fussed overhead before landing in the field nearest me. I watched them for perhaps an hour as they paced up and down, their red caps tilted forward, like rakish English schoolboys. They fed greedily, fattening themselves for the exacting flight ahead. By the time the cranes returned next year, they'd once more be the biggest birds around. Every sign suggested that the ostriches and the people who'd pursued them here would be gone for good.

Then two cranes began to dance. They leaped straight up, nine, ten feet off the ground. They threw back their necks and crowed, while thrusting air towards each other with flapping wings and bouncing up and down. Their performance seemed contagious; soon other cranes joined their minuet. It is said that when the pioneers first saw this dance they believed the birds were leading them in prayer.

Chapter Forty-three

I left the Willcox cranes behind and headed onto Interstate 10. I planned to spend my last few Arizona days near Tucson, eighty miles to the west. It was between Willcox and Tucson that my father and Gaffy finally acquired a sketchy history. I'd been doing so much rummaging through other people's histories that I'd begun to feel the need, with an intensity I never had before, for a deeper private past. After some prompting, my mother had sent me a tape with whatever snatches of family memory she could recall. So on the outskirts of Willcox, I put on her tape and listened as I began the descent towards Tucson and the Sonoran Desert proper.

Dad, it turned out, had narrowly escaped a desert death fifty years before, while serving as a World War Two signalman in North Africa. Although he'd grown up near the Karoo's northern extremity, in the cauldron town of Kimberley, nothing could compare with the Saharan heat. His body had revolted against the blistering temperatures and bad food, erupting into so many boils he was immobilized. Three days after his admission to a Cairo hospital, Tobruk fell. The Germans captured the remainder of Dad's regiment and held them in a POW camp, where many of them died. Dad spoke of the incident to my mother only once. Although he added, after the war was won: 'At least it's over now. And I never had to kill a man.'

The night we killed our priest together, my father did something that I didn't know until now. After the police apprehended him for questioning, he didn't go straight home. He had a job to do: one of his duties for the evening (in addition to reviewing the Feather Market concert he'd been unable to attend) was to find out if there had been any crimes or accidents that his newspaper needed to report. So he went directly to the office and rang the police station he'd just left to get official details of his crash. He wanted, I suspect, to show that he was still responsible.

At the office, he sat down and wrote a dispassionate account for the *Herald* of the death of Father J. Keats, the much-loved pastor of St Mary's, on his way to evensong. The driver of the vehicle, a tan-coloured Opel Kapitan, was a Mr R. R. W. Nixon. Mr Nixon had been charged with culpable homicide. Dad filed the story and – job done – returned home to his family.

I remember the article's impact lucidly. At five a.m., next morning, my little brother heard the newspaper land on our veranda steps. Andy ran to fetch it, to see if the accident was there; to see, perhaps, if it had really happened. A front page article (without a byline) proved that it had. We all clustered round Dad's bed while Andy read out the *Herald*'s story of our crash. When he'd finished reading, Andy's tears came flooding out: 'What are they going to do to my daddy?' Then he announced that Father Keats was the best priest who'd ever lived. How he'd given us both Easter eggs and shared his apple on the bus.

Dad was the only one, that morning, who knew we were listening to his words. He said nothing, lay there dead silently.

Where does anyone acquire such fidelity to the job? My father, I now learned, had left school early to become the mainstay of his family, after a younger sister had died. His mother, blaming herself for the child's death, had 'lost her mind' and gone semi-permanently to bed. Dad's Irish fireman father coped with this double loss by drinking, which soon pitched him into joblessness. As eldest son, Dad's task was obvious: to prop the family up. So he left school and found work odd-jobbing at the *Diamond Fields Advertiser*. He had a second, unpaid job: to set off each evening in search of his immigrant father, to bring him back from drink. Dad would trawl Kimberley, from bar to bar, father-hunting while his school mates were playing soccer. Then he'd sling his limp father over his back and trudge on home, past the neighbours' stares.

In adulthood, Dad pursued respectability with all his energy. Married, had five children, used his wife's ancestors to swell his home with extra people. The past was awkward, useless – ancient history. Besides, the hungry present grew all-consuming. Soon he was the sole breadwinner for nine mouths demanding bread.

I remembered that Dad never said: 'I've got work to do.' It was always: 'I've got a *job* of work to do,' a note of fearful pride discernable beneath his urgency. Behind him, hung the spectre of his father's joblessness. So once he found work at the *Herald* he clung to it, stayed put, sending roots down deep. I'd seen the evidence at the funeral: 2,000 consecutive Wednesdays' worth of 'Growing Things'.

About thirty miles from Tucson, I heard my mother explain for the first time Gaffy's murderous rantings which had so haunted me as a child. A murderer, a murderer twice over? My first encounter with uncomprehending fear.

'The murders,' Mom said, 'if you can call them that, were both in the family.' One day in Biggar, Gaffy had taken his eldest son to a curling game. His son kept nagging him; he was freezing, wanted to go home. But Gaffy was keen to see the game through to the finish. The son was struck down with double pneumonia. A week later he was dead.

Wracked by guilt, Gaffy decided it would be better if the family moved. He wanted to escape his memories, held to the illusion that he could out-migrate the past. A neighbour had returned from fighting in the Anglo-Boer War. South Africa, he said, was a land full of opportunities – a dry, hot country where a painter-decorator like Gaffy could work all year round. So Gaffy and his wife set sail for Africa, with two daughters and their remaining son.

Gaffy was too old to fight in World War One; his son, George, was two years too young. But because South African education proved inferior to the Scottish schools he'd left behind, George had been promoted two standards on arriving in Johannesburg. When war broke out, all his eighteen-year-old classmates started signing on. 'George was a boy,' Mom said, 'who at sixteen looked big enough to be a man.' He pleaded with his father to let him go, to fabricate his age. Gaffy, fearful, refused.

Then one day George got shown the feather – the white feather reserved for cowards. A woman in the street thrust one in his face. George raced home in a frenzy of shame and rage. 'Dad, I have to go.' Gaffy finally relented and signed his boy up as a man.

So in 1916 George went off to fight in German East Africa. He never saw any Germans. All he saw was mud. Month after month, rains prevented supplies from getting through. George wrote a letter saying they were reduced to boiling stones and grass in a pretence at making soup. He died there of starvation. After the war was over, George's commanding officer paid Gaffy a visit. Less to commiserate than to berate him for lying about George's age. 'Your son was the first to go,' the officer rebuked. 'His bones weren't set yet. He was still a growing boy.'

Mom paused: 'Gaffy had kept his daughters. But he always felt he'd killed off both his sons. He was such an unforgiving man. Especially towards himself.' His wife – Granny's mother – agreed with him, that he was entirely to blame. After their second son's death, she refused to speak to Gaffy again, although they stayed married and shared a house for another fifteen years. This became Granny and her sister's job: to ferry messages between mother and father, from one end of their silent house to the other.

A jumble of saguaro cacti, trailer parks and tract housing signalled Tucson's approach. Truckers in their eighteen-wheelers thundered by. Through it all, I could still hear Gaffy's rumbling tirades of murderous self-rebuke; and hear, echoing up above him, his all-remembering parrot, bellowing the old man's guilt to the world through a curtain of falling feathers.

Chapter Forty-four

Tucson is the only city in the world that stands at the centre of both a desert and a forest. Botanically speaking, 'forest' accurately describes the city's dense stands of tree-sized plants. But the saguaro forests unsettle our expectations of that word. Certainly, there's nothing around Tucson by way of woods that Little Red Riding Hood could comfortably get lost in.

The saguaros resemble huge green forks, plunged handle first into the earth by some fee-fi-fo-fum giant above. They are the largest cacti on the planet. They can rise to forty or fifty feet and weigh three tons. But even when thickly congregated, they offer little by way of leaves, branches or shade. The forest they create is naked, see-through four seasons of the year.

Like enormous index fingers, the saguaros point the eye away from the desert floor up towards the pale-domed sky. Each finger has blemishes – the maroony-yellow spots of an eighty Marlboro-a-day man. Close up, these stains reveal themselves as calloused cavities. They're all part of the cactus's intricate hidden life. Gila woodpeckers begin the process, excavating nesting holes from the saguaro's pulpy flesh. Other creatures then jostle for possession of these cactus pits: sparrow-sized elf owls, kestrels, purple martins, bats and lizards.

Saguaros may live for two centuries. They appear as solid as monuments. But they're changing – swelling or shrinking – on the inside all the time. After rain, they can drink and drink until they're ninety-five per cent water. They become fluted water-towers, held together by waxy skin. We, of course, can't boast much more solidity than that – seven tenths of us is fluid. But if we lose fifteen per cent of our water, we're dead, while saguaros can survive far more radical forms of metabolic retreat. During a drought, they can shed eighty per cent of their water and remain alive beneath their crusty residue.

Few saguaro seedlings survive to any height. Most wither within seven weeks. Their vulnerable period is long: to reach six inches takes them fourteen years. For all that time, they need cool shelter. Outside Tucson's Saguaro National Park, overgrazing has thinned vital mesquite and paloverde cover. It's not just the bushes that disappear, but with them, the desert's most precious life-force after water, the tiny pools of shade.

The rare saguaros that survive to a sturdy adolescent height turn mercilessly on their protectors. Often a saguaro that has grown up in the kindly shadow of a mesquite will slowly, cuckoo-like, overwhelm its host. The juvenile cactus's greatest asset is its refusal to take root with any depth. The roots remain so close to the surface they virtually pluck rain from the air. Each tree-cactus sends out a superficial fibrous skein that can sprawl one hundred feet from the stem. As a result, saguaros are maestros of the pre-emptive strike: neighbouring trees and bushes wait in vain for rainwater to trickle down through the soil. Slowly, the saguaro kills them. They die from a deep-rooted thirst.

On my penultimate day in Arizona I decide to drive one last time through the saguaro forests I love. On a whim, I stop off at the Arizona-Sunora Desert Museum nearby. I have no special expectations of this modest-looking place: a lowslung ochre building that defers to the desert's horizontal lines à la Frank Lloyd Wright. 'Museum', it turns out, is a misnomer. All the fauna and flora here are very much alive. This 'museum' is a cross between a botanical garden and a zoo.

But the place isn't like any urban zoo or arboretum I have

known. Instead of exotic samplings from around the globe, the collection embraces only desert life. The walls here feel nominal: if they crumbled, most of these plants and creatures would blend straight back into the surrounding world from which they've come.

A winding corridor leads me underground, allowing me for the first time to travel beneath the desert floor. As a child, I often dreamed of vanishing, like some dry country Alice into that magic netherworld. Now I can wander past dim tunnels which reveal in cross-section the desert's burrowing things: kit foxes, pouched kangaroo rats, black widow spiders, tarantulas, Gila Monsters, giant hairy scorpions, giant desert centipedes, tiger salamanders, desert spadefoot frogs and horned toads which, when annoyed, are apt to squirt blood at you from their eyes.

By day, the chimera of the dead desert holds. The place looks empty. Most mobile life has headed for the bunkers to wait out the killing heat. But by night, the evacuees abandon their burrows and disclose themselves. The surface once again becomes a crowded place.

But it's the burrows that interest me. I'm astonished by how much living goes on underground. In the prairie dog cities, for instance, which dwarf any human maze. The largest colony on record – in Texas – was 250-miles long, one hundred miles wide, and held 400 million prairie dogs. Population-wise, that's roughly equal to 120 upside-down Manhattans towering beneath the earth. And like Manhattan, those hidden cities are rife with unseen crime.

As I pass their colony, the museum's prairie dogs look pictures of innocence. They bounce about and squeak like fluffy toys. But in the breeding season, their homes become slaughterhouses for infanticide. Most prairie dogs die young and brutally at the hands of the mom next door. Maternal devotion is principally expressed by bumping off the neighbours' kids and eating them before they grow into daycare competition.

The surface life on display at the museum seems no less

punishing. The garden bristles with Horse-crippler Barrel Cacti, Cat Claw Cacti, Eagle Claws, Devil Chollas, Jumping Chollas, Spiny Strawberry Hedgehogs, Many-spined Fishhooks, Bonker Hedgehogs and Crucifixion Thorn. The names suggest plants which, to the first white settlers, must have seemed not just strange but actively malicious. The Jumping Cholla, a man-high cactus ringed by creamy thorns, testifies to the frontier suspicion that desert plants could be evil-minded. Disgruntled victims ascribed to this cholla improbable powers of ambush. The thorns, it was said, would leap out at you without waiting to be touched.

From the museum's perimeter, I gaze south over the Sonoran basin that stretches as far as the Mexican mountains – the Santa Ritas, the Huachucas, the Pajaritos – eighty miles away. Nothing, it seems, is moving between me and those distant peaks. Except the flailing ocotillos straining at their roots. Each ocotillo sends up forty or fifty thin arms from ground level, each arm ten to fifteen feet long. They writhe and grope in the slightest breeze like trapped spirits, wretchedly alive.

The ocotillo's thin whippy branches, laced with thorns, make this a punishing plant. Nature's gift to masochists. The Penitentes, a New Mexican desert sect, have long sought the ocotillo's assistance in their quest to mortify the flesh. During spring, before self-flagellation starts, the Penitentes remove the sumptuous flaming blossoms from each ocotillo tendril tip. These they replace with jagged bits of iron to supplement the natural pain of thorns.

Sometimes, like today, the wide desert floor gives off a subaqueous aura. In this shimmery underwater light, the ocotillos' waving evokes the tendrilled world of seaweed and octopi. There's something poignant about a flailing ocotillo, as if the plant were stirring still to the memory of some long-retreated ocean current.

And indeed, I discover, this was once a sea. The Sonoran's harshness gives it the illusion of great age. But it is a shallow, recent thing. Signature plants like the saguaro and ocotillo

282

only migrated into the area 8,000 years ago. Before that forest reigned: junipers, pines and pinon oaks. And before that – 250-million years before – the desert floor was a warm ocean bed, brimming with life forms that survive only in rich fossil sediments. The sea of the desert is a cliché. But in southern Arizona, it harbours a geologically sound memory.

The Karoo was also once submerged. Two hundred and fifty million years ago as well. I didn't learn that from a museum guide or a book. One day, when I was ten, I was scuffing my shoes in the dirt on an ostrich farm when I accidentally unearthed a stone with a twirly shell in it. I asked my father how it got there. He put one hand on my shoulder and looked around him with a far-sighted gaze. 'In the olden days,' he said, 'standing here we would have drowned.'

It was one of those startling, upside-down discoveries which touch children very deeply. That the world I thought I knew could be so strange seemed quite impossible. I stood there on that thirsty Karoo farm, surrounded by nothingness, listening and listening for the breaking waves of an evaporated sea.

I eat lunch sitting on the museum's dividing wall. On the far side, the desert floor stretches to the border and beyond. It's all distance – leading first the eye then the heart away. I feel a strange fellowship with this place: this oxymoronic world of arid oceans and treeless forests. It matches my own uncanny sense of being a returnee to this spot in the guise of a first-time visitor.

After lunch, I find something that I hadn't realized I've been looking for. A rocky pathway leads me to an alcove. It is filled with desert plants demonstrating the principle of convergent evolution. The plants are grouped in pairs of dead ringers. Yet these are twins that share no common ancestor, that have grown towards each other without any genetic bond. I look closer at the labels: each pair consists of a Sonoran Desert plant and a matching plant from the Karoo.

In these two great scrub deserts, continents apart, life forms have had to contend with almost identical environmental pressures. The conditions – sun, wind, geology, temperature and humidity – mirror each other so closely that natural selection has nudged plants to adapt convergently. So, over millions of years, these paired plants have developed the same survival strategies. And in the process, have become almost indistinguishable.

The cacti and succulents before me could be lining up, two by two, for some botanical rescue sequel to Noah's Ark. Here a euphorbia rises out of the filmy distance of childhood to join its doppelganger, a plant I've never seen before. An African milkbarrel squats low and round in spiky clusters. I close my eyes and its name drifts back: *Euphorbia horrida major,* one of my father's favourites. What child schooled in veld Latin could ever forget a majorly horrid name like that? Flush against the milkbarrel sits its Arizona double: *Echinocactus platyocanthus.* And so the parade continues: tall Sonoran agaves and African aloes, both bare-stemmed, fleshy mandibled and lined with alligator teeth. Sonoran and Karoo ironwoods, so heavy they sink in water. Another Arizona cactus poses alongside *Euphorbia ferox,* an old acquaintance that stood guard on the edge of our hoopoe lawn. I stand staring for a while at these local plants, these transplants, side by side. My eyes skip from one to the other, jumping continents of time.

My favourite non-genetic family reunion brings together a Sonoran stapelia and a *Euphorbia Jansenvillensis,* both waxy, tubular succulents that hug the ground. Jansenville is the ultimate one-mistake town, a nothing hamlet on the Karoo road leading from Oudtshoorn to Port Elizabeth. Blink while tugging at a bit of ostrich jerky as you drive through and you've missed it, Jansenville is gone. But right now, it's here and there, in a state of half-seen, half-remembered visibility.

Nothing is perfect in this world – not even metaphors. Dead ringers are never truly identical. The plot line of every film, play and novel on the subject moves towards the ex-posure of the flaw: the moment when a mole between the thighs, the angle of tooth, a memory blank or a fractured voice betrays some trace of difference. For these mirror plants that moment of exposure comes each spring.

Flowers are more complex than stalks, roots, thorns and leaves. For blooms evolve not just in response to weather, soil, humidity, but in tandem with their living pollinators – birds, butterflies, moths, bats and bees. Over hundreds of thousands of years, desert flowers have developed interdependently with their pollinators. And these pollinating creatures differ widely in the Sonoran Desert and the Karoo. So of all the parts of the plant, the flowers prove most resistant to co-evolution's convergent pressures.

If I stayed on into spring I could watch these desert doppelgangers diverge, their masquerade stripped by rain. Suddenly, one twin will erupt into a swollen crimson flower, the other send out through its thorns a delicate, orange bloom.

But I'm in no rush to wrench these worlds apart. I'm happy to witness these convergent strangers enact their mimicry. In this stony garden, there is no New World and no Old. This is a place without origins, without an Eden, without the deadweight of the single family tree. Just things from here and there, coexisting in the deep present of this shrine to the familiar yet new.

I feel my father's presence here with unexpected force. This would have been his dream spot, the perfect column for next Wednesday's 'Growing Things'. Well worth a trip back from the dead. And if he can't make it back, I'll have to ghostwrite it for him. I've never published a word about plants – things with roots have always bothered me. But this feels different, part of a dawning curiosity.

Dad was an uneasy traveller. He preferred places that knew him as well as he knew them. But he would have blossomed in this spot where, 10,000 miles from anything familiar, his alien knowledge could have passed as local expertise. He could have travelled here and kept his roots in place.

For reasons of first politics, then geography and money, I saw my father only intermittently in his last decade and a half. When he died his long-distance death, I was in London at the time and hadn't seen him in two years. Arriving at Port Elizabeth airport for his funeral, I felt a jabbing memory. What came back to me was the departure I'd made from that same airport twelve years before. At the time, in 1980, it was called not the Port Elizabeth but the H. F. Verwoerd Airport. I remember standing there, waiting for the plane to take me from South Africa and staring at the sign that spelled H. F. Verwoerd. The sign helped. It confirmed my sense I had to leave.

I was going – for good, for all I knew – clandestinely. I'd told my parents and my girlfriend, that was it. The plane was late. Dad kept pacing up and down and losing things – his camera, his wallet, his keys. He'd discouraged me from going. That morning, he'd taken me aside and said: 'You're being reckless, my boy. You're throwing your life away. You don't want to turn yourself into an exile. It's always a mistake to cut yourself off from your roots.'

Part of me must have known that his words were spoken out of love. But I was angry in my silent way, angry and afraid.

Proust said it perfectly: 'People do not die immediately for us, but remain bathed in a sort of aura of life. It is as though they were travelling abroad.' I didn't bury my father at the funeral; I was waiting first, for his return. In the hope that there were things that could be said.

I've been searching in the years since for a way, a place, to mourn him as deeply as I wished, to put his memory to rest. My desert travels on two continents have taught me to see things I couldn't see before. What I'd always sought was severance. But I'd been living in denial, refusing to notice how deeply my father's vision of things, especially natural things, had imprinted me.

Here in this Arizona alcove, I feel I can strike some truce between his values and my own. His belief in an anchored commitment to one spot and my restlessness, my need to live more shallowly in a wider world. The company here feels right: Dad's ghost, *Euphorbia Jansenvillensis*, *Horrida major* and their Arizona doubles. For a moment, his far-off world and mine briefly converge. I've stumbled on a place that makes some intimate sense to me and so I take the chance to grieve.

It is dusk by the time I leave this place of confluence. The light liquefies to a distant lavender, then moves through mauve towards magenta. Soon the mountains are reduced to crinkly outlines shaped by a child's snipping scissors. As I wind my way back through the dark saguaro silhouettes, they look even less like a forest now. More like a forest remnant of which nothing has survived except blackened trunks left standing after a blaze.

Chapter Forty-five

O n my last night in Arizona, a wind raged, hour after hour, sawing out tunes that kept me teetering on the precipice of sleep. I lay on my motel bed listening to the wheezy whistlings, the melodic moans. Through them, I heard another desert wind from many years before. I was a child, travelling with my father in a distant part of the Karoo. We were sleeping outside on a farm; the night was big with stars. I'd fallen asleep, then woken and couldn't go down again. The darkness felt alive, noisy with unfamiliar tunes. I shook my father: 'Listen: is that just the wind?'

We listened together carefully. 'Yes, it's the wind,' he said, 'but I'm hearing something else. The wind has company.'

Then he told me a story. 'There was a farmer called Fourie who lived not far from here. When the feather crash came, Mr Fourie opened his gates and let all his birds run off into the desert. But he didn't know that one of his inquisitive, hungry ostriches had been prowling around the yard. It had seen his mouth organ glistening in the sun and swallowed it. The mouth-organ must have gone down sideways and jammed in the darn bird's throat. Long after his ostriches had all vanished, Mr Fourie would sometimes sit sipping coffee on his stoop and hear that hungry bird playing his lost harmonica.'

'Farmer Fourie died long, long ago. But some people around these parts still swear they can hear that ostrich running up and down, breathing music as it goes. An ostrich, as you know, my boy, can live to be very, very old.'

I listened. And heard on the wind, I was sure of it, the same sad-tuned ostrich that farmer Fourie had heard. Less tuneful than Granny's mavis, but for an ostrich its sense of melody wasn't bad.

Back then, I had no reason to doubt that what my father said was true. I lived, like every child, differently in time. The crash had happened long ago, but stories all around me made it seem just yesterday, kept it totally alive. My watch had vanished down an ostrich, why not a mouth organ too? Besides, I was at an age when I would have swallowed anything myself, so long as my father told it to me with the right music in his voice.